A CHARCUTERIE DIARY

www.acharcuteriediary.com.au

THE DEDICATION

For Helen, Amelia-Rose, Nicholas
and
Sue, who sadly, did not get to read the book.

THE CONTENTS

THE PROLOGUE

I am not a chef, either by training or inclination. This humble book, therefore, may suffer from a lack of professional training and expertise.

Several years ago, I became interested in charcuterie. The first products were, frankly, inedible. After reading as widely as I could, I spent several years experimenting with recipes and techniques which were suited to my circumstances.

This book is a record of my experience and drawn from a diary in which I kept recipes, observations and results over the past four years. Hence, the title to this book. It is not intended to be a scholarly work nor a literary one. Neither is it intended for commercial use in which I understand premixes of spices and cures are common place. It may, however, provide some assistance to those who are interested in some homemade charcuterie. It was written primarily because the books that were available to me I did not find helpful. They were either based on imperial measurements (not metric) or just really old. Some of the books used products which I could not source reliably or at all (*"saltpetre"* for example) or which I did not understand (*"Boston butt"* comes from the front end of the pig not the rear end, for God's sake!). Some of them were predicated on equipment or conditions which I could not possibly replicate at home (*"...incubate at 27℃ and 85%RH for 12 hours then increase humidity to 95℃ and reduce temperature to 14℃ for the next 12 hours..."*); or suppliers who would not supply to me, on the other side of the world. Most of all they usually did not explain exactly what was going on in the process of charcuterie, a matter as to which I became intrigued just because they did not explain it or explain it to my satisfaction. All these things made me write this book. It is written by reference to my conditions and access to supplies and suppliers in Australia in 2017. Hopefully it is relevant to you.

I cannot commence without reference to the simple eloquence of Elizabeth David, writing in 1960 of a stall at a French market, *"...big bowls of pale amber-green and gold choucroute, and stalls bulging with sausages, the special smoked ones to go with the choucroute, ... terrines and pâtés of pork, duck, tongue; and deep dishes in which pieces of pork lie embedded in crystal clear jelly; this turns out to be the famous porcelet en gelée, an elegant brawn of suckling pig which makes a fine hors d'oeuvre; then there are trays of highly flavoured salad made from pig's head..."*. She is the standard to which any writer, even of cookbooks, should aspire.

As an aside David received an OBE in 1976, a CBE in 1986 and in 1977 was appointed as a Chevalier du Merite Agricole. The latter is the Order of Agricultural Merit of France and is bestowed on those who have made an outstanding contribution to agriculture. A Knight (Chevalier) of the Order is one who has provided at least 15 years of such service and is the most senior award. It is second in precedence in the French honours system to the Legion of Honour. However, perhaps most surprisingly (or not as the case may be), David was elected as a Fellow of the Royal Society of Literature in 1982.

As for vegetarians (so called) and vegans, to both of whom I have a special antipathy, I say pigs, cattle, fish and goats are mainly vegetarians. Bourdain had something to say about vegetarians which should not go unnoticed:

> *"To me, life without veal stock, pork fat, sausage, organ meat, demi-glace, or even stinky cheese is a life not worth living. Vegetarians are the enemy of everything good and decent in the human spirit, an affront to all I stand for, the pure enjoyment of food."*

As Rayner put it *'I like vegans but I couldn't eat a whole one'*.

In my view, vegetarians, vegans and the like are largely consumed and motivated by, fear and loathing.

I acknowledge that this book may be somewhat idiosyncratic but I figured that it was undesirable to write an anonymous cookbook. No doubt others will judge whether I was correct. This has been much more work than I expected it to be, but satisfying nonetheless.

I note at the earliest moment, charcuterie is serious stuff and best done in some place where the negative vibrations and comments emanating from family are left behind. Charcuterie is thousands of years old. It is important that you, a torch bearer of the traditions, have a place where you can practice your traditional beliefs and culture. If you have the opportunity to practice the arts in a place like a shed then you will feel much better and the process will be all the more purer for it. *"The shed is the man's natural hiding place. It is just like the pub, except nearer to home"*, *The Shed*, Hazeley and Morris.

Next, I must thank a number of people. First, thank you to my family for their good humour in relation to various charcuterie experiments and eccentricities. Especially to my wife Helen for her editorial expertise and encouragement. I appreciate the diligent typing of this manuscript by Nikki and subsequently, by Karen and Mary. Sebastian, gastronome and man about town, a thank you for agisting a prosciutto called *"Kevin"* under his house during some unseasonably warm weather. No. 1 Daughter spent quality time in a final, often quite hurtful, editorial proof read, thank you. To Dr Flower and The Hairy Nephews for being crash test dummies with a variety of charcuterie I am appreciative. Glen, who rode shotgun on matters legal, also deserves mention. Lucy[1], the black dog, benefited from some failures, although that is a secret. To The Rat[2], an evil Jack Russell Terrier for whom I have no regard, I say nothing. No. 1 Son assisted in his own special way.

I add a disclaimer, first because His Glen-ness told me that I must, but secondly due to the nature of the things and processes described in this book.

Read this stuff carefully. Be careful. Be hygienic.

Following these recipes and directions is no guarantee against mistakes or serious, lethal risks to your health. This is serious stuff. Be scrupulously vigilant concerning mould (especially nasty coloured mould), temperature and ingredients. Those following these recipes, directions and techniques do so at their own risk.

Do all these things and you should not get sick and die. That is what I did. I am still here. Why should you be any different? I have learned by trial and error. If this book is about anything, it is that self-teaching in cooking is OK. Time will tell. Not that it matters, but all that follows is true. It is a record of four years of trial and error, fear and loathing.

Thank you to Krystyne for outstanding proofreading. To Gina, whose tireless typesetting made it all possible, thank you.

Finally, a word from Fergus Henderson, *"Do not be afraid of cooking, as your ingredients will know, and misbehave."*

Meat the family.

P.J.B.
Melbourne, 2017.

---

1   Her real name, see also The One True Dog, (The Black Labrador).
2   Its real name.

THE ESSENTIALS

THE HISTORY

The Oxford English Dictionary attributes the origins of the word *"charcuterie"* as being derived from the French words *"char"* and *"cuite"* meaning cooked flesh and defines *"charcuterie"* as, *"Cold cuts of meat, esp. pork, ham, sausages etc. Also, a shop that sells goods of this kind."* Further, a charcutier is defined as *"a pork butcher; a preparer or vendor of charcuterie"*.

Accordingly, if you "prepare" some charcuterie, you are entitled to call yourself a charcutier, so says the Oxford English Dictionary.

Charcuterie, as it is known today and has been for centuries, is nothing if not part of a deep culinary history.

Ruhlmann, in *"Charcuterie"* observed that whilst the Romans were most likely the first to turn pork butchery into a trade, it was the French who brought the greater ingenuity to pig preparations. Whilst the Italians, German and Polish are well known for charcuterie, remember it was the French that really developed it. Indeed, the word charcuterie is a French word. French preparations for charcuterie are many and varied but other cultures such as the Germans, Polish and Italians have all contributed impressive products. They should not be overlooked. I have tried to include them where possible.

Grigson observed that, from 1476 AD, French charcutiers had the right, pursuant to Royal Edict, to sell cooked pork as well as raw pork fat but nothing else. However, they did not have the right to slaughter the pigs they needed *"...which put them at the mercy of the general butchers until the next century."* However at the beginning of the seventeenth century, charcutiers gained the right to sell all cuts of uncooked pork, not just the fat. Interestingly during Lent, when meat sales declined, the charcutier was allowed to sell salted herrings and fish from the sea. By the nineteenth century the charcutiers began selling tripe, formerly the exclusive domain of the tripier.[3] In the twentieth century, noted Grigson *"...all those categories (charcutier, tripier and traiteur[4]) have become blurred at the edges and interdependent"*.

---

3   Those who prepared and sold tripe, not a favourite of mine.
4   One who bought raw meat of all kinds and sold it cooked in sauces as ragouts.

In 1873, Zola unforgettably described a charcutier's window in Les Halles, the great produce market in central Paris:

> *"There were vast quantities of rich, succulent things, things that melt in the mouth... nicely rounded, golden with breadcrumbs, and adorned at the knuckles with green rosettes. Then came the larger dishes – stuffed Strasbourg tongues, with their red, varnished look, the colour of blood next to the pallor of the sausages and pigs' trotters; strings of black pudding coiled like harmless snakes; andouilles piled up in twos and bursting with health; saucissons in little silver copes that made them look like choristers... great cuts of veal and pork, whose jelly was as limpid as crystallized sugar. Towards the back were... large tureens in which the meats and minces lay asleep in lakes of solidified fat...strings of sausages and saveloys hung down symmetrically like the cords and tassels of some opulent tapestry, while behind, threads of caul were stretched out like white lacework...".*

The charcutier's wife, Madame Quenu, Zola observed, somewhat more prosaically had the *"... fine thin and pinky white complexion of those who spend their lives surrounded, by fat and meat ..."*[5].

Elizabeth David described visiting a charcutier in provincial France in the 1960s. She went '... *into Montagne's beautiful blue and cream tiled shop, hidden away in a narrow, unprepossessing street in Lamastre.'* Inside '*... besides the sausages and the hams, the patés and the local ardechois specialities called jambonnettes, cayettes and rosettes there were all sorts of special things for the fetes. There were trays of snails, their shells almost bursting with fresh-looking parsley butter, and Sunday hors-dóeuvres of cones of raw ham alternating with little chicken liver patés molded in sparkling aspic jelly ...; ... the paté made largely with grattons, the little browned scraps which are the residue after the pork fat has been melted down, and which were also the original ingredient of the renowned rillettes de Tours'.* She recounted a conversation with the charcutier's wife, Madame Montrayne who '*... told me how the jambonnettes are cut from the knuckle end of a ham, boned, stuffed with fresh pork meat and sewn up into a fat little cushion shape, how the rosette is called after the particular kind of sausage skin in which it*

---

5   Zola, E. – 'The Belly of Paris' (*'Le Ventre de Paris'*).

is encased, a thick and fat skin which, during the curing process, nourishes the meat inside and gives it its characteristically fresh and moist quality...'.

Charcuterie began as a method of preserving meat during times of plenty so that it could be eaten when times were not so hospitable. Remember that during the early 1800s ice was the only means to store fresh food. It was not until 1911 that General Electric produced a gas powered domestic refrigerator, an electric version not being manufactured until 1927. Putting aside the relative unavailability of electricity outside major cities, why did charcuterie not become obsolete after the invention of refrigeration? The answer is because charcuterie had become, and continues to be, a method of transforming meat into something which is different and enjoyable in its own right.

Charcuterie is nothing if not about history, and to some extent, literature. At least, I like to think so.

THE INGREDIENTS

There are really only three ingredients of any significance in charcuterie namely; pork, pork fat and salt. Everything else is just seasoning and, in reality, not much of the other things are used. The stars of charcuterie are, and always will be pork, pork fat and salt. Understand them and one will go a long way to understanding charcuterie. The only other things to understand are time and patience. Successful charcuterie is the result of careful preparation, obviously, but in fact it is time and air drying which transforms raw meat into quite a different product. However, one should always remember that charcuterie (save for hot smoked products) is raw meat. Treat it with respect. If you do not, then you will regret it.

The Pig

The most important ingredient in almost all charcuterie is fresh pork. Although there have been some times and people who do not agree *"Pork in every form, is indigestible and should never be eaten by persons of weak digestion, by young children, nor by the old and feeble."*[6]

Similarly, Mrs Beeton clearly did not like pigs. She referred to the pig, in a chapter entitled *"General Observations on the Common Hog"* as being *"... known for his gluttony, laziness, and indifference to the character and quality of his food"* and as having the ability to *"... turn with equal gusto to some carrion offal that might excite the forbearance of the unscrupulous cormorant"*. Further, that his *"... coarse and repulsive mode of feeding ... has in every country and language, obtained for him the opprobrium of being 'an unclean animal'"*. If that were not enough, Mrs Beeton went on to state *"From the grossness of his feeding, the large amount of aliment he consumes, his gluttonous way of eating it, from his slothful habits, laziness, and indulgence in sleep, the pig is particularly liable to disease, and especially indigestion, heartburn, and affections of the skin"*. Somewhat grudgingly, after such an excoriation of the poor pig, Mrs Beeton went on to say, *"... no other animal yields man so many kinds and varieties of luxurious food as is supplied to him by the flesh of the hog differently prepared; for almost part of the animal, either fresh, salted, or dried, is used for food; and even those viscera not so employed are of the utmost utility in a domestic point of view"*. I think Mrs Beeton should have spent more time getting to know our porky friends.

---

6   The Picayune's Creole Cook Book (1901).

However, Mrs Beeton described other livestock in glowing terms. As to quadrupeds, to which it seems she referred only to cattle, she opined that they afford '... *food ... shoes ... clothes ... drinking vessels, knife handles ... combs, and boxes ... glue ... venison ... suet, fat, and tallow ... butter and cheese ... This is every part of this animal valuable to man, who has spared no pains to bring it to the highest state of perfection.'*

As to lamb or 'sheep' she said '... *of all the wild or domesticated animals, the sheep is, without exception, the most useful to man as a food, and the most necessary to his health and comfort...'.*

Charcuterie is dependent upon and, would not be as diverse as it is, without the pig. Such a noble creature, loyal and true. Winston Churchill famously said of pigs, *"I am fond of pigs. Dogs look up to us. Cats look down on us. Pigs treat us as equals."* I agree with Mr Churchill. The pig has given us its all for centuries and continues to do so. As is often said, one can use every part of the pig except the squeal. Interestingly, the modern pig is a result of cross breeding the European pig with the Chinese pig. The European pig of the Middle Ages was a *"lean, ridgy and rangy pig beast with bristles down his back."* The Chinese pig was *"small, plump and short legged."* The cross breeding was undertaken by one Robert Bakewell in Leicestershire in about 1760 resulting in the predecessor of today's commercial pig.[7]

Most of us will purchase pork from a retail butcher. It will be of excellent quality albeit somewhat lean. Grigson noted that it was considered that the original cross breed *"... should be too fat to walk more than 100 yards."* She later observed that in the nineteenth century, changed consumer tastes and habits meant the decline of high fat diets. Thereafter the pig *"...grew smaller...now his weight is watched as carefully as any film stars."* A great pity in my veiw. In the end, the pig gives its all, '... *the pigs are strung, in rows, open-mouthed, dignified in martyrs deaths. They hang as stiff as Sunday manners ...'*[8].

Use organic meat if you choose, although its expense may make it uneconomical for the amateur at the outset. I find that perfectly acceptable results can be achieved using non-organic meat but that is a matter for you. Certainly homemade charcuterie will surprise you and be better than much (if not most) mass produced charcuterie. It

7   See Grigson.
8   Topping, A. – *'The Butchers Shop'*.

is, after all, at its best an artisan product produced by artists (one of which you will soon become).

If you have access to your own pigs or boutique pork producers then I am sure the products will be even better.

Insofar as you may be considering purchasing larger quantities of pork or butchering your own pig it may be useful to have some guidance as to the meat quantities which will be produced. Hasheider, writing of commercially available pork in the USA, observed that a 200lb (95kg) animal will dress (i.e. have a carcass weight) at about 72% resulting in a carcass of about 145lbs (65kg). The yield of meat (excluding skin and bone) will be about 60% thereof or 110lbs (50kg). He noted that the largest part of the carcass is the ham which can be about 23% of a live carcass or 18% of a dressed carcass. The side or belly and loin represent about 15% of the dressed carcass.

I assume these figures to be roughly true of commercial pork in Australia. Although, I note "The Australian Pig Annual" (2013-2014) recorded the average pig slaughter weight in Australia as being between 70.3kg and 77.3kg (depending on the time of year), perhaps slightly larger than the carcass upon which Hasheider bases his calculations. Nonetheless, Hasheider's figures may be of some guidance if you are dealing with whole pork carcasses.

In my purchasing experience, a leg of pork will weigh between 10-15kg (including the hock and trotter but before trimming and shaping for prosciutto). A pig's head can weigh in the order of 5kg.

As to how to butcher a pig (if you intend to do so) it is not my area although I confess that I have done a little bit and find it strangely satisfying. Even if I was proficient, which I am not, it is an art which cannot be described adequately by words on a page. It is best to watch butchery as it takes place and the internet is alive with videos of all types of techniques insofar as butchery is concerned. There are many websites but consider videos by Scott Rea[9] or Camas Davis of Portland Meat Collective. Alternatively, Hasheider's book contains very good step by step photographs.

At all events, I have assumed that you are not intending to kill and butcher a pig yourself. The reason being that it is probably best left to the experts. However, if you

---

9   www.youtube.com/user/TheScottReaproject.com

are intending such intrepid activities, I note that Livingston has a very useful tip, *"Scratch the hog down with a corncob until it starts to snore, then dispatch it quickly"*.

He notes that one should not *"... chase the hog or otherwise rile it up before the slaughter"*.

Sounds like a plan to me, but I do not intend to find out if it works.

Reluctant as I am to leave the pig, I defer to Noel Coward:

> *"Any part of the piggy is quite all right with me.*
> *Ham from Westphalia, ham from Parma, Ham as lean as the Dalai Lama.*
> *Ham from Virginia, ham from York, Trotters Sausages, hot roast pork.*
> *Crackling crisp for my teeth to grind on bacon with or without the rind on.*
> *Though humanitarian I'm not a vegetarian.*
> *I'm neither crank nor prude nor prig.*
> *And though it may sound infra dig, any part of the darling pig is perfectly fine with me."*

Prior to concluding in relation to the pig, I should point out that not all charcuterie is pork based. There are recipes for salami made with pork and beef, products using venison and the like. As to these non pork products, Rayner, a British food critic and writer put it very well:

> 'Other animals provide material for charcuterie and cured goods. There are salamis and sausages made from beef and lamb. Of course there are. Some are worth being introduced to. Some are even worth eating, once or twice'.

Salt

The next most important ingredient is salt.

Common salt (sodium chloride, NaCl) is the principal ingredient in the process of meat preservation, in its various forms. It is a method which has been used for centuries. Kurlansky, in his marvellous book *"Salt"*, noted that the ancient Egyptians may have been the first to cure meat and fish with salt. He went on to refer to the earliest written record of preserving fish dating from about 2000BC.

Undoubtedly, salting meat and fish was a method of preserving which was practised well prior to the invention of refrigeration, freezing and canning. Without modern food preservation techniques, the seasonal abundances could not be stored for harder times. Salting and drying fresh produce provided a way in which the product could be available all year round.

Curiously, the process of salt preservation also altered the flavour of the fresh product to a different, and often better, product. As Kurlansky wrote in *"Cod"*, it was a way to transport an abundant product but also changed the product dramatically. Indeed there is a preponderance of recipes for salt cod in Europe due to the fresh product being rarely available in times past.

I deal later with the various types of salt and other related matters.

Fat

Not to be forgotten, is fat. It is essential in sausage and salami production. Salami and sausage production requires fat in order to lubricate and flavour the product. Without fat, or adequate fat, the sausage or salami will be extremely unpalatable.

Pork fat comes in several types, only perhaps four of which are of relevance to a charcutier (of which you are one or soon will be).

Let me turn to the types of fat in a pork carcass.

First, the intramuscular fat present in pork shoulder or pork neck (the latter is pork shoulder but a particular and well defined muscle within the shoulder musculature).[10] This intramuscular fat, when minced as part of the shoulder or neck, gives the correct mixture of fat required for sausages. Although, as you recall, modern commercial pork is bred to be quite lean. Some of the recipes you will find presume by using pork shoulder that a good percentage of fat is present and no fat needs to be added. In my view these recipes are either older and written in a time when pork was indeed much fattier or written in other countries where the product is quite different. Recipes which rely solely on shoulder to give the required ratio of fat are often based on pork carcasses which are not available in Australia (at least on a retail basis). Lean pork

---

10   Books written by our North American cousins call this pork *"butt"* or *"Boston butt"*. I do not know why.

shoulder needs additional fat. The fat: meat ratio required for successful sausage and salami production is about 20 : 80 or 25 : 75. This can be achieved by adding pork belly as a source of fat to pork shoulder if you do not think the shoulder has sufficient fat content. A ratio of pork shoulder/neck: pork belly of 80 : 20 or 75 : 25 will work.

Smaller or boutique pork producers sometimes offer much fatter pigs, referred to as prosciutto pigs or charcuterie pigs. They are not difficult to locate with some modest research. I understand that such products usually attract a significant premium from normal retail pork. I have not used such products often but may well do so in the future.

Flare fat is the fat layer within the abdominal cavity of a pig. It is soft and quite yielding. It appears as a layer inside the rib cage and is easily removable as a single piece. It renders well and is used to seal preparations like rillettes against oxidization.

Caul fat is the diaphanous veined membrane which lines the abdomen of a pig. It is prized for wrapping pork for roasting in such dishes as the English *"faggots"* or Cypriot *"sheftalia"*. It shapes, bastes and protects the meat. A quail wrapped in caul fat and roasted is something not to be overlooked.

Back fat is the most prized fat for charcuterie and is essential for dried sausages and salami production. It is the layer of fat on the back (spine) of a pig. It is hard and pure white. It is the reason why salami has the large white pieces of fat which gives it the visual appeal and unctuous taste. You will have seen it many times without understanding its true utility. It is the layer of fat on pork rib chops which is usually discarded when they are cooked. The thickness of the layer will vary depending on the provenance of the pig. Commercial pork will have back fat of maybe about 1cm if you are lucky. It is not a readily available product because it is reserved for use by butchers in smallgoods preparation. It can be ordered from good butchers without difficulty. In the trade, it is often referred to as *"fatback"*. It freezes very well. If you obtain some from the butcher, get more than you need and freeze the remainder. Cut it into small pieces before you do, so it is easier to dice by hand or to mince.

Interestingly, Grigson wrote that the French identify six different types of pork fat:

- La panne (flare fat).
- Lard de poitrine (hard belly fat under the skin).
- Gras dur (back fat);
- Gras mou or fondant ("*the poorer quality fat immediately touching the lean pork*").[11]
- Crépine (caul fat).
- Grillons ("*the solid scraps remaining after the fat has been rendered from lard*"). [12]

Clever people, the French.

However, for your purposes, intramuscular fat and hard back fat are the only types of fat which really matter.

I cannot conclude without reference, again, to Mrs Beeton. Somehow, Mrs Beeton managed to overcome her significant antipathy to the pig, and after listing the benefits of porcine products such as "*hide, horns and hoofs*", she wrote "*Besides so many benefits and useful services conferred on man by this valuable animal, his fat, in a commercial sense, is quite as important as his flesh, and brings a price equal to the best joints in the carcass. This fat is rendered, or melted out of the caul, or membrane in which it is contained, by boiling water, and, while liquid, runs into prepared bladders, when, under the name of lard, it becomes an article of extensive trade and value*".

Well done Mrs Beeton.

---

11 Grigsons' words, not mine.
12 Grigsons' words, not mine.

THE OTHER THINGS

Whilst on the subject of ingredients, and because they really do not fit in any other sections, let me deal with casings and mould. You have been waiting for this, I just know it.

Casings

Sausages and salamis are all simply minced, salted, seasoned meat in a casing. What then is a *"casing"*? Let me be realistic. *"Casings"* are a euphemism for animal guts. The term also refers to synthetic casings, but real charcutiers (of which you will soon be one) only use natural casings, which brings me back to where I started. Guts.

Thankfully they are cleaned, rinsed and salted before you get them. If not, then I do not want to know about them and neither do you.

They come in different sizes, that is to say, different diameters. Pork and sheep casings are the small intestines of the respective animals. They are the diameter commonly associated with sausages. They are of about 20-30 cm in diameter. Beef intestines, often called middles, are much larger. They are of about 40 cm in diameter but will vary.

There are other products. Sheep 'bungs' are the appendix (caecum)[13] of the animal and are a single, one ended pouch which is used for cotechino or other larger salami type products.

Beef bungs are similar, but larger and used for casings in the matter of bologna, mortadella, culatello or similar. The home charcutier will probably not need to go past sheep/pork casings or sheep bungs.

Sometimes other parts of animal intestines are traditionally used as a casing for the meat. Culatello, for example, is traditionally cured inside a cow or pork bladder. Sadly, bladders (whether of cow or pork) are very difficult to source in this country, which brings me to the next type of casing, namely collagen *"wraps"*. Wraps are sheets of

---

13   As near as I can tell.

natural collagen which, after a brief rehydration, can be used to protect the outside of a product. They are usually secured by an elasticised netting or tied with string.

Regardless of the type or diameter, all casings keep well in the refrigerator if kept in salt and vacuum packed. They also freeze quite well.

Casings are available online and in specialist shops. Your local butcher will also have a supply. He/she will usually be happy to sell whatever length you require. Normal sausage type diameters require about one linear metre of casing to accommodate about 1 kilogram of minced filling.

In this book I generally refer to sausage diameter casings. There are several reasons for this. First, they are easy to handle. Secondly, they use less meat. If you have one link that fails, then you lose less. Thirdly, they are easier and quicker to cure and dry than larger diameter casings. As a beginner you need to know the bad news sooner rather than later. Lastly, because they are more reliable and less likely to fail than larger diameter casings. Try and fill them quite hard such that there are no air pockets inside. Air pockets inside are not a good result. The casings are surprisingly tough and will expand quite a good deal.

Mould

During the dry curing process, the meat will often (but not always) develop an exterior coating of mould. If the curing process has been done correctly and the ambient conditions are correct (temperature and humidity) this is both normal and desirable. The mould which is desirable is a white, chalky, mould which is a form of penicillin. It is a good mould which prevents other moulds from developing and imparts some flavour to the product. It is the white mould of happiness (**WMOH**).

If conditions are not good, other evil moulds will develop. They can be green, red, bluish or even black. These are the moulds of many colours (**MOMC**). They are evil bad moulds and are not to be trusted, they are not your friends and will do the wrong thing by you. Don't you worry about that.

Watch the product carefully to see if mould develops and what colour it is. Any MOMC should be wiped off immediately with cloth using (sparingly) some white

THE OTHER THINGS 21

vinegar diluted with water[14]. If it persists or if the MOMC returns, discard the product. Finding the MOMC on your meat is like breaking wind in a spacesuit – there is nowhere to go. It is in all likelihood spoiled and unsafe to eat. Certainly you do not want to find out if it is safe to eat.

Similarly, a sticky or 'tacky' coating on the meat is not at all good. In all probability it is a film of bacteria and your cure has not worked properly. If you are game enough, try washing it with water or wine and dry it thoroughly. If the sticky coating returns, then the patient is lost. Discard the product immediately.

The WMOH can be wiped off or removed with a nail brush (nylon bristles not metal) if you wish. I prefer to leave it, the WMOH looks authentic and makes one feel like a proper charcutier. However, even with WMOH if it starts to go sticky, then all may not be lost. Give it a wipe with a vinegar solution. This can sometimes happen if the product is stored in the *"crisper"* of your refrigerator. It is too humid for them and they do not like it. Vacuum seal and/or freeze.

You will find that, over time, your curing chamber becomes inoculated with mould (hopefully). This means that after about one week or so, the meat will show signs of the mould. This is either good news or it is bad news. If your chamber is inoculated with the WMOH it is a joyous thing. If the chamber is inoculated with the MOMC it is not so joyous. If the latter then you should clean the curing chamber carefully with a solution of vinegar and water (say, 50:50) to ensure that the MOMC is discouraged. If the WMOH seems to be living in your curing chamber then treat it with respect. It is your friend, wipe off any spillage drips, or excess salt with some warm water. Nothing more.

Treat any mould with a significant degree of caution.

---

14   About 10% vinegar: water solution by volume. Not too strong or your charcuterie will taste like vinegar.

SALT PRESERVATION

Salt preservation of meat is successful because it creates an environment in which bacteria find it difficult to exist. As you are well aware, bacteria acts upon meat to spoil it for human consumption. The process of air drying further creates an environment in which bacteria cannot survive, by reducing the water content of the meat.

Salt both reduces water content in meat and creates an antibacterial environment by osmosis. Osmosis is the process by which the lower salt environment in meat cells migrates across the cell membranes into the higher salt environment of the brine or salt cure. In so doing, liquid from inside the cell is transported into the brine or cure. This is the reason for the liquid which accumulates in the container during a salt cure.

In time the salt concentration inside and outside the cell wall is equalised, or equilibrated. However, if this is allowed to occur, the meat will become as salty as the brine or salt cure. This is usually an undesirable result, except in the case of hard dried/salted meat like beef jerky or salt cod. The products become completely stiff and inedible. They require rehydration over several days to leach out (by osmosis) the salt in the meat.

Therefore care is taken in most recipes to avoid the meat becoming too salty. Different recipes call for different curing and brining times as required.

McGee explained the effects of salt at a molecular level. He opined that high salt concentrations cause the normally tightly bunched protein filaments in the muscle cells to separate into individual filaments, which are too small to scatter light: so the normally opaque muscle tissue becomes translucent. The same unbunching also weakens the muscle fibres, while at the same time dehydration makes the tissue denser and more concentrated: hence the close but tender texture. Some of the muscles' biochemical machinery survives intact, in particular the enzymes that break flavourless proteins down into savory peptides and amino acids, which over the course of months may convert a third or more of the meat protein to flavour molecules. The concentration of mouth-filling, meaty glutamic acid rises ten to twenty fold, and as in cheese, so much of the amino acid tyrosine is freed that it may form small white crystals. In addition, the unsaturated fats in pig muscle break apart and react to form hundreds of volatile compounds, some of them characteristic of the aroma of melon (a traditional and chemically fitting accompaniment to ham!), apple, citrus, flowers, fresh cut grass and butter. Other compounds react with the products of protein breakdown to give nutty, caramel flavours normally found only in cooked meats (concentration compensates for the subcooking temperature).

Gerrard, an English master butcher wrote many books on butchery and smallgoods during the 1960s. His honorifics read as follows; *"MBE, F. Inst. M, M. Inst. R, M.R.S.H."*. He is described in one book as '*Gold Medallist of the Worshipful Company of Butchers; Diploma of the National Federation of Meat Traders; Past President, The Institute of Meat*'. A bloke that knows his stuff. In one of those books[15] he described the process of salting meat. He observed that, when a piece of meat is placed in a strong solution of salt the fluids in the meat begin to flow out and mix with the salt solution. Meanwhile the salt has begun to penetrate the meat and to bring about changes within the meat. These changes slow down the outward flow of fluid from the meat, and finally the flow is reversed. Water as well as salt now flows into the meat from the strong salt solution. The stronger this solution the longer it takes before the reversal of flow takes place. If solid salt or solid sugar is used, no action takes place until they have dissolved in the fluid exuding from the meat. Thereafter the changes are similar to those occurring when meat is immersed in strong solutions but occur more slowly, the rate depending upon the speed at which the fluid can exude from the meat.

Gerrard's explanation may be more approachable than that of McGee, but it is the thought that counts.

Generally speaking, charcuterie requires a salt cure of between 2.5% and 3.5% by weight to be successful. I prefer 3% in order to be sure that bacteria cannot survive in the preparation. This does not give an overly salty result but there are many recipes which use salt at a rate of 2% to 2.5%. In my view, anything less than 2.5% is just seasoning. In time you will adjust the percentage of salt to suit your taste but I think 2.5% to 3% is a good place to be.

The accurate calculation of salt and Curing Salt is critical. Recipes will often refer to the amount of salt as a measure (e.g. tablespoons). This is confusing and apt to produce unsatisfactory results. I prefer, and this modest book mainly uses, salt and Curing Salt quantities by reference to a percentage of meat weight.

---

15   "Sausages and Smallgoods Production".

Example 1: 3% salt means calculate the ratio of salt to meat by reference to the weight of meat in grams. 1kg of meat = 1,000g. Therefore, 3% salt = 1000 x .03 = 3g.

Example 2: If the meat is not exactly 1kg – say, weight of meat = 1.65kg = 1,650g. Therefore, salt at 3% = 1650 x .03 = 4.95g.

Depending upon the type of product being prepared, you will either need a small or large amount of salt. The first issue is what type of salt to use. Salt is available in many forms but they are all exactly the same product, sodium chloride (NaCl). The common varieties in Australia are fine sea salt, flossy salt and coarse sea salt. Let me deal with each in turn.

Sea salt usually has no additives and comes in either a relatively fine form or in a coarse form. Flossy salt is a salt with a medium size, flaky crystal. These are the three main salts used for charcuterie. It is a matter of preference which is used. The larger crystals are sometimes used when curing pieces of meat for longer times. It is said that these do not penetrate the meat as well and therefore the meat will not become overly salty. Whereas the finer sea salt may give an overly salty result. 'Table salt' (the type you normally buy at the supermarket) is a fine crystalline sea salt which may contain iodine and an anticaking agent.

American, and to some extent, European books mostly refer to kosher salt. I understand that Kosher salt usually has no additives and is of a larger crystal size than table salt. It can be difficult to source in Australia. The equivalent is probably Flossy salt.

I have used different types of salt depending on availability, including table salt. I have not found a discernible difference in the resultant product.

> NOTE: If you are curing a pork leg for prosciutto, you will need more salt than you might think. A 10kg pork leg will require (depending on the size of your container) up to 20kg of salt to completely cover it. Accordingly, use the smallest container which will accommodate your meat covered completely in by salt. You can purchase salt in 20kg or 25kg bags from specialist suppliers (see suppliers). Try and use the smallest container that you can. All that matters is a good coverage of salt.

Methodology

The methodology of salt preservation and curing is simplicity itself. The meat is either rubbed in salt, or completely immersed in salt or brined in a salt and water solution. Each produces slightly different results and each is used to achieve slightly different products.

Salt rubs and salt immersions are often used when the product is to be air dried. Brines are often used when the product is to be smoked, in order to avoid excessive desiccation during the process.

A salt rub technique is best achieved in a resealable plastic bag so the meat can be overhauled[16] (turned) daily.

Salt immersions are best undertaken in a rigid food grade container such as a plastic container with a sealed lid. The meat does not need to be overhauled due to the amounts of salt used.

Brines are best achieved in a rigid plastic container to avoid liquid leakage. They do not need to be overhauled. However, the meat needs to be weighed down to ensure complete immersion in the solution. A bag of water or a freezer ice block will work quite well.

> *NOTE: Do not re-use salt or brine after an immersion has been completed.*
> *It is now contaminated by meat juices and cannot be re-used safely.*
> *Salt is very cheap, discard it and use fresh salt for the next preparation.*

---

16   See 'Techniques'.

How much salt

Modern diets eschew the use of salt, and it may be said that salt cured meat, like charcuterie, is an undesirable part of today's diet. In that regard I note that A.D. Livingstone wrote (over 30 years ago) of the traditional American salt pork breakfast:

> *"These days we are constantly told that animal fat is not good for us. If you tend to eat too much of a good thing and have no self-control, or if you are under a doctor's orders, proceed at your peril."*

The answer, it seems to me, is that salt consumption is a question of moderation. Salted meat may have once been a large part of diets but it is not now. These products are a fascinating part of history and a culinary triumph. Taken in moderation, they are unlikely to do you any harm. Sadly, I do not do moderation very well.

As a rule, I have used 3% salt and 0.3% Curing Salt by reference to the weight of meat. I reckon that is about right. It is a matter for you.

Nitrates and nitrites/Curing Salts

The use of nitrates/nitrites in charcuterie has had some recent controversy. However, prior to dealing with the controversy (insofar as I can), let me explain what they are and how they work.

Kurlansky in *"Salt"* observed that as early as the 16th century, nitrates were used in cured meats to make them a reddish colour. Nitrates were found in some salt (as an impurity), in gunpowder or in its other form, called saltpetre. Historically, nitrates and nitrites have been used in charcuterie, whether deliberately or not, for thousands of years.

Meat colour is as a result of a protein, myoglobin, present in red meat. Once exposed to air, the protein binds to oxygen to create oxymyoglobin, which is a bright red colour. Further oxidization of oxymyoglobin results in metmyoglobin which is a brownish colour. This is the colour associated with red meat which is not as fresh.

Nitrates and nitrites change to nitric oxide which binds with myoglobin and gives meat the pink colour seen in cured meat. Nitrates and nitrites also create an environment which is hostile to bacteria, notably clostridium botulinum. Clostridium botulinum is extremely toxic and is the organism which causes botulism when contaminated food is consumed. Nitrates and nitrites also retard the development of other harmful bacteria like salmonella and listeria.

Nitrates and nitrites also retard rancidity by inhibiting lipid (fat) oxidation. The concentrations used are extremely low, usually at a rate of 0.3% by weight.

Nitrates and nitrites are naturally occurring in many foods which are consumed. Celery for example, is rich in natural nitrates and nitrites. Celery salt or celery juice is sometimes used to cure meat and which results in a similar product as with nitrate/nitrite salts. You will now treat with some scepticism products which proudly proclaim to be "nitrate free" but which are full of celery juice.

Sodium nitrite and sodium nitrate are sold under various names – Curing Salt, Prague Powder or Pink Salt to mention a few. The products are a mix of sodium nitrate or sodium nitrate and salt. They are dyed a pale pink colour to avoid confusion with normal sea salt (hence they are referred to as *"pink salt"*). In this book I refer to them as Curing Salt No. 1 or Curing Salt No. 2 respectively.

There are two types of Curing Salts, Curing Salt No. 1 or Curing Salt No. 2. Curing Salt No. 1 contains 6.25% nitrate. Curing Salt No. 1 is used for shorter term products. Curing Salt No. 2 contains 5.67% nitrite and 3.63% nitrate. Curing Salt No. 2 is used for longer cured products such as salami or prosciutto. The reason being that sodium nitrite is the active ingredient in the preserving process. It is converted from sodium nitrate. Curing Salt No. 2 provides a longer term cure by conversion of sodium nitrate into sodium nitrite over time.[17]

In some countries the more concentrated form of nitrate known as saltpetre is available. It was originally the source of nitrates for preservation of food. In Australia it is not widely available and difficult to purchase because of its role in explosives manufacture. If you try and buy it, I think stern men in dark suits and official business will quickly come your way. Good luck convincing them you are not

---

17   See Ruhlmann's *"Salumi"* for a very technical explanation.

a backyard terrorist. Recipes from Europe or North America (usually the older ones) refer to saltpetre being added (see for example Grigson *"Add a pinch of saltpetre"*). They are not helpful to an Australian charcutier in 2017. Whereas Curing Salts are available online in Australia, and other less fortunate countries , quite readily.[18]

A word of warning, some salts are naturally pink coloured, for example, *"Murray River"* pink salt or *"Himalayan"* pink salt. They are not Curing Salts, they are just naturally pink coloured salt. Whether they contain nitrates or nitrites, I do not know. Neither do I know why they are naturally pink coloured (if indeed they are). However, they should not be used as a substitute for Curing Salts. They are not Curing Salts. If you use them as a substitute for Curing Salts, you may get sick and die. It is a matter for you.

As an aside, because I am interested in such things, crustacea, molluscs and shellfish do not have red blood. Why, I hear you ask? The answer is because they use a copper based molecule for oxygen transport. Mammals (like pigs) use an iron based oxygen transport system (haemoglobin). However not all animals evolved to use an iron based oxygen transport system. Haemocyanins are the proteins which transport oxygen in many invertebrates (notably insects (arthropods), crabs/prawns, (crustaceans) and shellfish (molluscs)). These consist of two copper atoms which bind to a single oxygen molecule. The unoxygenated form is colourless whereas the oxygenated form is a blueish colour. That is the reason why crustaceans, molluscs and arthropods do not have red blood. Their blood being based on copper not iron, is colourless or has a bluish tinge. There are a number of reasons why this was a good evolutionary decision for arthropods, crustaceans and molluscs. There are a number of reasons why it was not. But I digress, let me return to nitrates.

None of the above explains how some cured meats, which do not use nitrates/nitrites achieve the pink colour associated with the use of Curing Salts. I was puzzled by this but assumed that it was a result of naturally occurring amounts of nitrates in salt. As usual, and as with most things, I was wrong. McGee put that theory to rest as follows: *"Sea salt does contain nitrate and nitrite impurities, but not enough to affect ham color. Recently, Japanese scientists found that the stable red pigment of these hams is not nitrosomyoglobin, and its formation seems associated with the presence of particular ripening bacteria (Staphylococcus carnosus and caseolyticus)".*

---

18   See Suppliers.

The debate about nitrates

The addition of nitrites and nitrates to food has recently (in the last 40 years) been somewhat controversial. Apparently, this controversy follows a study in the 1970s which identified a link between nitrates and cancer.[19]

Sindelar provided a useful summary of the debate and subsequent quelling of the controversy in a scientific paper entitled, *"Human Safety Controversies surrounding nitrate and nitrite in the diet"*.[20] Sindelar pointed out that after the controversial 1970s study, there were a series of other studies including one by an Inter-Agency Working Group convened by the United States Food and Drug Administration ("**FDA**"). The Inter-Agency Working Group responded to the FDA in 1980 *"...that no demonstration could be found that the increased incidence of nitrites in* [tumours in rats] *were induced by the ingestion of sodium nitrite."* Sindelar also pointed out that during this period a special National Academy of Sciences ("**NAS**") committee was created to comprehensively review the available literature and risk assessments and information on nitrate and nitrite. This extensive review resulted in two reports by the NAS entitled *"The health effects of nitrate, nitrite and N-nitroso compounds"* and *"Alternatives to the current use of nitrite in foods"* published in 1981 and 1982 respectively. Sindelar noted that these two exhaustive reports addressed the concerns of nitrite usage among regulatory authorities. After the release of these reports and a change to USDA regulations, the public and regulatory controversy around nitrite *"subsided"*.

Some authors of books in this area use nitrates and nitrites. Some do not. Those who use Curing Salts include Boetticher, Ruhlmann, Kowalski, Marianski, Kutas, Turan , Cottenceau and Weiss. Wildsmith, Vecchio and Grigson use saltpetre. Lamb and Livingston do not use nitrates at all. Most books in this area acknowledge that in high quantities, nitrates and nitrites can be toxic. All who use them do so to avoid bacterial contamination of their products (amongst other things). Boetticher referred to the 1970s study as *"... the nitrate scare ..."*. Ruhlmann observed that *" ... the evidence suggests that in limited quantities, nitrites are not a substantial health concern ... "*. Weiss quoted the American Medical Association who opined that the *" ... risk of developing cancer as a result of consumption of nitrite-containing food is negligible ... "*. Marianski wrote that that studies referred to above *" ... started a lot of unnecessary panic in the 1970s about the harmful effects of nitrates to our health ... "*.

---

19   See W. Lijnsky, S. S. Epstein, *"Nitrosamines are environmental carcinogens"*, Nature 225 (1970) 20.
20   Nitric Oxide 26 (2012) 259-266.

As with all things, sodium nitrite can be toxic. If you ingest enough of it, it will kill you, don't you worry about that. The human toxic dose of sodium nitrite is 71 mg/kg. This means a person weighing 100 kg would need to ingest 7.1g of sodium nitrite to administer a potentially lethal dose. Remember that most of the recipes in this book use 0.3% Curing Salt No. 2. That means if you consumed 1kg of the product in one sitting, you would ingest 3g of Curing Salt No. 2. Curing Salt No. 2 contains 5.67% nitrite. Accordingly, 1kg of product using 0.3% Curing Salt No. 2 contains 0.17g of sodium nitrite. You would, therefore, have to ingest in excess of 123.45kg in one sitting to achieve a lethal dose of 7.1g/kg for a 100kg person. Putting aside metabolic rates, solubility, and all the other stuff; it can be seen that a charcuterie plate is not a health risk, at least insofar as sodium nitrite is concerned (unless it is a really, really big plate of charcuterie).

Make up your own mind.

I note that, somewhat surprisingly, Grigson writing in 1967, observed:

> *"French saltpêtre, nitrate de potassium, is important in the making of brine because it gives meat … an attractive rosy appearance, when otherwise it would be a murky greyish brown. It has no value whatsoever as a preservative, and should be used in tiny quantities as it will harden the meat, a tendency which is counteracted by the addition of sugar to the brine."* [21]

Vecchio, in 2013, in promotion of the use of saltpetre, wrote as follows:

> *"The ancient designation of potassium nitrate is the traditional and still preferred curing agent in combination with salt and a small quantity of sugar. The natural curing process implies bacterial activity and time. In faster modern techniques it can be replaced, directly with nitrite of sodium, acting without the intervention of the curing flora. The modern shortcut, though, is lacking in aroma and flavour. There is nothing like the good old saltpetre, bacteria and time for quality."*

---

21   I note that Grigson, and Vecchio (following), refer to the curative agent as potassium nitrate. It is sodium nitrate.

You can choose to use Curing Salts or not. I use them because I am an amateur charcutier without access to expensive curing chambers, pH meters and laboratory testing. I do not want to take any chances and do not want to get botulism or anything else for that matter.

As near as I can tell, it is safe to consume products which have been produced using small amounts of Curing Salts. It is a personal choice. For my part, I just do not want to get sick and die. It is a matter for you.

SMOKING

Some of the recipes in this book require the charcuterie to be smoked. Many books in the area discuss smoking either by reference to *"cold"* smoking or *"hot"* smoking. Smoking of meat has long been used to flavour and preserve meat. It is a useful technique, albeit a bit tricky. How does it work, I hear you ask? Well, chère Reader, I am glad that you asked. McGee observed that burning wood transforms the components (chemicals) into a variety of compounds which are flavourful. He noted that the sugars in cellulose and hemicellulose break apart into many of the same molecules found in caramel, with sweet, fruity, flowery, bready aromas. The interlocked phenolic rings of lignin break apart from each other into a host of smaller, volatile phenolics and other fragments, which have the specific aromas of vanilla and clove as well as a generic spiciness, sweetness, and pungency.

Further, McGee went on to state that wood smoke contains many chemicals that slow the growth of microbes. Among them are formaldehyde and acetic acid (vinegar) and other organic acids, thanks to which the pH of smoke is a very microbe-unfriendly 2.5. Many of the phenolic compounds in wood smoke are also antimicrobials, and phenol itself is a strong disinfectant. The phenolic compounds are also effective antioxidants and slow the development of rancid flavours in smoked meats and fish.

So much for the technical stuff. The question remains, what temperature should I smoke meat at, either internally or externally, so that it is safe?

The United States Department of Agriculture (**USDA**) publishes safe internal temperatures for various meats as follows:
- beef, pork, veal and lamb – 62.8℃;
- ground meat – 71.1℃; and
- ham (fresh or smoked) – 62.8℃.[22]

---

22   http://www.fsis.usda.gov/wps/portal/fsis/topics/food-safety-education

McLagan in *"Cooking on the Bone"* also usefully provided internal temperatures for cooking meat as follows:

- Pork – loin 65℃; other cuts 68-71℃.
- Poultry – duck 82℃.
- Lamb – 68℃.

Allow me to briefly explain the smoking process and the difference between *"hot"* and *"cold"* smoking.

Cold smoking

Cold smoking is a technique for imparting flavour and curing the meat at temperatures below 30℃. Some cold smokers operate at even lower temperatures, say, between 20℃ or 30℃. The design of the smoker is such that the smoking chamber is not heated. The smoke is generated externally (usually) to the chamber by a duct such that it is cold when entering the chamber.

Many cultures and countries have a rich history of cold smoking. However the risk with cold smoking is that the process does not generate sufficient heat to kill bacteria and pathogens which may be present in the meat.

Harmful bacteria like listeria monocytogenes (listeria) which causes listeriosis and clostridium botulinum (botulinum) which causes botulism, will be destroyed if the meat is cooked to the temperatures involved in normal cooking. Cold smoking is risky because it does not achieve these temperatures. The (USA) National Center for Home Food Perseveration in its *"Guide and Literature Review Series: Smoking and Curing"*[23] stated that *"Most food scientists cannot recommend cold-smoking methods because of the inherent risks..."*. It is best left to the experts and I do not recommend it to the amateur charcutier.

Hot smoking

Hot smoking on the other hand, both cooks and preserves meat. As noted above, the internal temperature of the meat is critical to the success of the process. If the meat does not achieve an internal temperature sufficient to cook and kill bacteria, then it

---

23   http://nchfp.uga.edu/publications/nchfp/lit_rev/cure_smoke_rev.html

will not keep and will not be safe. The requisite internal temperature for hot smoking will depend upon the meat.

I have included recipes for hot smoked pork which generally require an internal temperature of at least 71°C. This is a minimum which you should achieve, a bit more is probably good. Remember that, in all probability, your thermometer may not be as accurate as that used by the USDA. Therefore, give yourself a bit more leeway, just to be safe.

Hot smoking both cooks and flavours the meat with very acceptable results. It is useful for meat and fish. The meat or fish is brined first in a salt/sugar solution together with the desired aromatics for additional flavour. The reason the meat/fish is brined is to ensure that the product is safe even though it is *"cooked"* during the process and that it does not dry out too much.

Conclusion

Leave cold smoking to the experts.

Hot smoking can be a bit tricky and is somewhat time consuming. However, the results are spectacular and quite different from unsmoked charcuterie. It is well worth the effort and the modest investment in a smoker.

If you are prepared to give it a go, hot smoking will open up a completely different world of charcuterie.

THE EQUIPMENT

Not a great deal of equipment is required for charcuterie. Most of it is common household kitchen equipment although some is a little specialised. Fortunately the equipment, even if specialised, is readily available and can be found in domestic versions.

Emilé Zola[24] described the equipment and kitchen of the charcutier, Madame Quenu, at Les Halles in 1873. He wrote that the walls of the gaslit room were covered with blue and white tiles to the height of a man's head. On the left stood the big cast-iron stove with its three holes across the top on which three squat cooking pots were firmly set, their bottoms black with soot. At the end was a small range fitted with an oven and a smoking-place; it was used for grilling. Above the oven, high over the skimming-spoons, the ladles, and the long-handled forks, a row of numbered drawers contained grated crusts, both fine and coarse, soft breadcrumbs, spices, cloves, nutmegs, and peppers. The chopping block, a huge mass of oak, leaned heavily against the wall, its hollowed surface covered in cuts and indentations. Several items of equipment were attached to it, an injector pump, a stuffer, and a mincing machine, all of which, with their cogs and cranks, gave the place a strange, mysterious appearance, suggesting some devil's kitchen. Then, all round the walls, on wooden shelves, and even under the tables, were piles of pots and pans, dishes, buckets, plates, various tin utensils, a battery of deep saucepans, wide-mouthed funnels, racks of knives and choppers, rows of skewers and needles – a whole world downed in fat.

You will observe that the equipment from 1873 is not substantially different from that which I describe below. This is timeless stuff. You are a custodian of history.

Knives

Good knives are important but not essential. If you are intending to undertake some basic butchery and/or mince your own meat, you will require good knives. On that assumption, the basic knives required are at least a 20cm butcher or chef knife, a 12-15cm curved boning knife, and a 8-10 cm paring knife. A 15-18 cm skinning knife is a useful tool if you intend to remove a lot of pork skin.

---

24   Zola, E. *"The Belly of Paris"* (*'Le Ventre de Paris'*)

There are many brands of knives and many different qualities and prices. Buy the best knives that you can afford. However, the most expensive are not necessarily the easiest to use and to keep sharp. The harder the steel (measured on the Rockwell scale "**HRC**") the more expensive, usually, is the knife. The good news is that hard steel knives wear very well and keep an edge well. But the bad news is that they are very difficult to sharpen, unless your technique is very good. Even so, a mechanical knife sharpener is usually required. Knives made from softer steel may not wear as well but will wear perfectly adequately for domestic use. They will keep an edge well and are very easy to sharpen with a sharpening steel. I prefer knives which are easier to keep sharp. The good news is that they are much cheaper than knives made of really hard steel. My favourite knife at the moment is a cheap mild steel knife; it is not made of stainless steel. It gets a bit rusty but is easily cleaned and after one or two passes on the sharpening steel it is razor sharp.

I like knives. I have lots of them. I have many good cooking knives. They are all German. They are heavy and made of the hardest steel. They will last a lifetime. The problem is that they are used and abused by evil persons in my family who do not appreciate them. They are used until they are so blunt that they require professional sharpening to become useful once more. I am not happy about this. To that end, I purchased six butchers knives of various sizes and shapes. They are very good stainless steel knives but not of the hardest steel. Accordingly, they can be sharpened quite easily. They live in a secret place that only I know about. I retrieve them when I am undertaking serious butcher stuff. I use them and then I sharpen them. Then I wash them and return them to their secret resting place. This is the stuff of happiness.

Knife sharpeners

A sharpening steel is essential. Again, buy the best quality you can afford. Diamond steels are quite affordable and give the best results but do wear out, contrary to what you may think. The diamond dust with which they are impregnated separates from the steel and they become 'blunt'. Ceramic sharpening *"steels"* last longer than diamond steels but are brittle and can get notches or nicks in the surface in normal use which impairs their function.

If you are really serious about sharpening your knives, consider a whetstone. Whetstones, or stones, are manufactured rectangular composite blocks of abrasive grits. They usually have a coarse and a fine side. The knife is rubbed along the block in a continuous motion which sharpens the edge. Water or oil is used for lubrication. They are somewhat old fashioned but very satisfying to use. The quality of the edge which results from honing on a whetstone is unsurpassed in my view by any mechanical sharpening, including using a steel. My father showed me how to hone a knife using a whetstone when I was young. My pocket knife and fishing knives were like razors as a result. A little too sharp sometimes. I still have one of his whetstones and really enjoy using it.

Real charcutiers do not use electric knife sharpeners. Not ever.

Meat mincer

If you intend to mince your own meat, fat or skin, then you will need a mincer.[25]

Manual mincers are cheap and readily available. Mincing meat by hand is quite laborious, particularly if you are mincing a reasonable quantity of meat, fat or skin. It is satisfying nontheless.

Domestic electric mincers (say 300-600w) are not very expensive and are much easier than manual mincing. In my experience they will perform an adequate job of mincing meat provided it is cut into manageable cubes (not more than 2.5cm). Sadly, they find skin and fat to be somewhat more challenging but can do it if cut small enough to start.

Mincing attachments for food mixers (not food processors) are also available but can be less efficient in my experience. I have one. I used it once or twice. It was less than satisfying.

Small commercial quality mincers (about 0.5 hp)[26] are more expensive than their domestic counterparts but perform the tasks easily. They are significantly more expensive than a domestic mincer. It all depends on how much you intend to mince and how much you are prepared to invest in your hobby. Do not be tempted to use a food processor to mince meat. You will regret it. It will pulverise the meat into a

---

25   Described by our North American friends as a 'grinder'.
26   For some reason commercial mincers quote power in "horsepower" not "watts". Whereas domestic mincers are rated in 'watts' of power.

paste. The easy solution is to ask your butcher to prepare the meat, fat and skin for you. They are generally pretty obliging chaps and they need your support in these troubled times.

Scales

It is very important to weigh the meat and the ingredients carefully. The meat must be weighed because in many recipes a basic test for completion of the air drying process is when the meat has lost at least 30% of its weight. The ingredients must be weighed because, especially for salt and Curing Salts, the ratio of salt and Curing Salt to meat is critical.

There are several types of scales which are useful, each having a different utility. Large kitchen scales of the mechanical type are good for weighing larger quantities of meat. These are scales which will weigh, say, up to 5kg with a large, easy to read dial. Larger pieces of meat can be weighed and the large dial makes it easy to record the weight.

Digital scales are very useful and will also usually weigh up to 5kg. However, they are more difficult to read and large pieces of meat will often obscure the dial of the scales. They are very accurate and great for measuring dry ingredients or smaller quantities of meat.

Smaller digital scales, which measure in 0.1g increments (often only up to 1kg) are also useful. These are sometimes called jewellers scales. They are especially useful for weighing Curing Salt. The amount of Curing Salt is calculated by reference to the weight of meat. It is undesirable to overuse the Curing Salt. Amounts can be precisely calculated using the jewellers scale.

Spring scales or hanging scales are scales which are suspended from a fixed point and have a hook underneath. They come in all sizes. Butchers use really big ones for weighing meat carcasses or pieces thereof. For your purposes a small one which weighs up to, say, 15kg is useful weighing a whole pork leg when making prosciutto. The pork leg will be too large for normal kitchen scales but a spring scale (slip a wooden spoon through the top ring to hold it easier) will do the trick nicely. They are inexpensive and readily available.

Kitchen scales, both mechanical and digital, are readily available from cookware suppliers and are quite inexpensive. Jewellers scales can be found online, they too are quite inexpensive.

Smokers

It is not necessary to have a smoker in order to make charcuterie, although some types of charcuterie do benefit from the smoking process.

At its most basic, a smoker is a chamber into which the meat is placed, thereafter wood smoke is introduced into the chamber.

A cold smoker is one in which the smoke is usually generated externally to the chamber. Smoke is introduced to the chamber at very low temperatures (between 20℃ to 30℃) by ducting or a conduit. By the time the smoke reaches the chamber it has lost its heat, hence the term *"cold smoking"*.

A hot smoker is one in which the temperature of the chamber is at least about 85℃. The smoke too, will be at around that temperature. Hence the term *"hot"* smoking. The smoke generator is within the smoking chamber. Accordingly the smoke is at approximately the same temperature as the ambient temperature within the smoking chamber.

A smoker can be purpose built for larger operations or constructed using an old refrigerator, filing cabinet or steel garbage bin. A kettle barbeque makes a simple smoker using a small steel smoke generator (a container to hold some wood chips or wood sawdust). Small smokers are also available from fishing equipment retailers. They are small stainless steel boxes which use sawdust. They are usually heated with a methylated spirit burner used under the smoking chamber. They are perfectly good for small quantities of fish or meat. They do not cost much to purchase. If you really want to, you can use a domestic oven or a wok for hot smoking. The principles are the same, you need a heat source and a smoke source. However, it will make your oven or wok smell like smoke for a very long time afterwards. It is not something that I am in a hurry to try, nor should you.

Alternately, there are purpose built domestic smokers available. These operate on gas or electricity and are about the size of an under-bench refrigerator. They are reasonably expensive but not out of the question for a domestic charcutier (which, of course, you yearn to be). Those using electricity have the ability (usually) to quite accurately set the temperature. That is a very good feature. Whereas, gas powered smokers are not as easy to control regarding temperature. Retailers of barbeque equipment will be able to guide you depending on your needs.

I use a basic electric smoker which produces very good results. It has a digital temperature controller which works well. The built in thermometer is augmented by the addition of a digital thermometer with a probe. Digital thermometers are cheap and very accurate for domestic purposes.

The types of commercially available wood chips can vary quite significantly but do tend to be European varieties rather than Australian timbers. Certainly strongly aromatic wood like Eucalyptus should not be contemplated. Wood chips are available online or from barbeque equipment retailers.

The basic types of wood chips and their differences are as follows:
- Pecan (a subtle flavour) – poultry, fish and beef.
- Hickory (quite strong, good with bacon) – poultry, pork and beef.
- Apple (light and quite sweet) – poultry, pork and beef.
- Oak (quite strong, good with beef) – poultry, pork and beef.
- Mesquite (quite distinctive flavour) – poultry fish and pork.

Insofar as Australian timbers for woodchips are concerned they are too strong, in my view.

You can use trimmings from your fruit trees or grape vines if you wish. Just make sure the wood is completely dried and not green. However, as an amateur, I think it is best to stay with commercial wood chips.

Meat thermometer

A digital meat thermometer is required for measuring the internal temperature of meat when hot smoking. Rather than open the door of the smoker to check the temperature [27], a thermometer with a probe is best. The probe will constantly record

---

27   The heat loss slows down the process dramatically and should be avoided.

the temperature. It can be checked either from a base unit outside the smoker or with a remote device. The remote devices are great and mean you can check the temperature from inside the house, often up to 20-30 metres away from the smoker.

These products are available from barbeque shops and online. They are not expensive and well worth the small investment.

Hygrometer

A small, digital combined thermometer and hygrometer (the latter measures relative humidity) is essential to measure ambient conditions (temperature and humidity) in a curing chamber. These devices are available at specialist brewing suppliers, salami making suppliers or online. A good one will record the current conditions as well as the historical highest and lowest temperature and humidity. It is very useful to know if there are significant variations in your curing chamber. They are not expensive and provide some peace of mind as to the ambient conditions.

Meat slicer

An electric meat slicer of the type used in a delicatessen, is an investment worth considering. The charcuterie you will produce is often best consumed when thinly sliced. It is possible to hand slice the charcuterie. A knife will produce inconsistent results, is very time consuming and apt to end up in tears. An electric slicer produces better, quicker results. It is also safer than trying to cut paper thin slices.

Unfortunately, there are no other devices which can replicate the thin slices produced by a meat slicer. A mandolin, used for thinly slicing vegetables, will not achieve the same results.

Electric meat slicers are reasonably expensive, a good domestic quality slicer may cost up to $500-$600. A substantial investment perhaps, but one you will not regret.

Meat slicers can also be beautiful pieces of industrial art. The manual flywheel meat slicer is a thing of beauty and desire. Well, they are for me, at least. They are best described as "retro" pieces of industrial art. They come from Italy or Germany, they are usually red in colour (they go faster than other coloured slicers) and I really, really, really want one.

If you purchase one, then I know that the two of you will be very happy together.

Make sure I can come too.

Sausage filler

The seasoned meat mixture, whether for sausage or salami, must be squeezed into a casing. The process cannot be achieved without specialist equipment. A funnel and a length of casing, for example, will not work no matter how hard you try. Happily, there are several choices when considering such equipment.

A sausage filler consists of a round chamber and a mechanical piston. The piston can be driven electrically but is usually manual for domestic sausage fillers. The piston forces the meat from the chamber into a nozzle which is loaded with casing. They are available in several sizes depending on the amount of meat to be placed in the chamber. A 3 kg size filler is adequate for small production. They are reasonably expensive, say $300 at least, but make the process extremely easy. This can be important at the end of a long day butchering, mincing, mixing and seasoning.

Sausage fillers come in two different designs. Vertical fillers in which the chamber and pistons are vertical and the meat is extracted horizontally. Horizontal fillers are designed so that they operate in a horizontal fashion. Both appear to function perfectly well, although a horizontal filler uses more bench space. I use a horizontal sausage stuffer mainly because I have one. Although it just seems to me that a 90 degree bend in the whole mincing process, with the pressures involved, is not a happy thing.

My sausage filler is of 4kg capacity but it is Italian and, most importantly, it is red. We have enjoyed quality time together. No more need be said.

There are alternatives, however. Electric mincers will also perform the same function. All that is required is that the blade and die are removed. The seasoned mixture is fed through the mincer (without the blade or plate (die)) which forces it into a casing loaded on a nozzle. This works well, albeit considerably slower than the dedicated sausage stuffer. It is quite acceptable for small quantities of meat (say, 1 kilogram) but may be tiresome for larger amounts.

Spice grinder

Spices can be purchased in ground or in whole form. The whole form tends to keep its flavour better but must be ground depending upon the recipe.

Spices in small quantities can be ground quite easily in a mortar and pestle. Good stone mortar and pestles can be found at Asian grocery suppliers for modest amounts. They are really good, but very heavy.

Alternately, small electric spice grinders make quick work of grinding tough woody spices and achieve better results. They are available from kitchenware suppliers and are inexpensive. I have such an appliance and we are very happy together.

Curing chamber

Finally, the elephant in the room. Once you have butchered, minced and seasoned, how do you air dry or cure the final product? This was the problem which I became very troubled by. In Europe, where traditional charcuterie is well known and understood it can be undertaken successfully in ambient conditions. The books in the area usually avoid confronting this issue, for good reason. The authors assume that you have a perfect place to cure the meat. Sadly, much of Australia does not lend itself to such techniques. Happily, some places in Australia may have correct conditions. If so, the product can be hung in a shed or in an area under the house with great effect. If not, then alternatives must be considered. Allow me to assist.

A domestic refrigerator will not produce air dried charcuterie. There are two reasons for this. First, they operate at very low temperatures, usually less than 5°C. This is too cold for charcuterie to mature during the air drying process.

Secondly, and most importantly, they are designed to operate at extremely low humidity. The air is too dry and will dry out any charcuterie far too quickly and completely. You will be left with a rock hard product within a few days which has not matured and will be no good.

Commercial curing chambers are available from specialist suppliers. They operate by controlling both temperature and humidity to pre-set levels. They are available in various sizes, the smallest about the size of a domestic refrigerator. They are expensive and probably beyond the reach of most amateur charcutiers. I really, really want one.

An acceptable curing chamber can be fashioned from an old refrigerator. The refrigerator provides a contained area which is well insulated and relatively airtight. However, as noted above a refrigerator runs far too cold and dry to produce charcuterie. The product will not mature properly and will dry out far too quickly. Modifications need to be made. First something to regulate the temperature to acceptable levels. Secondly by adding components which allow the humidity to be controlled. The internet is replete with blogs and other sites in which amateurs go through the step by step process of constructing such a device. I did not go down that road.

A more elegant solution, in my view, is to hand. A wine refrigerator, not a bar refrigerator, is designed to maintain temperatures between 10℃, and say, 18℃. The desired temperature can be set and will be maintained automatically. The device also draws in air from outside, unlike a refrigerator. The drawing in of outside ambient air gives a more humid environment than a refrigerator. The result is that charcuterie can be matured at a set temperature (12-14℃) and at a more humid environment than in a refrigerator.

If the wine refrigerator is inside the house it will probably maintain a relatively stable humidity. Although this will depend on whether your house maintains a relatively stable temperature and humidity. Try putting the wine refrigerator in a place which is dark and reasonably cool, certainly not a place which is well heated.

I have used a wine refrigerator as a curing chamber for a number of years with reliable success. It is in a cupboard in the laundry, a room which is not heated. I recommend that you give a wine refrigerator a try.

Dry ageing bags

Dry ageing bags are a relatively new product which may be useful to the home char-cutier. These plastic bags are made of a semi-permeable membrane which allows water vapour to escape but not air. The bags are used in conjunction with a vacuum sealer such that they form a tight contact with the meat. In time the plastic bonds with the meat and the transfer of water vapour is enhanced.

The benefit of this product is that dry ageing, apparently, can be achieved in a normal refrigerator rather than in a specialised curing chamber. It is said that they achieve a result which is not dissimilar to traditional dry ageing.[28] These bags could be used to dry age charcuterie, however I have not tried them. The whole thing looks too much like wet ageing for me.

Gloves

Disposable latex gloves help maintain hygienic conditions. They can be purchased from cookware suppliers and medical suppliers online. They are inexpensive. I use them for as much of the process as possible. In between various steps I either wash and dry gloved hands or discard the gloves and re-glove for the next step. It may be obsessive but you would be surprised how much bacteria is happily living on your skin. Cleanliness is critical. A real charcutier does not make friends with critters. They are not your friends.

Meat hooks

Stainless steel meat hooks are useful to hang the products in the curing chamber or curing area. They are reasonably expensive. If a true meat hook is not required (i.e. one with a sharp end), cheaper alternatives are 'S' hooks available from hardware suppliers. They work just as well but do not have a sharp end to pierce the meat. If the meat is suspended from string, which it usually is, then these work just fine. Just loop the string through the 'S' hook. They are also good to use when drying a number of pieces of charcuterie, just use a length of wooden dowel between two meat hooks. Thread the charcuterie loops onto the dowel and hang for the desired time.

String

Butcher's string, or food grade twine, is needed to tie the meat for drying. Tying the meat helps keep its shape and also allows a loop to be fashioned for hanging. Do not use garden twine or plastic twine. You will regret it.

---

28   For a more detailed discussion see: M. L. Ahnstrom et al, *"A novel method to dry age beef by using vacuum pack-ageing"*, Beef Cattle Research 2006 60; R.D. Smith et al, *"Dry versus wet ageing of beef"*, Meat Science Volume 79, Issue 4 631-639; M. L. Ahnstrom et al *"Dry ageing beef in a bag highly permeable to water vapour"*, Meat Science Volume 73, Issue 4, 674-679.

Labels

Labels are useful to record the type of product, the 'wet' weight and date upon which it was made. Small paper or light cardboard luggage labels are ideal. They can be written upon in pen and are available from stationary suppliers. They are really useful because you will not remember the date, weight or anything else in a few weeks' time after completing the initial steps. Get some.

Vacuum sealer

Once the charcuterie is cured and dried it can be consumed immediately. However, you may need to keep it for longer.

If it is left in the drying chamber then the air drying process will continue and over time the product will become unsatisfactory.

Some charcuterie can be frozen with varying degrees of success. Chorizo and bacon, for example, freeze very well. A good solution is to vacuum seal the charcuterie and keep it in the refrigerator. It will keep for a very long time.

Small domestic vacuum sealers are available from kitchenware suppliers. They are relatively inexpensive and are a worthwhile investment.

Plastic containers and plastic bags

Whether for brining or immersing in salt, a non-reactive sealed container is required. A range of different sizes is useful so that not too much room is taken up in the refrigerator. Plastic "take-away" containers are very convenient. They can be purchased cheaply in quantity from cookware suppliers. Once used, they can be discarded.

In that regard, resealable plastic bags are extremely useful. They do not take up much room in the refrigerator. They are great, particularly if the process does not require complete immersion in salt and overhauling. Once the process is completed they can be discarded.

Pricker

Sausages and salamis which are to be dried need to be lightly pricked all over to allow any air which may be trapped in the casing to escape. This can be done with a needle but a sausage pricker is a quicker way. These are small, round, plastic instruments with a large number of spikes. They give a quick and easy result. They are available from butchery suppliers. Life is too short to use a needle in a champagne cork.

Muslin

Muslin or cheesecloth is a light open weave cotton fabric which can be wrapped around meat which is air drying. The benefit of muslin is that it reduces the rate of desiccation of the product and thereby improves the end result. Meat which is dried too quickly can develop a hard exterior which prevents the interior from drying. This is called case hardening and often means that the product will spoil.

Muslin also discourages critters from interfering with your meat whilst it is drying. It is difficult to describe the desolation one experiences when discovering that the lovingly prepared prosciutto is now running amok with tiny livestock. Critters in charcuterie are bad, try and avoid them if you can. Prosciutto is often wrapped in muslin if air drying is to take place outdoors or in areas to which critters may have access.

Muslin is available from fabric retailers at modest prices. A few metres (say 4) would be sufficient to wrap a large prosciutto. Wrap tightly so that several layers of muslin protect the meat. Tie both ends to prevent critter access.

Netting, socks and tying

Elasticised tubular netting in various widths is available from specialist suppliers. Netting comes in a continuous roll and is sold by the metre of linear length. It is often used in commercial charcuterie for presentation purposes.

The meat is inserted into the netting with the use of a hollow tube over which the net is threaded, the meat slides into the expanded netting, it is then tied at both ends and cut from the length.

The net cannot be used without the hollow tube. They are a little expensive, if you wish to economise, a length of plastic piping from the hardware shop in the required diameter will do the job. But it has to be acknowledged that this solution is not as good as the specialty product.

Whilst the end result is visually appealing, it is not necessary if you are economising. You may choose to disregard the use of netting and tie the meat in shape with string. However, they do a very good job, the netting looks professional and you will feel like a real charcutier (which of course you are, or soon will be).

Another useful product is a fine elasticised cotton tubing often used to wrap hams and prosciuttos. It looks somewhat like a white stocking and is sometimes sold as *"ham sock"*, for obvious reasons. It is stretched over the meat (ham or prosciutto) and tied at both ends. It is a very useful product which can be obtained from online butchery suppliers.

The alternative is to tie the meat to hold its shape and to give a loop for hanging. It is easy and a good way to learn and practice a basic butchery technique, namely the butcher's knot.

A word about spices and lard

A word about spices; the amounts required are usually quite small (with the possible exception of chilli). They provide subtle flavourings to enhance charcuterie and care must be taken not to overpower the product with a particular flavouring. In *Larousse,*[29] you will find a recipe for *"home-salted pork"* which recommends *"... a few garlic cloves, peppercorn and a bay leaf may be added,* **but not to excess.***"*[30] Clever chap, that Larousse. As a rule, be sparing with the spices because once added they cannot be removed. Over time you will no doubt come to a view as to what amounts are pleasing for you. In the end, the process of curing and preserving meat is, I find, quite rewarding. It is a matter of not so much technique, but as in all cooking, a matter of touch. As A.D. Livingston wrote, *"Guidance is needed, but not in the form of magic cures and gadgets. Those people who think that the problems can be solved with*

---

29   Larousse Gastronomique, *"Meat, poultry and game"*.
30   Emphasis added.

Prague Powder and brine injection pumps are wrong.". Clever chap, that Livingston, except the bit about Prague Powder.

Most supermarkets will stock the range of spices which are required. Asian grocers have a very wide range of spices in many forms (whole, cracked or powdered) and in many sizes (from small to ridiculously large). Some of the more esoteric spices like powdered garlic, powdered onion and fenugreek can be obtained from Asian grocers.

Lard can be hard to source. It is rendered pork fat. Once widely available from butchers, it is, in my experience, now only available at some supermarkets and even then, quite sporadically. If you can find it, it is sold in 250g blocks and stored in the refrigerated section of the supermarket together with butter and the like. Its use in charcuterie is to prevent exposed (not covered by skin) areas of meat from drying out too quickly. It is applied liberally, mixed with cracked pepper to discourage critters in open air situations. In order to cover the exposed area of a prosciutto leg, about 350-500g is quite adequate. Do not be tempted to use beef dripping, rendered beef fat or suet. If, indeed, you can find them. They are all made from beef fat and the flavour will not be conducive to good pork charcuterie. If you use them, you will regret it.

Starter cultures

Charcuterie, especially salami production, is assisted by the addition of microbial starter cultures to the mixture. Do not be afraid of them. On the contrary, they may well be your friends. They assist in the fermentation of salamis. As a novice, they are really useful. Starter cultures come as a dried powder, like yeast for baking, and they must be kept in the freezer until required. A small amount of the starter culture is dissolved in distilled water or rainwater. Pure rainwater or distilled water with no additives like chlorine must only be used. Tap water, which may contain chlorine or other additives depending upon where you live, is not suitable. The chemicals, like chlorine, interfere with or kill the starter cultures. That is very bad and you do not want that. Starter cultures are available under various trade names and have various properties depending upon the salami being made. It is best to contact a supplier (there are several online suppliers in Australia) to discuss your needs. Order them in the cooler months so that they are not damaged during the delivery process and store them in the freezer immediately.

Similarly, penicillin moulds can be purchased online, and after dissolving in distilled water, are sprayed or wiped onto the surface of the salami or sausage (or any charcuterie for that matter) to facilitate WMOH production. They are available from the same suppliers as starter cultures.

In either case, do not purchase them from overseas suppliers, in all likelihood they will have spoiled by the time they arrive in the post. You do not want to find out several weeks or months later, that the inoculation did not work.

THE TECHNIQUES

There is not much in the way of technique in charcuterie but there are some things which I can usefully share with you.

Temperature

Meat, casings, equipment and everything else must be really, really cold. There are several reasons for this. First, it prevents critters from participating in the process. You do not want critters in your charcuterie. Secondly, lower temperatures prevent fat from "smearing" or dissolving in the process of mixing and mincing.

Put the mincing equipment in the freezer prior to use. Chill the meat until partly frozen. Mince into a bowl over ice. Fill casings into a bowl over ice.

Put everything into the refrigerator if it does not need to be on the bench.

In between various steps, return the relevant meat, equipment and casings to the refrigerator or freezer as the case may be. Everything must be as cold as you can get it. If not, then you will regret it.

Hygiene

Hygiene is critical in charcuterie. The whole point of charcuterie (that is to say, salt curing) is to create an environment in which bacteria find it difficult to survive. It is unhelpful if you add extra bacteria to the process or create conditions in which they thrive. You must respect the process. If you do not, then you will regret it.

There are some simple rules:
- Always work in the cooler part of the day.
- Always work out of direct sunlight.
- If it is warm, use an air-conditioner or fan to reduce the ambient temperature.
- Preferably work on a cool or cold day rather than a hot day.
- Wear disposable gloves. Indeed you may use several pairs in one preparation.
- Use plastic cutting boards. They are much more hygienic than wooden chopping boards.
- Wash everything well and rinse well to remove soap and detergent residues.

- Have plenty of clean, dry tea towels or disposable wipes available.
- Disposable kitchen wipes are essential. Paper towels are not great because they tend to dissolve with too much moisture and thereafter to adhere to meat surfaces. A porous woven type kitchen wipe is preferable. Have a large roll available and use it liberally to wipe up spills and to dry wet meat. Discard after each use and use a fresh piece for each wipe down or clean up.
- All machinery, bowls, meat and casings must be as cold as possible. **This is absolutely critical.**

Mincing

If you are mincing meat, fat or skin, it is important that the meat, fat or skin is extremely cold, almost frozen. This will make it easier for a domestic mincer to do its job. First, however, the meat, fat or skin must be cut into small pieces. If it is almost frozen, it will not be very difficult to cut it into small pieces. Frozen meat, fat or skin must be thawed slightly if it is to be cut prior to mincing.

Put the mincing parts like the die, mincing blade (or knife) and head of the mincer in the freezer for several hours before they are needed. They must be extremely cold, or the meat will become too soft to mince well and the fat or skin will smear rather than mince.

Remember that the meat, fat and skin will warm up quickly in the mincing process.

Take the meat, fat or skin out of the freezer/fridge at the last moment. It will warm up and soften very quickly in most ambient environments, especially the fat.

> *NOTE: Place a bowl of ice under the bowl into which the meat will collect upon exit from the mincer. This will keep it cold until it is returned to the refrigerator. Once the meat, fat or skin is minced, return it to the refrigerator immediately. It is a fertile ground for bacteria if it becomes warm.*

Mixing

Once the minced meat and seasonings are combined it is very important to mix the filling very well. It should be vigorously kneaded, like bread, for at least 3-5 minutes, possibly up to 15 minutes. This not only evenly distributes the seasonings but also changes the texture of the meat. The meat will develop a very sticky quality. The sticky character of the meat is due to the release of myosin, a meat protein, which becomes extremely sticky.[31]

Somewhat unusually, myosin is soluble in salt (or more precisely a solution of salt at about 6%; although its solubility commences in a salt solution of about 2% and increases thereafter). However, mincing the meat and adding salt (usually much less than 6% but greater that 2%) will assist in transforming the myosin into a more soluble form. This takes some time and is a good reason to mince, salt and season the meat the day before it is put into casings. Keep it refrigerated in a sealed container or a plastic bag overnight. It will bind much better the following day.

The next day, the myosin will be in a more soluble form and the meat will become sticky in a much shorter time whilst requiring less effort on your part. The reason being that after interacting with the salt overnight the myosin becomes sticky. The latter is certainly a good thing. What happens is that the dissolved myosin when mixed creates a gel which is quite sticky. When cooked, the gel is also what assists in retaining water into a sausage and holds the *"fat globules in a rigid web"*.[32] It is what contributes to the juiciness of a cooked sausage.

Further, without this *"stickiness"* the resultant sausage or salami may not be cohesive and will be crumbly when cut. The mixing can be done with an electric mixer using the paddle attachment. Do not be tempted to use a food processor, it will only turn the mixture into a paste, a most undesirable thing unless making an emulsified sausage like mortadella. It can also be done by hand, like kneading bread. Although that is a pretty hard piece of work.

---

31 Myosin, together with actin (another protein), are responsible for the contractile properties of muscle.
32 Gauri, S. – *"Structural changes in meat emulsions during cooking at various process conditions and formulations"*, Food, Agriculture and Environment Volume 2 (1), 116-121; see also Xiang, D.S. & Anor – *"Factors influencing gel formation by myofibrillar proteins in muscle foods"*, Comprehensive Reviews in Food Science and Food Safety Volume 10, 2011, 33-51.

Once kneaded, you will need to discern whether you have done enough work to achieve your purpose.

A way to test whether the mixture has achieved the desired consistency is to scoop a small handful into the palm of your hand. Invert your open hand such that it is palm side down. If the mixture falls from your palm it is not sticky enough. If it adheres to the palm of your hand it is good to go.

Casings

The casings which you purchase will be preserved in a coarse salt preparation and perhaps vacuum sealed. Cut the required length of casing. Remove the excess salt. Rinse the casing well and run water through the casing (carefully) to remove any salt or brine. Repeat this several times and allow the casing to sit in cold water in the refrigerator for about an hour before use. Keep it really, really cold.

Filling

Fill the casings as quickly as possible and, preferably, use a very cold canister if using a sausage filler (put it in the freezer beforehand). Certainly, fill the casings using a really cold meat mixture into a bowl over ice. When you have finished filling a length of casing, put the filled casing into the refrigerator.

Linking and tying

Salamis and sausages which will be individually dry cured will need to be separated and tied individually. It is easier to do this as you fill the casings like so:
- Fill one length.
- Tie a bubble knot at the end; leaving enough string for a loop (for hanging).
- Push back the meat in the "unfilled" casing for, say, 6cm.
- Tie a bubble knot at the start of the "meat part" of the casing; leaving enough string to make a loop for hanging.
- Cut the section of casing between the two links and trim. You now have two links, tied at each end, both ends with loops for hanging.
- Repeat the process.

The process which I have described will be a bit time consuming but easier, and less prone to bursting casings, than trying to do it once an entire length of casing has been filled.

Fresh sausages are not commonly pricked to remove air because they will leak valuable juices whilst cooking. However, sausages or salamis which are to be air dried must be pricked to remove any air which is caught in the casing. You can do this with a small tool (pricker) which has a large number of sharp needles, obtained from a specialist supplier.

Overhauling

Overhauling is the practice of turning the meat daily during its curing time. This gives the meat a more even exposure to the salt cure mixture. Obviously it is irrelevant to brines or meat which is fully immersed in salt.

Pellicle

Smoking of meats, whether sausages, whole muscle or fish, benefit by allowing them to stand uncovered in the refrigerator overnight or for up to one day. During this time the surface of the meat will develop a sticky coating. This is a coating of proteins which greatly assists the smoking process. What happens is that the salt interacts with the meat proteins and they unwind and dissolve, releasing a sticky material called exudate. This coats the surface of the meat and it becomes the shiny, sticky protein coating called pellicle.[33]

The smoke adheres to the sticky coating thereby increasing colour and flavour.

Dry cure

A basic dry cure which is rubbed onto the meat is as follows:
- Salt – 1 kg.
- Pepper (black, powder) – 2%.
- Fennel (cracked seeds) – 6%.

---

33 Marianski and Anor, 'Curing and Smoking Fish'.

Depending upon what you are curing, various aromatics can be added. For a sweeter cure (for say, bacon) add 20% brown sugar or white sugar; for something spicier (for say, pancetta) add 0.5% chilli flakes. Juniper berries, lightly crushed, are a welcome addition to any dry cure. Do not add too many, three or four should do.

> *NOTE: If you are intending to keep the product for some time, add a Curing Salt. I use Curing Salt No. 1 for short cures, and Curing Salt No. 2 for longer cured products like prosciutto. Both are added at about 0.3% by weight of the meat.*

Wet cure

A basic wet cure or brine can be used for a variety of different preparations. The mixture I use is as follows:

- Water – 1 litre.
- Salt – 10%.
- Brown sugar – 10%.
- Juniper berries – 1 tsp.
- Peppercorns (cracked, black) – 1 tsp.
- Bay leaves – 2.

To this a multitude of aromatics can be added; consider chilli flakes, cracked fennel, orange zest, lemon zest and crushed garlic. Use small quantities (say 1 tsp.) until you achieve the balance which you find pleasing. I add a Curing Salt if the product is not intended to be consumed immediately.

> *NOTE: Never re-use brine once it has been used to cure meat. Discard it.*
> *If you do not then you will get sick and die.*

Teaspoons and the like

Surprisingly enough there are differences between the size of imperial measurements as between the United Kingdom, United States of America and Australia.

This is one of the (many) reasons why metric measurements are to be preferred. Nonetheless if you are confronted by a recipe with imperial measurements you need to be aware of the differences, albeit that they are quite slight.

A useful guide is as follows[34]:

Measurement	AUS	UK	USA
1 cup	250 ml	250 ml	225 ml (but sometimes 240 ml)
1 tsp.	5 ml	5 ml	5 ml
1 tbsp.	20 ml	15 ml	16 ml

Another variable is whether the teaspoon is flat or heaped. My mother always said that a spoon measure is heaped not flat. I do not know what the British or Americans think as to this matter but I have never departed from her direction.

Temperature stalling when smoking meat

A common problem when slow cooking or hot smoking is that the internal temperature of the meat stalls for a long period. It is really frustrating and quite perplexing. What happens is that the internal temperature of the meat rises reasonably rapidly and consistently during the first 2-3 hours. The temperature stall occurs at about 50°C-60°C (depending on the thickness and type of meat) and lasts for hours. During this time the internal temperature does not rise and may even fall slightly. Thereafter, and it can be four or five hours later, the temperature will rise reasonably rapidly. This happened many times, much to my unhappiness.

What on Earth was going on? I simply did not know.

First, I checked all the hardware. There was no problem with the temperature probe (although they can fall out, so you should check it) nor had the batteries failed (but do check them). After some research, I discovered that the temperature stall is a physical phenomenon associated with slow cooking at low temperatures.

Blonder,[35] an American physicist (and American style barbeque aficionado), has a theory which explained the phenomenon as being caused by *"porous bed free*

---

34   See Appendix 5 for more detail.
35   http://www.genuineideas.com/ArticlesIndex/stallbbq.html

expansion cooling". He explained that when water molecules evaporate from the meat in this temperature band they cool the surface of the meat. The rate of cooling is such that it balances the heat input. In other words the meat starts to sweat which reduces its temperature. He further concluded that the stall is more rapid in dry environments and more prolonged in a humid environment. This may explain the stall and its duration - the hot smoker creates a relatively low temperature but humid environment. Blonder's theory sounds pretty compelling although I have read other theories to deal with collagen rendering and fat breakdown.

At all events, the solution is quite simple. Once the meat hits the stall zone, increase the temperature in the smoker to about 95℃. Once the temperature is increased, the internal temperature should continue to rise. All is good again.

Let me give you a recent example. I was smoking two rainbow trout, very nice fat fish of about 750g each. They had been in a quick brine of salt and sugar for about one hour, then washed and dried. After about another hour in the refrigerator the skin was sticky (the pellicle had developed) and they were ready for the smoker. The smoker was at a steady temperature of about 85℃. The fish were placed in the smoker at about 11am. The internal temperature of the fish at the beginning of this process was 6℃. The internal temperature rose nicely until it reached about 55℃, approximately 3 hours later. The temperature then stalled for the next 5-6 hours. Ultimately I got tired of waiting and raised the smoker temperature to 95℃ (this is a good reason to purchase a digital smoker, so that temperature changes are reasonably accurate). After 30 minutes or so, the temperature started rising again, until it reached 76℃ after about another 30-45 minutes. The fish were a good colour and very moist.[36]

Another solution is to wrap the meat in foil when the temperature stalls. The foil will prevent evaporative cooling of the meat and does overcome the stall. The downside, of course, is that meat wrapped in foil is unlikely to take up smoke effectively if at all. This may not matter depending how much smoke has been taken up prior to that point. Although after a few hours it probably has taken up sufficient smoke for your purposes.

The alternative is to wait it out, but it can (and does) take a frustratingly long time.

---

36   This phenomenon is not confined to fish but occurs with pork, beef and lamb.

A note on knots

There are only two knots you need to know, a bubble knot and a butchers knot.

A bubble knot is a double knot used to seal the ends of a salami such that the contents will not escape during the drying process. It is very simple. Tie a normal granny knot over the end of the filled casing. Tie it tight. Do not cut off the ends of the string. Cut the unfilled end of the casing about 5cm from the knot. Pass the cut end of the casing over one of the strings. Tie another granny knot. This leaves a small section of casing between the two knots. The section of casing between the two knots usually form a small bubble due to the trapped air, hence the term bubble knot. It is a very secure way of tying the end and also stops air entering the meat inside the casing.

A butcher's knot is different and is used to securely tie meat into a desirable shape. Cut a good length of string, say 25cm long. Pass it under the meat, tie a knot in the end furthest away. Tie a slip knot using that end around the other end of the string. Pull the knot tight with a back and forward motion. The slip knot will run down and lock onto the knotted end of the string. Tie another knot to lock the whole thing down tight. Cut off the ends neatly. It will not slip and is very strong. It really is the only way to tie meat securely into shape that is why all butchers use it. It is a little difficult to describe in words but there are many good videos online (as with a bubble knot). Practice on a rolled up tea-towel or a tin can. Once mastered, it is strangely satisfying.

Senses

Finally, use your senses of smell, sight, touch and taste in order to come to a view about whether the product is ready or is no good. A whole muscle charcuterie, sausage or salami will either look good or not. It will be a good colour, and when cut, should be of even colour and consistency.

It should be reasonably firm, almost hard, and dry. External sliminess is not good. It should smell like ... charcuterie, not like 'napalm in the morning'. The smell is difficult to describe, sometimes called funky, it is not unpleasant, nor meaty, but savoury, sweetish and perhaps slightly yeasty. If it smells bad, you will know immediately. Get rid of it.

Taste it yourself before anyone else, especially when starting out. Consume a small piece and see if, 24 hours later, all is still well. It is a far, far better thing to inflict it on oneself than upon others. If the charcuterie has passed the assessment by sight, touch and smell, it is most unlikely that anything will be wrong (especially if a Curing Salt is used).

Mould, a subject dealt with separately, can be either good or bad. Generally, one should be very suspicious of mould. Once again, use your sense of smell, sight and touch. If in doubt, throw it out. My late neighbour, Bill said "...*machines are like horses, they are always trying to kill you...*". He was speaking in relation to tractors, a common interest and was correct, of course. I interpolate that mould (save for the WMOH) is exactly the same.

> *NOTE: Charcuterie has had a successful history for thousands of years but it does have limitations, notably that you must follow some basic rules. No doubt those whom did not respect its limits are legion. You do not want to be one of them.*
>
> *Treat the process and the products with respect and hopefully with the aid of this book, they will respect you.*
>
> *Do not be the one to give charcuterie a bad name. There will be nowhere to hide if you do.*

THE STORIES

There are many stories from the Diary, some are good; some are not so good. There are some that I can tell you, there are some that I cannot. Allow me to share a few. Not that it matters but they are all true.

In the beginning

The joyous decision that resulted in the commencement of sausage and salami production was accompanied by gritty determination and quiet enthusiasm. Perhaps gritty enthusiasm and quiet determination. I cannot recall, but at all events I was a very serious young insect about the whole damned thing. Some might say that I still am. I watched videos on the internet pertaining to the subject. I watched them again. I purchased specialised books, often from overseas suppliers. I read the books. I read them again. I was armed with knowledge.

All my sources were telling me that I must, unequivocally, start with whole cuts of meat on the bone, preferably a whole pig. It must be butchered by me, and minced by me, so the purity of the experience could be retained. To do otherwise was to undermine the sanctity of the salami and the purity of the pig. Naturally, I decided that it was the only way to approach the whole thing. To do otherwise was to undermine the sanctity … etc, you get the picture.

I purchased a pork shoulder, on the bone, of course. The butcher (not Frank The Butcher) inquired what I was going to do with it. I told him, proudly, it is to make salami. He said why not buy the mince, already prepared? No, I said, I want to get it just right. He was silent. I assume others had been before. Many are called but few are chosen.

I brought the meat home. It was very heavy. I separated meat from bone. It was very satisfying.

I chopped the meat into mincer sized bits. I had earlier purchased the mincing attachment for the expensive American food processor (you know the one). I set it up. I added the meat to said attachment (maybe a bit warm but I make no admissions). The mincer did not like it. Not one little bit. The mincer attacked the task with enthusiasm. In the beginning, at least. Things got a bit heavy going. The mincer slowed down. The mincer made a comeback. The sinew in the meat blocked the auger in the mincer. It was getting pretty bad. The mincer had to be taken apart and cleaned. This occurred many times. I decided that I needed reinforcements.

I drafted No. 1 Daughter to form a Coalition Of The Unwilling. She was overqualified.

No. 1 Daughter was enveloped in grim silence, for my part, I found it all quite stressful and difficult. I was not very adult about things, but that is not unusual. I was vocal, but The Mumster was not around so it was OK.

I worked through it. Surely this was what everyone does. It took a very long time to mince the meat. I did not know how much meat I had (on the bone purchases do result in a lot less meat after butchering). I weighed the resultant mince. It was an uneven amount. My recipes were based on 5 pounds of meat. I did not have 5 pounds of meat, in fact I had a lot less. I made rough adjustments for seasonings. The recipes were all based on 5 pounds of meat and in imperial measurements. Things were starting to go bad. They were about to get worse. Much worser in fact. I needed help to fill the salami casings.

I formed a second Coalition Of The Unwilling (I bribed No. 1 Son to help). The problem was that No. 1 Daughter would only help on the basis that she would not touch the meat (it is a teenage girl thing).

We proceeded. No. 1 Son had no such qualms. Well, not as many as No. 1 Daughter. It was not a happy coalition. The meat was getting warm. The fat was getting soft. Things were not good. We finished. It had taken hours. The results were less than satisfactory, crumbly in texture and poor of flavourings. No. 1 Son and No. 1 Daughter retreated to their rooms in grim silence; as is their want.

I gave the sausages to The Hairy Nephews. They said they were really good. However, as full time tertiary students, they are omnivores and are always looking for free food. I did not place great store upon their opinion.

This was probably the turning point. I decided that the whole charcuterie thing would not beat me. Nonetheless, I decided that it was better to buy mince from the butcher for a number of reasons. First, it is a whole lot easier than making it yourself. Secondly, it is not much more expensive than meat on the bone. Thirdly, if you do not think it has enough fat, ask the butcher to mince some pork belly or back fat. They are generally very obliging chaps. Of course if you start with your own pig, it is a different matter and you need to get a big electric mincer. Lastly, one does not have to enter into a Coalition Of The Unwilling (well, not so much anyway. One does need help with filling the casings). In any event, in my view, Coalitions Of The Unwilling, usually end up in tears.

A prosciutto called Kevin

I turned to whole meat charcuterie. I was determined that this charcuterie thing would not beat me. Frankly, I had mixed success. For reasons which I do not now recall, I decided to jump into the deep end and embark on a prosciutto. I certainly did not understand what I was doing, but it felt good nonetheless. I was becoming a charcutier, (well sort of) although I did not know it at the time.

It just seemed like a good idea at the time.

Kevin was the start of the more scientific approach.

If you feel the need to apportion blame for all that has followed, then most must fall to Kevin.

Although, you already knew that. But I digress.

Kevin was the first prosciutto. I asked Frank The Butcher[37] when it would be good to start preparing a prosciutto. He said "*When you see me wearing a beanie in the shop, then it will be time*". It sounded pretty scientific to me. I waited. I waited some more. Frank The Butcher did not wear the beanie until mid-June, to my mind a bit late. In any event, I did what he said.

When I saw the beanie being worn, I attended the shop to purchase a leg of pork. Frank The Butcher trimmed the leg of pork for prosciutto and I was all set to start the journey. After careful consideration, it was decided that the inaugural prosciutto would be called Kevin. Kevin was lovingly rubbed with a mixture of salt and Curing Salt and put to bed in a salty sleeping bag (a big plastic tub actually) for 2 days/

---

37   His real name.

kilogram. Far too long as it turned out but it seemed like a good idea at the time. Thereafter Kevin was put into some nice muslin pyjamas for the big sleep. Kevin was hung high up on the veranda out in the direct sun but with good airflow. I checked Kevin every few days and things were good. Kevin was happy. I was happy.

As things transpired, there were some unseasonably warm days in August. That was a problem because things got quite warm on the veranda up under the eaves. My thermometer told me so. Accordingly, I put Kevin in the fridge for a few days. Kevin seemed happy enough. When things cooled down a bit I returned him to the veranda. Sadly the days got warmer more often. Kevin still had so much time to spend maturing that I decided drastic action needed to be taken.

I decided to relocate Kevin to Camp Otway, on the west coast of Victoria, about 3 hours' drive from Melbourne. Kevin was left in a cupboard in the house which is situated at 300 metres above sea level with plenty of breeze. It seemed like a good idea at the time. Indeed it was a good idea until, once again, things got warm. I got nervous and decided that I had to check on Kevin. I travelled for 3 hours to Camp Otway to see how Kevin was progressing. Nervously, I opened the door, expecting to see Kevin watching my television and drinking my wine. All was good, much to my relief. Kevin was happy and so was I. Nonetheless, I figured that it was not good to be so far away from Kevin, so we returned to Melbourne together. The question now was what to do, the weather becoming warmer each day. I suggested that Kevin might enjoy time in my modest cellar. Kevin agreed. Sadly, although the temperature was good, the humidity was too high. Things went bad very quickly. We fought off the MOMC bravely together. It was a close run thing. What to do?

The answer was at hand, Sebastian (a local gastronome), has a cellar. Well alright, it was just a space under his house, but which had more airflow than my modest cellar. Kevin was agisted at Chez Sebastian quite happily for much of the remainder of his days. Kevin ended up being a remarkable success, especially as a first time effort (albeit a bit salty, a point I return to later).

A prosciutto called Julia

Let me take you to the following winter.

Julia was second in line for the prosciutto throne, following Kevin. My theory was that more veranda time was needed and we just had to tough out any warm days. I obtained Julia from Frank The Butcher in mid-June; just like he said that I should. I prepared Julia as I had done with Kevin. However, after my problems with Kevin, I was apprehensive about Julia. It was only natural.

In the event Julia spent time on the veranda together with some little friends, a capocollo and a pancetta. I really should not have included them, but as with all little friends they were very insistent. I wrapped Julia in the white pyjamas as I had done with Kevin. I did not wrap Julia's friends. I cannot remember why, perhaps I was out of muslin, perhaps I thought they did not need it because they would not be there for very long. Certainly I trusted them not to require wrapping. In any event, I was wrong. All little friends need to be strictly controlled and are not to be trusted. All of a sudden, the little friends were overrun with many tiny livestock. (Little friends are want to do that). Even more importantly, the tiny livestock had migrated to Julia, as tiny livestock are want to do.

Quel desastré.

Julia and her little friends were consigned to history and rightly so.

A prosciutto called Tony

Allow me to advance to the third winter.

Tony was the third in line to the throne, following on from Julia and Kevin. I was more enlightened and obtained Tony from Frank The Butcher in early May, much to Frank The Butcher's unease. However, I figured Tony needed more cool weather time if Tony was to make the grade.

The usual followed, time in the salty sleeping bag (1 day/kilogram this time – because I asked Frank The Butcher how he prepares his prosciutto. He asked his dad, who said 1 day/kilogram is good enough. I followed Frank The Butcher's dad's advice).

Then I gave Tony a day in the refrigerator to dry off the surface a bit. The white muslin pyjamas followed. This went much better, indeed the winter was longer and cooler. However, it was not long enough. By this time I had a theory about using a wine fridge to air dry or mature the prosciutto. When the weather got too warm for Tony's liking, we agreed he should spend time in the fridge. It worked, maybe not as prosaic as a limestone cave deep in the Pyrenees', but it did work. At the time of writing, a prosciutto called Malcolm is doing time in the wine refrigerator. Time will tell as to whether he makes the grade. We hasten with faint but eager steps.[38]

Dad and Son Salt

A by-product of the charcuterie process is left over salt and dried spices, sometimes quite a lot. At any given time, I have considerable amounts of both, which has turned out to be a good thing on several occasions.

No. 1 Son[39], aged 10 years at the time, wanted a new smartphone and computer game console. They were very expensive. I pointed out that he had insufficient funds to purchase such devices. No. 1 Son opined that I should buy them for him if I was any sort of a Dad.

I informed No. 1 Son that he must earn a part of the money himself. This was met with surprising enthusiasm. The difficulty then became everything that he was asked to do around the house (e.g. put out garbage bins) became a negotiation as to the price for the task. Indeed, he embraced the concept of item remuneration so well that we decided that a plan needed to be devised. The result was *'Dad and Son Salt'*, a range of flavoured salts.

No. 1 Son and I figured that it could not be hard to do and it would use available resources (in part), namely excess salt and spices. No.1 Son conducted some technical research (internet based only, as is today's practice). It transpired that the use of fresh herbs is frowned upon due to spoilage. Good, we had plenty of dried spices.

Next, No.1 Son conducted some market research as to the desired flavours (he

---

38   Bach Cantata BWV 78 *'Jesu, der du meine Seele'; 'Cantata for the Fourteenth Sunday after Trinity'* – *'Wir eilen mit schwachen, doch emsigen Schritten'*.

39   Not his real name; entitled because there is only one. In the same way No.1 Daughter is entitled.

discussed it with a marketing panel comprising of No.1 Daughter[40], the One True Dog and The Rat).[41] Thereafter he gave his three flavours appropriate names – *'Lamb's Best Friend'*, a cheeky herbaceous salt with garlic undertones; *'Tangy Herb'*, a fiery but subtle combination and *'Brain Buster'*[42], a pugnacious mix of everything No.1 Son found in the pantry.

The salts were made, they were put in nice containers (originally small salt shakers, in subsequent production runs small cardboard 'noodle' type boxes) labels affixed, and orders taken.

The salts were marketed to friends, family, colleagues and a few teachers from school. They were all good and generous enough to support the project.

After two production runs No.1 Son made sufficient funds to purchase (with a substantial subsidy from Management) a smartphone and then some type of game console. Sadly, his creditors (namely, Moi) are still awaiting full reimbursement.

The problem with bottarga

Recently, I found a recipe for bottarga, the Italian air dried fish roe which is used as a condiment on pasta, amongst other things.

It spoke to me. I knew that I had to do it.

But there were issues to deal with.

I do not live in Italy, and it follows that I sadly do not live near Cabras, the lake in Sardinia from which the most famous bottarga is sourced. I do not have access to the female thin lipped grey mullet, from which the best bottarga is, apparently, made.

However, I did recall that my parents, not renown gastronomes, would crumb and fry any fish roe (egg sacs) which were to be found in fish which were prepared for the table, usually flathead (*platycephalidae*, of various types).

---

40   Not her real name.
41   Not their real names.
42   Originally named *'Bum Burner'* but it was decided that The Mumster would not like it, so it was changed.

Accordingly, I knew that, fish roe could be found in fish with which I had some familiarity and to which I had access. The problem was that the fishmongers to whom I had access, did not seem to value these fish offal products. Indeed, my inquiries were met with very blank looks (at best).

Fortunately, I did find a fishmonger who had, earlier that day, come across trevally roe of significant proportions and which he was happy to sell. As an aside, he was from New Zealand (not that it should be held against him) and he said that salted overnight and smoked they were a great delicacy. How would one use such a product, I inquired? Like salami he said, "... cut thin and eat on toast or bread".

Clever people these New Zealanders.

In the event I prepared the roe as described later in this book.

A word of warning, do not cure anything else in the same vicinity at the same time. The roe has a very strong fishy odour as it dries and one that will taint everything else (unless dried in open air, as the Italians do). In fact, I had to thoroughly wash the curing chamber afterwards with a vanilla solution to get rid of the fish smell.

Happily, I did not use the curing chamber which I use for other charcuterie, because the wash down would have, I assume, removed the WMOH which had inoculated the chamber (I now have a second wine refrigerator for use as a curing chamber).

Nonetheless, the bottarga was a success.

I think the above shows that these recipes are adaptable and it does not matter where you live. With some perseverance you can do what other people have been doing for hundreds or thousands of years.

You just need to have some confidence and give it a go.

The curing chamber

The idea of charcuterie is really simple. Kill the beast. Salt the meat. Maybe add some flavourings. Sit back and wait. Enjoy the view over your vineyard as you do. Partake of last year's wine and charcuterie. Drive to the local boucher in your Citroën

2CV and discuss meat issues. Think happy thoughts. The only problem is where to accommodate the salted meat whilst one waits. A shed high in the Pyrenees would do nicely. A limestone cave in southern France would not be bad either.

Sadly, tragically, I did not have access to any of the above. I decided to place my thoughts elsewhere and do what the books said namely, '*... then hang the [product] in a well ventilated place for [12 months]*'.

As you expected, it did not go well. In fact it all ended up in tears.

The weather conditions in Melbourne, where I live, are not consistent enough for a sufficiently long period for the charcuterie to air dry properly. In particular, the weather is insufficiently consistent for the thing that I really wanted to create, namely prosciutto. Other things worked to a greater or lesser extent.

I tried a variety of things as follows:
- the pantry – the bresaola went hard and dry. I gave it to The One True Dog[43] and The Rat[44].
- the cellar - the MOMC invaded within a few days.
- the cellar again - this time with a fan to move the air and reduce humidity – not much better, the MOMC came again (just a bit later).
- under the eaves on the front veranda (north facing) - things got too hot when the sun came out even though the charcuterie was high up out of the direct sun.

The refrigerator was not even worth a try - I knew it was too cold and dry.

What to do?

The other problem was that one can only really expect to do this successfully during winter. It can get to 40°C in a Melbourne summer, don't you worry about that. A Melbourne winter, cold as it is, only reliably goes from late May until late September. Not long enough to air dry a prosciutto. Accordingly, the window for experimentation was not very long.

---

43   Not her real name.
44   Its real, evil, name.

I did not have the inclination or space to convert a refrigerator into a curing chamber, even if The Mumster would let me (which She would not). I came to the view that a wine fridge might just do the trick. I purchased such a product. It seemed to me that if it would operate at a warmer temperature than a refrigerator and at a higher humidity, then it might just work as a curing chamber during a Melbourne winter.

The wine fridge was set at about 16°C, and put in a cupboard in an unheated room in the house (the laundry). The manufacturers' booklet said that it drew air from outside and it ran at (not quite) ambient humidity.

Inside a house is a relatively humid environment, especially in an unheated room during a (wet) Melbourne winter. No one was more surprised than me when it worked. No MOMC. No tiny livestock. No slime. No bad smell. Hallelujah.

I have since used it for relatively short air drying during summer for products like capocollo, lonza and pancetta.

It has also been successful insofar as longer term dried products are concerned, for example prosciutto.

I have purchased a second wine fridge to expand production capacity. Interestingly it was put in the garage. Sadly, it does not seem to be able to maintain a stable temperature and is very affected by the diurnal variations in the garage. The next project is to find a nice dark cupboard in the house in which to relocate it (secretly).

Standby.

Guanciale and I

I had made pancetta with some success. Both kinds, in fact, that is to say, pancetta tesa and pancetta arotollata. They had both been received to some acclaim, if I do say so with all modesty.[45] The books said that guanciale was much better than pancetta in its various forms. Naturally, I had to make that as well.

Here is the thing.

---

45   It is a relative thing.

Pork jowl is not something on the butcher's radar in the leafy suburbs of Melbourne, or anywhere else in Melbourne for that matter. Requests for it will be politely deflected to pork belly or to oxtail. The latter is a kind of non sequitur but butchers do not speak Latin. One is asked what one is wanting it for. One explains. Blank looks follow.

Part of the problem is that butchers are in sharp decline and the culture of butcher shops in my vicinity is not that of European charcuterie. I travelled further afield in order to seek out new worlds of guanciale. Sadly, the further I went, the blanker the looks were in relation to the subject. The closest I got was sliced "pork cheek" or "pig face". Neither was satisfactory. The pork cheek was mostly fat and nasty bits, the pork face was a deboned head without nasty bits or any meat. The alternative was a pork head. Readily available, I hear you say. Indeed.

However, the retail pig head is cut very short on the neck (just under the jaw bone) and has little jowl, just cheeks full of nasty bits. Nasty bits do not cure at all well. In a moment of desperation, I purchased sliced "pork cheek" (in truth, sliced bits of pig face with skin, fat, nasty bits and not much meat). It looked like it might do the job in the shop window. When I unwrapped it at home, it was much more dubious. I knew that I had been dudded. Nonetheless, I figured that it was worth a try. It was salted, spiced and treated with respect – as one should do with any piece of meat or fish. It was washed, weighed and hung to dry in the curing chamber. It was inspected regularly. It did not go to plan. It became not nice and decidedly unusual looking. I thought it might improve. I gave it some more time. I was wrong. It got worserer and worserer. It was the damned glands and other nasty bits.

The pork cheek (I cannot call it guanciale) was consigned to the big pork failure bin in the sky. One learns from one's mistakes.

Beware the nasty bits.

The truth about offal

The truth is that I do not like offal. Not one little bit.

There are many who identify charcuterie as being synonymous with offal. In fact, nothing could be further from the truth; they just like offal.

I know that a lot of people like offal. Leopold Bloom was a character in Ulysses[46], a novel by James Joyce. Sadly, Bloom's favourite foods were all offal. He is described by Joyce as follows:

> *"Mr Leopold Bloom ate with relish the inner organs of beasts and fowls. He liked thick giblet soup, nutty gizzards, a stuffed roast heart, liver slices fried with crustcrumbs, fried hencods' roes. Most of all he liked grilled mutton kidneys which gave to his palate a fine tang of faintly scented urine".*

It sounds all good. Until you try and eat the stuff.

I have tried to like offal. I really have. Sadly I just cannot do it. It is a textural thing for me. I cannot abide the texture. Just like raw oysters. I tried to like them for years. Everyone else liked them. Why shouldn't I? The reason is that they are nasty slimy suckers and I just cannot eat them. Not even Hemingway, a bloke who knew a thing or two about food, can make me eat them. He wrote about oysters as follows[47]:

> *"As I ate the oysters with their strong taste of the sea and their faint metallic taste that the cold white wine washed away, leaving only the sea taste and the succulent texture, and as I drank their cold liquid from each shell and washed it down with the crisp taste of the wine, I lost the empty feeling and began to be happy and to make plans."*

Hemingway is entitled to his view regarding oysters, wrong as it clearly is. Smoked oysters, however, are an entirely different matter. But I digress.

Charcuterie is about fresh meat which is cured, dried and preserved. It is not about nasty, slimy, slippery bits. Charcuterie is not about bits that animals have been thinking with, eating with, digesting with or "you-know-whating" with. It is about meat. Only meat, fat and skin (sometimes) but definitely not nasty bits.

Nothing else. Not under any circumstances. Ever. Hence, The Rule Against Offal.

---

46   Joyce, J. – *'Ulysses'*
47   Hemingway, E. *'A moveable feast'*.

Charcuterie is a labour of love whereas, in the past, it was a matter of survival. The modern iteration of charcuterie is all about good food and has little to do with preservation for preservation's sake.

Which brings me to offal once again.

I do not like it, not one little bit. Allow me to tell a story which is both on point and against myself, something that I do not do very often.

A recent family holiday to France was outstanding.

One day, No. 1 Son, No. 1 Daughter and Moi[48] were without adult supervision. We decided to eat at one of the many bistrôt. The menu was in French. They were concerned. I told them that I could deal with it. They were even more concerned. Their concerns were well founded as things transpired.

They had onion soup (soupe a l'oignon) and chippies (pommes de terre frites). I was somewhat more adventurous, I decided to have sausages because I could decipher (I thought) such a dish on the menu.

I vaguely remembered the name, andouillette, although I could not quite place it in English ("*en anglais*" as we Francophiles are want to say). The meaning of the word was strangely familiar, it was so close, but yet so far. I knew it, but could not quite recall it. As soon as they arrived and I smelled the dish, I remembered what it meant, Andouillette = tripe sausage. "*Quelle dommage*", in fact big "*dommage*" because Parisians like tripe "green" which to you and I means not washed very well. Not a good day for Moi on the French culinary scales.

I was made to eat lamb's fry (liver) and brains as a child and did not like them. Not one little bit. Although I concede that they both came with bacon. Bacon was not something that we were given very often and even then not without offal "*quelle dommage*". I think that Charles Dickens felt about lawyers like I do about offal, who can forget his descriptions of lawyers? Mr Vholes, in "*Bleak House*" – "*... a sallow man with pinched lips that looked as if they were cold ...*", "*... dressed in black, black gloved and buttoned to the chin ...*", "*... so eager, so bloodless, and gaunt ...*",

---

48   We were in our French phase, not our real names.

"... always looking at the client as if he were making a lingering meal of him with his eyes; Sampson Brass from the *"Old Curiosity Shop"* – *"A tall, meagre man, with a nose like a wen, a protruding forehead, retreating eyes and hair of a deep red with a cringing manner and a harsh voice"*. His face being *"... one of nature's beacons warning off those who navigated the shoals and breakers of the world, or of that dangerous strait, the law*; Uriah Heep in *"David Copperfield"* – *"... was a red eyed cadaver"* whose *"lank forefinger"* when he reads makes *"clammy tracks along the page ... like a snail"*, also, *"... he had a way of writhing when he wanted to express enthusiasm, which was very ugly"*; finally, he wrote that other lawyers infest dimly lighted, mouldy offices *"... like maggots in nuts"*.

I am confident that Dickens was about to move on to offal with equal opprobrium. A great pity that he did not.

However, I digress. Offal is all about, and only about, nasty bits. It is sufficient to say that if you are looking for offal, this is not the right place – save for pig head, trotters, fish roe and a few other things – they are well known exceptions to The Rule Against Offal.

I do not do blood, tripe, liver, lungs and all the other nasty bits. There are an abundance of recipes using these things. You can easily find recipes for liver sausage (liverwurst), lung sausage (salsiccia de pulmone), blood sausage (boudin noir, black pudding, bloodwurst) and everything in between. In fact, for those of you who are interested Hashheider has recipes for brain rissoles, heart goulash, pig stomach soup, pig pâté, pig bladder and not to be overlooked, stir fried pig uterus. It is a matter for you but if that is what you want, then off you go, just do not call it charcuterie and do not involve me. Make as much of it as you want. I am happy for you, but also disgusted. It is not charcuterie as I know it. The childhood memories are too strong.

You will observe that there are no recipes in this book for lung salami (salame de pulmone), tongue salami (linguale), liver salami (salami di fegato), or the like. Nor will there ever be on my watch.

At its core (I was tempted to say, heart) it is a textural thing for me. I cannot abide the slippery, gooey, primal, slimy character of offal. And, before you say it, oysters are in the same category. They are nasty, slimy, slippery little suckers and I cannot abide them. It is all offal to me.

Do it yourself.

Proper charcuterie is another matter. Read the book and set aside your evil, offal, ways. Henceforth and hereafter the foregoing is defined as The Rule Against Offal.

Porkathon

I was invited to join Michael and others for a porkathon. The idea was that you gather a lot of friends, one pig and end up with a great deal of sausages, salamis and charcuterie at the end of the day. It is a good idea and one which has worked well for centuries.

Michael had collected the pig from the farmer the previous day. The pig had been butchered into primal cuts. It was huge, a live weight of about 220-240 kilograms and a dressed weight (which really means very undressed) of about 200 kilograms.

I arrived early the next day, expecting to find many amateur charcutiers, or at least those who wanted to be.

However, the only persons to attend were myself, Michael and Boris The Blade, a former SAS operative. Nonetheless, we were unfazed.

The pig was magnificent. The back fat was at least 5cm thick, the meat a dark rosy colour that resembled yearling beef. In short it was nothing like a commercial pig with which I was familiar.

We attacked the pig with much zeal. We were busier than Baghdad builders. We were a symphony of motion. We moved with the liquid grace of finely tuned athletic machines, (not surprisingly, because we were just that) and the speed of a thousand gazelles. To our surprise, in about four hours, we had prepared bacon for smoking, loins for curing, hams for curing, capocollo for curing, diced meat and fat for salamis and sausages. For the technically minded amongst you, the predicted weight of meat can be accurately calculated as follows:

4 hours x <u>one really big pig</u> + (6 cappuccinos and some very nice cake) - (the kids' help)
　　　　　　3 blokes　　　　= a massive amount of meat, skin, fat and bones

The timing of kids' sport and other weekend obligations meant that the next part, sausage and salami making, had to be adjourned. The meat was frozen, so as to make it easier to mince and we packed up. Beers may have been involved, but I make no admissions.

Early the following Sunday, I attended to resume proceedings. This time, it was a false alarm. The electric mincer had technical troubles. Well alright, the mincing knife had been assembled backwards and broke. But it was not my fault. Further, Boris The Blade was nowhere to be seen. We were adjourned again.

Third time lucky. Once again it was the two amigos. Boris The Blade was nowhere to be seen. Clearly on a mission in a dictatorship in some foreign country. The type of mission which he could tell you about, but if he did then he would have to kill you afterwards. (Not that he would be troubled by that.) We were confronted with 36kg of meat and 18.5kg of back fat. Michael had a serious meat mincer. By this time I had invested in an equally serious meat mincer. It would be wrong to describe this as mincer envy, but I am pleased to say that mine was larger than his. Marvin The Mincer is 1.1 hp of pure power and he acquitted himself very well. But I digress.

After two hours we had a really big pile of minced meat and minced back fat. It was really outstanding.

The casings were a problem, but that is another story; maybe next time. Standby.

Regarding butchers

I have always liked butchers and butcher shops. I do not know why. As for butchers perhaps it is their cheery demeanor or their plain honesty. As for butcher shops, perhaps it is the rosy reds and pinks of the meat and the promise of a good meal. I do not know. When I was young the meals were based upon red meat, namely lamb and beef. They being much more affordable than the farmed chicken which was a luxury, so much so that it was only partaken of on special occasions, like birthdays hence the appellation 'Happy Birthday Chicken'. The rarity only made chicken so much more important and therefore desirable.

My mother grew up on a sheep grazing property. She was handy with a knife. When I was young, she would purchase large cuts of beef or lamb (cheap in those days) from the wholesale butcher or the retail shop at the abattoir. Thereafter there was much cutting, chopping and freezing. For some reason, meat was not to be eaten or used fresh. It, apparently, had to be frozen in the gigantic freezer before it was used. This was the way of the 1960s and 1970s when I grew up. Nonetheless, I can work through a carcass or a portion thereof of and I can chop and dice. More importantly I can sharpen a knife on a butchers steel relatively efficiently, although not as fast as my late mother.

But I digress.

If you are interested in domestic charcuterie then the butcher is your best friend. He will obtain the cuts of meat that you want. He will cut the meat as you want it to be cut. He will source things that you need – whether it be fat, back fat, a pig or lamb for a spit roast, sheep bungs, beef middles, or sausage casings. He knows everything. He is your new best friend. Let me give you an example.

No. 1 Daughter's 18th birthday dinner was to be at home. The menu had been settled for several months. Forty eight hours prior to that time, No. 1 Daughter wanted to change the menu. I spoke to Sean The Butcher[49] about sourcing a particular cut of chicken; not a usual product. It is called Supreme of Chicken to some, to you and I it is the cut with the boneless breast and shoulder with the bone. It is used for Chicken Kiev although this cut retains the bone. All that was needed, said Sean The Butcher, was 24 hours' notice, and Sean The Butcher would provide. A supermarket could not do that.

Let me give another example, in the early days of charcuterie experimentation, I needed casings. Most butchers would not supply them. A few did, and I have stayed with them. It was the same with back fat and caul fat. So too, was the case with suckling pigs or milk fed lamb. They also give advice about all sorts of stuff. Remember, they are the experts. You will learn a lot of good stuff from them. The butcher is your friend. The real problem is that he or she is becoming an endangered species.

---

49   No relation to Frank the Butcher.

Dickins, who did not like lawyers at all, clearly was rather fond of butchers. In *'Martin Chuzzlewit'* he wrote:

> *"To see the butcher slap the steak, before he laid it on the block, and give his knife a sharpening, was to forget breakfast instantly. It was agreeable, too – it really was – to see him cut it off, so smooth and juicy. There was nothing savage in the act, although the knife was large and keen; it was a piece of art, high art; there was delicacy of touch, clearness of tone, skilful handling of the subject, fine shading. It was the triumph of mind over matter; quite."*

Angela Topping[50] whom I suspect does not like butchers all that much, described the butcher quite differently:

> *"The butcher smiles a meaty smile, white apron stained with who knows what, fingers fat as sausages...".*

Over the last 40 years I can count the local butchers who have closed their doors permanently in my area. That count would now occupy two hands. It is a sad thing, but reflective of our modern lifestyle. For my part I think the days of butcher shops with sawdust on the floor are things to be missed.

The title and first sentence are everything

I have long been impressed by the first sentence of a book. It is like The Three Minute Test for a film. If you are not interested in the film after the first three minutes, then it is unlikely that you will be interested thereafter. I have a short attention span, what can I say. It is the same for a book. Hence the term The Three Minute Test.

I have shared this with No. 1 Daughter and No. 1 Son. They seem little interested in this observation; as with much of my observations. As to first sentences, there have been some really good ones. Melville *"Call me Ishmael"*[51], or Dickens, *"It was the best of times, it was the worst of times"*[52]. There are many more.

---

50   Topping, A – *'The Butcher Shop'*.
51   *"Moby Dick"*.
52   *"A Tale of Two Cities"*.

I tried to think of one. I really did. But there was nothing to be had. It was more achievable to think of a book title. This was a more realistic opportunity.

There were a few contenders:

- "*A prosciutto called Kevin*" (a hot contender which missed out by a whisker);
- "*A pig called Bill*" (maybe save that for next time – if there is one);
- "*The big mince*";
- "*A few good salamis*";
- "*You can't handle the prosciutto*".

All received careful consideration and natural justice. The merits of each were assessed. Each was accorded procedural fairness. Many were called but only one was chosen. In the end, there would be only one. The title, and these stories are all true. I note again, not that it matters, but, they are all true.

On capitalisation and writing the book

When writing this book, one thing amongst all others was more troubling than most. That is to say, one thing, was more vexing than everything else. It was not the tense in which to write. Clearly when one is describing events which have passed, one must write in the past tense. Similarly, when one is referring to books which have already been written, one is obliged to write that the author said, opined, observed, noted and the like. The tense is quite properly that of things which have passed. It is quite incorrect, in my view, to write that the author has written of matters as if they are occurring in the present moment. Further, one cannot assert that something is 'said' by an author. It quite obviously is not, the written word is not to be confused with the spoken word. But I digress.

These were not matters which I spent any time considering, well not much anyway. The really vexing issue was whether names should be capitalised or not. For example, Pinot Noir, or pinot noir; Calebrese or calabrese. My natural inclination is that they should not be capitalised.

In my view proper nouns only are capitalised, for example '*John went to New York*'. The sentence capitalises the person's name as well as the geographic name. There is little else which should be capitalised. I undertook some research on this topic, well, in truth it was for a seminar, and a different purpose. Nonetheless, it seemed like a good idea to include the results in this book. Allow me to share the results of that research.

It is very common to use capitals, particularly in headings where they are not required. Of course names, titles and places (C.S.I.R.O., Mr Smith and Canberra) require the use of capitals. However, other words rarely require capitalisation, nonetheless it is common to observe headings like *"The Defendant's Affidavit of Documents"*. For some reason which always escapes me, the word *"of"* is usually not capitalised in the example which is given. Insofar as I have been able to identify the source of this practice, it seems to have some antiquity. The Cambridge Encyclopaedia of the English Language attributed the origin of the process to John Hart, a grammarian who died in 1574. It is stated that he recommended his readers to use a capital letter at the beginning of every sentence, proper name, and important common noun. By the 17th century, the practice had extended to titles (Sir, Lady), forms of address (Father, Mistress), and personified nouns (Nature). Emphasized words and phrases would attract a capital. By the beginning of the 18th century, the influence of "continental books" had caused this practice to be extended still further (for example, to the names of the branches of knowledge), and it was not long before some writers began using a capital for any noun that they felt to be important. Books appeared in which all or most nouns were given an initial capital (as is done systematically in modern German) – perhaps for aesthetic reasons, or perhaps because printers were uncertain about which nouns to capitalise and so capitalised them all.

Apparently the fashion was at its height in the latter 17th century, and continued into the 18th. The manuscripts of Butler, Traherne, Swift, and Pope are full of initial capitals. However, the latter 18th century grammarians were not amused by this apparent lack of discipline in the written language. By this time, the proliferation of capitals was considered unnecessary, and causing the loss of a useful potential distinction. Thereafter rules of grammar brought a dramatic reduction in the types of noun permitted to take a capital letter.

So, as near as I can tell, it was a practice which originated in the 16th century and then fell out of favour, albeit 300 years later. The efforts of several professions including the legal profession, to re-establish it should be avoided.

Accordingly, you will not find Pinot Noir, Shiraz or the like in this book. You will not find Calabrese, or Tenderloin. Neither will you find Oregano, Thyme or Paprika. You can look as hard as you like. They are not there, at least I hope not. Hopefully, you will find short simple sentences without capitalisations.

Short, simple sentences are best. Use simple, plain English words. In my view each sentence should be no more than 8-10 words long. (Hopefully I have not breached the rule.) I think that each sentence should only make one point. Consider Winston Churchill's *"Blood, sweat and tears"* speech given on 4 June 1940:

> *"We shall go on to the end.*
> *We shall fight in France,*
> *We shall fight on the seas and oceans.*
> *We shall fight with growing confidence and growing strength in the air.*
> *We shall defend our Island, whatever the cost may be.*
> *We shall fight on the beaches.*
> *We shall fight on the landing grounds.*
> *We shall fight in the fields and in the streets.*
> *We shall fight in the hills.*
> *We shall never surrender"*

A symphony of simplicity. A speech which focussed on the subject matter with an economy of words.

Outstanding.

Capitals are not your friends.

They are the friends of the weak and ineffectual.

That is not you.

Eschew them whenever possible.

THE RECIPES

Many cookbooks in this area provide recipes based on unusual amounts of meat (say 5lb), with imprecise measurements (say, 2 juniper berries) or are in imperial measures (say 2 tsp. of sugar into 1 gallon of water). Indeed Grigson often referred to adding *"a pinch of saltpetre"*. All these things have some obvious shortcomings for those of us attempting charcuterie at home.

Importantly for an Australian and me in particular, these things are both frustrating and apt to produce a different result than that which was intended.

I decided that this was not good enough. In the event, I converted the recipes to metric measurements and the ingredients as a percentage of the weight of meat. This seemed to work and gave some consistent results. Certainly, I found this to be more acceptable. I was happy, well moderately satisfied at least.

In this book I have tried to base the recipes on 1kg of meat and a quantity of other ingredients as a percentage by reference to the weight of meat whenever possible. Some recipes do not lend themselves to a great deal of precision. Meat rubbed in salt or immersed (buried) in salt are examples. Traditional recipes, like corned beef, parfait or choucroute or those using salt immersions do not lend themselves to great precision nor have I attempted to do so. You should not either. Nonetheless, I have tried to give a guide to the amounts required. You can experiment to achieve a result which you find pleasing.

Hopefully this means that the recipe can be quickly adapted to your weight of meat. Indeed rarely will any cut of meat be available in exact multiples of 1kg. However, the recipes are not intended to be proscriptive (save for the amounts of salt and Curing Salt) and are a guide only.

Experiment with different amounts of seasonings and aromatics, if you prefer a hotter taste, then add more chilli. It is a matter for you.

Many of the books in this area, especially the older books, assume a high level of proficiency in the kitchen. Some almost assume a familiarity with the subject.

In my experience, various representations of culinary proficiency by kitchen colleagues are rarely true. These days I assume low level proficiency and a desire to self mutilate when I am cooking with someone else (on their part not mine). I find that I am rarely disappointed. I have tried to write in a narrative style which does not assume much kitchen expertise and is based upon those working assumptions.

I have tried to include a variety of French charcuterie recipes as well, but beyond the obvious such as paté, terrine and rillettes. There are several reasons for this. First, charcuterie is a French word and they need to be heard in this regard. Secondly, French charcuterie recipes are not readily available to me, at least not in English and, as stated above, they need to be heard. Thirdly, most of the books to which I have access to, in my language, focus on Italian or Central European (mostly Polish) recipes. I suspect that this has a lot to do with the authors being located in North America. At all events I wanted to give French recipes a voice in this book; after all the term for the whole process is French, not Italian, Polish or German.

I am a river to my people.

THE WHOLE MUSCLE CHARCUTERIE

The easiest way to start experimenting with charcuterie techniques and recipes is with whole muscle cuts of meat. That is where I started and where I had the most success for the least angst. What I mean by "whole muscle cuts of meat" is meat which is 'defined' within the musculature of the animal rather than minced meat. An example is pork loin. Pork loin is a single muscle running along the spine (back bone) which can be cut into manageable pieces for charcuterie. Whole muscle cuts require simpler technique because mincing and filling into casings is not required. They are also less prone to spoiling because bacteria are not likely to be present internally, unlike with raw minced meat. The curing times are quite short for small whole muscle cuts, although for a whole leg (prosciutto) it is the longest cure time in all charcuterie preparations.

This is where I started and, in my view, where you should start also.

Whilst charcuterie usually uses pork whole muscle cuts of meat, whole muscle charcuterie can use parts of beef, lamb or duck. They all give really good results and should be respected in their own right. I deal with recipes for each separately.

PORK

LONZA

Lonza is cured and dried pork loin. Lonza in Italian, lomo embuchado in Spanish; air dried and cured loin of pork in English. The meat is very lean and can dry out quickly during the curing and drying process, but creates a delicate and unique cured product. It makes a good addition to a charcuterie plate and is one which many have not come across before.

Pork loin (trimmed of fat and sinew) – 1kg.
Salt – 3%.
Curing Salt No. 2 – 0.3%.
Pepper (ground, white) – 1%.
Clove (ground) – 1/2tsp.
Juniper berry (crushed) – 0.2%.
Fennel (ground) – 0.5%.
Garlic (powder) – 0.5%.

Place the pork loin in a sealed, non-reactive container (a resealable plastic bag works well) together with all the ingredients.

Cure for approximately 1 day/kg and overhaul the meat twice daily.

Once cured, wash the meat with water or white wine (sparingly) or wipe off the cure. Dry and tie the meat like a rolled roast. Tying the meat helps keep its shape and makes it easier to hang. Tying the meat and practising the butcher's knot is also quite satisfying to do; at least I think so.

For some extra flavour, and to assist the drying process, the meat can be lightly coated with a finely ground dry spice or herb. Do not use a whole or coarse ground spice or herb. The delicate flavour of the loin is best complimented by a milder spice like white pepper but you may choose to use fennel, coriander or sweet paprika.

Weigh the meat and record the weight. Hang in a cool dry place until it has lost approximately 30% of its weight. This will take 3-4 weeks depending on conditions.

CAPOCOLLO

Capocollo (sometimes called coppa) is cured boneless meat from within the pork shoulder. It is a large muscle which can weigh 2-3 kg. It is often sold as pork *"neck"[1]* in Australia and has a good marbling of fat through the interior of the muscle. After it is cured it develops a deep ruby red colour with an attractive marbling of fat. Once sliced, the profile and colour is instantly recognisable. It has no rind or skin, so it can dry a little but unlike lonzo, its more significant diameter and intramuscular fat means it does not dry out too much.

Pork (neck) – 1kg.
Salt – 3%.
Curing Salt No. 2 – 0.3%.
Pepper (white, ground) – 1%.
Juniper berry (crushed) – 0.2%.
Pepper (black, cracked) – 1tbsp.

Place meat and dry ingredients in a resealable plastic bag or non-reactive container. Refrigerate for 1 day/kg, overhauling daily.

Thereafter, wash (sparingly) with water or red wine and weigh. Record weight.

You can lightly coat the meat in a finely ground dry herb or spice. The choice is up to your tastes. It assists with the drying process and imparts an extra flavour which is very pleasing. However, the nature of this meat will tolerate a more robust flavouring such as ground fennel, ground thyme, black pepper or paprika. Each will give a slightly different flavour.

Tie the meat like a roast to hold its shape, hang it for 4-6 weeks or until it has reduced weight by 30%.

---

1   Boston butt, for our North American cousins.

PANCETTA

Pancetta is cured pork belly, often smoked but not necessarily so. Usually the section of belly which is used is that which is not from the rib section, but the true pork belly. It is thinner and more fatty than the rib section and the part which has no bones. This is the part which is traditionally used for bacon and pancetta production.

The meat can either be left as a relatively thin, flat piece (pancetta tesa) or skinned and rolled (pancetta arrotolata). Flat pancetta is easier to make as a novice because it cures quickly due to its relative thinness. Flat pancetta is also less likely to spoil from the inside than rolled pancetta.

Pancetta can also be spiced depending upon your preference, either hot and spicy or more aromatic.

The skin (rind) of flat pancetta can be removed or not, whichever is your preference. If it is left on then the rind is usually removed before eating, much like with traditional bacon. I prefer leaving it on. It is quite pleasing to the eye particularly if the pancetta is smoked as part of the process.

The rind of rolled pancetta must be removed before it is rolled and tied. If not you will get rind within each slice of the finished product. A very bad result.

FLAT PANCETTA

Our Italian friends call this pancetta tesa.

Pork (belly, skin on, bones in if you wish) – 1kg.
Salt – 3%.
Curing Salt No. 2 – 0.3%.
Pepper (black, ground) – 1%.
Juniper berry (crushed) – 0.5%.
Bay leaves – 2.
Thyme (fresh or dried) – 0.15%.
Garlic (crushed) – 1tsp.
Sugar (brown) – 1.2%
For a hotter style, substitute the following for the aromatics (quantities of salt and Curing Salt No. 2 are the same as above):
Garlic (powder) – 1.5%.
Onion (powder) – 1.5%.
Paprika (sweet) – 1.5%.
Paprika (hot) or chilli – 1%.
Pepper (black, ground) – 1.5%.

Place meat and spice mixture in a resealable plastic bag or a non-reactive container. Refrigerate for five days, overhauling daily.

Thereafter wash, dry and weigh the cured meat. Record the weight. There is no need to tie the meat.

For ease of handling and drying, hang on a meat hook or make a loop of string through a corner to hang. Hang for 2-3 weeks or until weight has reduced by 30%.

ROLLED PANCETTA

Our Italian brothers and sisters refer to this as pancetta arrotolata.

1kg piece of pork belly. The skin (rind) **must** *be removed otherwise the rind will be throughout the finished rolled product. It will be difficult to eat.*

The ingredients are the same as with the flat pancetta. The only difference is the rolling.

Dredge the meat in the spice/salt mixture and then roll. The external fat (the side which formerly was covered with skin) must be on the outside of the finished roll. Tie the roll like a roast. Use a butchers knot.

Weigh the roll and record the weight.

Hang for 2-3 weeks or until weight has reduced by 30%.

PROSCIUTTO

Prosciutto, or air dried whole pork leg is quite simple to prepare and produces a fantastic result. It can be prepared using a whole (rear) leg of pork or smaller cuts like chump (with bone or without) or a rolled, boned leg. I will describe the process for each separately.

CLASSIC WHOLE LEG PROSCIUTTO

You will need a whole (rear) leg of pork. The best prosciutto is made from female pigs only, the male having a much stronger taste. This is referred to as *"boar taint"*. It arises due to the prevalence of male hormones and is quite unpalatable.

You (or your butcher) will need to prepare the pork leg in order to make prosciutto. The skin is left on to prevent the meat drying out too quickly in the process and to resist any critter attacks. The flesh on the cut side is trimmed to remove loose meat, fat and skin. These are places where bacteria can develop and spoil the ham. The ball joint needs to be well exposed so that the salt can penetrate close to the bone, a source of spoilage.

It is a matter of preference whether the trotter and hock are removed. In Spanish jamon they are left attached, in Italian prosciutto they are usually removed. I find removing them makes the ham shorter and easier to fit into a container for curing.

The meat needs to be well massaged to remove any residual blood from inside the meat, especially the large femoral artery. Usually meat purchased from retail butchers in Australia is well prepared and there is no blood, but check anyway. If you are butchering your own pork then ensure that the blood is completely removed. This is critical, blood will spoil the product.

Salt[55] – sufficient amount to completely cover the pork. A commercial leg of pork will be between 8-12kg. It will need at least 10kg of salt to cover it.
Curing Salt No. 2 – 0.3%.

Rub the exposed meat with a mixture of the Curing Salt and a few cups of salt. Work the mixture well into all exposed surfaces and close to the bone. If the hock has been removed, work the mixture well into the exposed hock end. The purpose is to ensure that the Curing Salt is in contact with the meat.

Use a non-reactive container large enough to cope with the meat and salt sufficient to completely cover. Place a layer of salt in the bottom of the container. Place the pork leg onto the salt, cut side down and at a slight downward angle, if possible. Cover the meat completely with salt.

Place a weight on top of the covered meat. For example, a plastic chopping board with a brick (wrapped in plastic) on top. Place the lid on the container.

The container must be kept in a dark, cool place whilst the meat cures in the salt. The time for curing is approximately 1 day/kg. It can be left for longer if you choose, if so, the end product will be slightly saltier and firmer in texture.

After the salt curing, remove the meat and brush off excess salt. A small nail brush is ideal for this purpose. The meat can be washed sparingly with water or wine (it helps as an antibacterial agent) but it is not essential.

---

55. The salt required is only sufficient to cover the meat. The Curing Salt should be more precise.

The meat is now air dried by tying a string securely around or even better, through the hock. Wrap the meat in muslin or a 'ham sock' to prevent critter attack. The air drying needs to occur in a cool, dark place. The temperature should be no more than 10-12°C and a relative humidity (RH) of 60-80%.

NOTE: The exposed meat will dry out faster than the meat covered in rind. To avoid the prosciutto drying out too quickly, cover the exposed meat in a mixture of lard and cracked black pepper. The lard seals the exposed meat and slows the drying process. The black pepper discourages unwanted attacks from critters.

Air dry for as long as you can, the product improves significantly with age. However, the prosciutto should be well cured and ready in about six months. Test it by pressing the meat, there should be some resistance to hard pressure but not a great deal. It should also smell like prosciutto, a certain musky, funky smell which is characteristic – but not an unpleasant odour.

When cut, the meat will have a familiar rose colour and soft consistency, the fat will be white in colour (remove any yellowish fat) and creamy in texture.

'MINI' PROSCIUTTO

Exactly the same result can be obtained by using a smaller piece of meat. The benefits are that air drying is much quicker and if it spoils, there is not as much to be lost. The latter is of some comfort to the novice.

The cut can be from the leg – for example, a rolled, boned leg 'roast' from the butcher. However, make sure that it has as much rind on as possible. This will stop the meat drying out too quickly. Another cut to use is the 'chump' end of the leg (on the bone).

The method is the same as for a whole leg. However, the salt curing time should be approximately 3 days/kg (rather than 1 day/kg for the larger piece). Thereafter, follow the air drying process until it is cured. This will probably take 2-4 weeks, depending on the size of the piece. The smaller the piece of meat, the quicker it will air dry. Watch it carefully, it will have a tendency to dry out too quickly.

NOTE: If it is drying out too much on the cut surface of the meat, apply a paste of lard mixed with cracked black pepper to retard dehydration. It is also useful to discourage critters, if you are dry curing outdoors.

CULATELLO AND FIOCCO

Culatello is prepared in much the same way as prosciutto but using a large muscle from the pork leg rather than the whole leg. Think of it as a boned prosciutto, which in many ways, it is. The butchery required is not difficult and any mistakes will be hidden when the meat is rolled and tied. Get your butcher to do it or, even better, have a try yourself.

Traditionally it is rolled, tied and dried inside a pig or ox bladder. However, pig and ox bladders are difficult to obtain; use a netting bag, a collagen wrap or a ham sock.

The boned out leg traditionally gives two pieces of meat. The larger culatello and a smaller piece – fiocco. Cure and dry fiocco in the same way as with culatello.

1 culatello. (The meat is rolled and tied into a roughly tear drop shape. I will describe how to butcher in the method section. Accordingly, if you wish to do this yourself (and you should), it will forgive some butchery mistakes).

Salt – 3%.

Curing Salt No. 2 – 0.3%.

Pepper (black, crushed) – 0.1%.

As an option, other aromatics can be added such as a few bay leaves, a pinch of thyme or marjoram.

The butchery required:

You will require one leg of pork. It does not matter if it has been trimmed for prosciutto, or if the femur end has been squared off for a roasting joint. The hock and trotter are not required and can be removed.

Lay the leg on the bench in front of you with the hock end facing away. Rotate the leg such that the leg bones are uppermost.

Feel where the bones are within the leg; they are not deep and their alignment can be easily felt. Note that the bones are not symmetrical within the meat. The right hand side is the larger "piece" of meat, the left hand side is the small piece of meat. They are roughly divided by the leg bones.

Dissect the leg by removing the bones (tunnel boning is not required). You will be left with the leg meat opened out like a book, but with the right hand side much larger than the left.

Cut longitudinally (in the same direction as where the bones run) to separate into pieces. The larger piece is the culatello, the smaller piece is called fiocco. Tie each into their natural shape, a roughly tear drop shaped portion of leg meat.

You now have a culatello and a fiocco to brine and air dry.

Outstanding.

Combine ingredients and rub the meat, after rolling and tying. Use a butchers knot. Place the culatello in a non-reactive, sealed container or in a resealable plastic bag. Keep in the refrigerator for 21 days, overhauling daily. Remove, pat dry and weigh. Record weight.

I note in passing that traditionally the culatello is placed in a pork bladder (an ox bladder will also do nicely if it is a large culatello). The bladder is sewn tightly such that the culatello is wrapped in the bladder. The resultant tear drop shaped piece is tied to keep its shape. Thereafter it is air dried in a curing chamber until the weight has reduced by at least 30%. For those who do not have an ox or pig bladder readily at hand, wrap the meat in collagen sheet. Place in netting or in a ham sock and into the curing chamber. The drying process will take about 6 months at least. The approximate guide for readiness is weight loss of about 30-40%.

BUENDNERSCHINKEN (GERMAN AIR DRIED HAM)

Buendnerschinken is cured air-dried pork from the leg of the pig. Any whole muscle cut would work, for example, culatello.

Pork (leg, boned and skinless, separated into the major and minor muscle groups, as with culatello and fiocco.) – 1.
Salt – 3%.
Curing Salt No. 2 – 0.3%.
Sugar (caster) – 0.5%.
Pepper (white, ground) – 0.2%.
Nutmeg (ground) – 0.15%.
Garlic (powder) – 0.15%.

Butcher the pork leg in the manner described for culatello and fiocco.

Use the larger muscle group, the culatello cut for this recipe.

Rub the meat well in a mix of some salt together with the spices, sugar and the Curing Salt.

Work it well into all the nooks and crannies where critters might like to live.

In a non reactive container place a layer of salt, put the meat on top, now cover with remaining salt and pack it well down.

Refrigerate for one week.

Remove the meat, repeat the process (but with the meat rotated so the top surface is now on the bottom) for a few weeks.

Repeat the process once more.

Remove and brush off excess salt.

Tie the meat like a roast or put into an elastic netting. Cover with muslin or a ham sock type cloth (an elasticised muslin).

Weigh and record weight.

Air dry until the meat has lost 30% of its weight.

NOIX DE JAMBON (FRENCH SMALL DRY CURED HAMS)

Noix de jambon (which translates literally as 'ham nuts'), is almost the same as cullatello or fiocco. Noix de jambon is closer to fiocco because both are smaller pieces of leg meat which are cured individually. Similarly to culatello and fiocco noix are quicker to cure than prosciutto. Also, if something goes wrong then it is better to find out quickly rather than wait for 6-12 month as with a prosciutto. This is a good way to start with a prosciutto style cured ham.

Salt – 3% (coarse or flossy salt).
Curing Salt No. 2 – 0.3%.
Pepper (black, cracked) – 2tbsp.
Thyme (dried, finely ground) – 2tbsp.
Bay leaf (dried and ground) – 1-2 leaves ground.

Start with a bone in leg of pork or boneless pieces – it does not matter.

First, decide if the rind is to remain. It is a matter of choice. Keeping the rind on prevents the 'noix' from drying out too quickly, but this hard rind must be removed prior to slicing.

Debone the leg. It is not necessary to be delicate with this process, the meat will be cut into pieces. Next separate the meat into muscles or groups of muscles. A leg of pork will yield between 6 and 12 'noix' depending on its size. What you want is a reasonably well defined muscle and a piece which is not too small. If it is too small it will dry out too quickly. If possible cut the 'noix' such that they are of a relatively even size, they will cure more evenly. Trim the 'noix' carefully, remove any external fat and sinew.

Rub the 'noix' well with salt and Curing Salt and place in a resealable plastic bag or a sealed non reactive container. Put this container into the refrigerator. Overhaul daily.

The trick to this preparation is how long to leave the 'noix' on the salt. Because they can be quite small they will have a tendency to become over salty. You will have to be the judge, but a minimum of 2 days will be required. A maximum of, say 4 days. You will feel that the 'noix' has firmed up quite well and observe a good amount of liquid has been drawn out. Perhaps in the order of 3 days would be an acceptable compromise, depending on the size. Also consider removing smaller 'noix' after 2 days and large 'noix' after a total of 3-4 days.

Once removed from the cure, pat the 'noix' dry and coat well in the pepper and herbs. The quantity does not matter, but use a ratio of equal parts pepper and thyme. Bay leaf is strongly flavoured; use about one bay leaf for a whole leg of pork. Tie each 'noix' to keep its shape or use elastic netting. Weigh each and record its weights. Air dry in a curing chamber or well ventilated cold place.

The noix will be ready when they have lost about 30% of their weight. This should take about 2-3 weeks. A very good way to become familiar with the process and not too disheartening if something goes wrong.

Bon courage.

NOTE: *Noix de jambon can also be smoked.*

If you intend to try a smoked product then interpose the smoking step before air drying. That is to say, cure, dry, coat in the pepper and herbs and then smoke the 'noix'. A light smoking for 3-4 hours at maybe 65°C would be sufficient. The smoking is not intended to smoke the meat, merely to give it a light smoke flavor. Thereafter hang the 'noix' as described above.

GUANCIALE (CURED PORK CHEEK)

Guanciale is made from the jowl or cheek of the pig. It is prepared in the same way as pancetta but produces a product which has a slightly different texture and flavour.

Pork cheek can be a little hard to source unless one purchases a whole pig's head (which I encourage you to do). Even so, the jowl extends down the throat beyond the head, so you are not getting all of the jowl. In truth, this is made from the throat of the pig rather than the cheek.

A butcher will help you but often Asian butchers will have pork cheek for sale, not the whole piece but in large chunks. This is ok if you cannot obtain a whole guanciale.

Pork cheek (the size will vary, it does not matter for this recipe) or some pork cheek pieces – 1kg.
Salt – 3%.
Curing Salt No.2 – 0.3%.
Pepper (black, crushed) – 10g.
Bay leaf - 1 (other aromatics can be added if you choose. Think of this as pancetta, use whatever aromatics you prefer).

If you have a whole pig head, remove the cheek from the head. In any event, keep the skin on and trim to remove loose edges. Try and obtain as much of the throat as you can.

Remove any obvious glands or nasty looking bits (a pig face contains quite a few glands which are not at all good to eat).

Place the cheek or cheek pieces into a sealed non-reactive container. Add salt, Curing Salt No.2, cracked black pepper and a bay leaf or two.

Place in the refrigerator, overhauling daily for 7 days.

Remove, wash and pat dry. Weigh and record weight. Hang in a cool place or curing chamber until it has lost 30% of its weight.

NOTE: After curing, the guanciale can be lightly coated in either white pepper, ground fennel, ground paprika or chilli. Either will assist the drying process and impart flavour. It is up to you.

SPEC TIROLESE

A prosciutto style cured boned leg from the Tyrol region of Italy, or so I am told.

Pork (leg-boned, rolled and skin left on) – 1kg.
Salt – 3.0%.
Curing Salt No. 2 – 0.3%.
Sugar (caster) – 0.5%.
Pepper (black, cracked) – 0.1%.
Rosemary (dried) – 0.1%.
Juniper berry (cracked).
Coriander (ground) – 0.1%.
Allspice (ground) – 0.1%.
Ginger (ground) – 0.1%.

Mix all dry ingredients together.

Tie the meat like a roast.

Rub the meat well with the ingredients.

In a non-reactive container lay the meat, exposed surface down, on a layer of dry ingredients. Cover with the remaining dry mix.

Seal the container and refrigerate for 1 day/kg, overhauling daily, wash lightly.

Dry cure until the meat loses 30% of its green weight.

JAMBON DE PARIS (PARIS HAM)

This recipe is adapted from Grigson. She referred to it also as jambon blanc or white ham. She described the method as an 'unsmoked ham using English brine'. It is a lightly cured and boiled "ham". I dare say that it is referred to as jambon blanc because her recipe does not contain saltpetre or nitrite for that matter. I prefer to use a Curing Salt for preservation and aesthetic reasons.

Pork leg (boned or bone in, rind on).
Brine :
Salt – 350g.
Sugar – 350g.
Curing Salt No. 2 – 0.3%.

Submerge meat into the brine solution. Refrigerate for 1 day/kg. (Grigson says 'at least ten days, at most thirty'.)

Remove the ham from the brine. Grigson instructs that next you should place in a pot of cold water and bring to the boil, simmering for 10 minutes. This is to be repeated several times (although not entirely clear). I suspect the point is to soak until the salt is leached from the meat. You can include this step if you wish. I do not.

Prepare to court bouillon (water, carrot, onion, salt, pepper, quatre épicés).

Place the meat in the court bouillon. Simmer until cooked.

NOTE: It can be seen that this recipe is not really what we would call ham today.
It is more in the nature of gammon or what I would describe as pickled pork.
Think of this as equivalent to corned beef.

CIDER CURED HAM

British recipes use a variety of flavourings, such as molasses or, as in this case, cider. The ham is wet cured (brined) and then boiled.

Sometimes they are also smoked but not in this recipe. You can use either a whole leg of pork or a smaller rolled piece. It really depends upon how much ham you intend to produce and whether you have a pot large enough to contain a leg of pork.

Pork leg (rind on).
Salt – 2kg.
Curing Salt No. 2 – 0.3%.
Apple juice – 1 litre.
Cider – 1 litre.
Water – 2 litre.
Sugar (dark brown) – 1kg.
Molasses – 1kg.
Juniper berries – 20 (lightly crushed).
Pepper (black peppercorns, whole, lightly cracked) – ¼ cup.
Bay leaves (fresh or dried) – 5.
Coriander seeds (whole) – 1tbsp.

Combine all ingredients to make a brine.

Heat it to dissolve if need be.

Transfer brine to a non reactive container with a lid.

Immerse the pork in the brine, use a weight to keep it submerged. Allow the ham to brine in the refrigerator for 4 days/kg. Turn it in the brine every few days.

Thereafter remove the ham and dry it well. Now the ham needs to be soaked in fresh water for 24-42 hours, changing the water frequently.

Next, boil the ham for 2-4 hours depending on its size until an internal temperature of 65°C is achieved. Alternatively it can be glazed and baked in a low oven until an internal temperature of 65° C is achieved.

JAMBONNEAU (PICNIC HAM)

This is a French quick cured pork knuckle or hock. It can be smoked but is usually made as an unsmoked boiled fresh ham. With the bone removed, rolled and tied it is known as jambonnette.

Pork knuckle (bone-in, skin on) – 1.
Water – 3-4 litres.
Salt – 250g.
Sugar (caster) – 300g.
Curing Salt No. 1 - 0.3%.
Wine (white, dry) – 350ml.
Bay leaf (fresh or dried) – 2.
Mustard seed (ground) – 2tsp.
Allspice (berry, lightly crushed) – 1tsp.
Cloves (whole) – 4.
Pepper (black peppercorn, lightly crushed) – 1tsp.
Juniper berries (whole, lightly crushed) – 1tsp.
Thyme (fresh or dried) – 1 tsp/1 sprig.

Make a brine with all the ingredients. Heat to dissolve if need be. Allow to cool completely.

Submerge the pork knuckle for 5-8 days depending on the size. Weigh if necessary so it is completely immersed. Thereafter remove and pat dry.

The cured meat can either be boiled (traditional fresh method) or roasted.

If you choose to boil then in a large pot, make a court bouillon with the usual suspects, add pork and a bouquet garni. Simmer for two hours. Allow to cool in the poaching liquor.

Chill, when cold it is ready to slice.

Insofar as it can be roasted, rub the meat with epices composes, sel-épicé or dried herbs such as rosemary, thyme and sage. Place on a tray in the oven at 200°C until the internal temperature is 65°C. Remove from the oven and slice.

BEEF

BRESAOLA

Bresaola is cured and dried beef, one of the few charcuterie products using beef. Although Grigson wrote *"...it varies a good deal but when not too dry makes a very good hors d'oeuvre."* Whilst it does have a tendency to dry out, it is a very good product.

Topside is usually the cut of meat which is used. The best topside cut of meat to use is the *"eye"* of the topside often sold in Australia as *"girello"*. The reason topside is used is because it is extremely lean, beef fat is not pleasurable once cured, unlike pork fat. A whole *"girello"* will weigh up to 3kg, but a piece will be sufficient if you want a smaller result.

Do not be tempted to use other cuts of beef. Other cuts of beef just will not work for this dish. They are either too fatty (scotch fillet) or are too soft (eye fillet).

The beef needs to be quite resilient in order to take the cure and still hold its shape. It is also important that it has very little fat. Fat will only go rancid. You do not want rancid beef fat. Accordingly, topside is really the only choice.

As an aside, one cannot write a book about charcuterie in Australia without using the national emblem, kangaroo, at least once. Farmed kangaroo meat is readily available in supermarkets. It is very lean with a good flavour. It is not at all strong tasting or gamey, although it has a more mineral aftertaste than beef. It would lend itself very well for a variation on bresaola. Simply substitute kangaroo meat for beef (fillet or rump are easiest to source, but eye of the round would be perfect if you can find it).

I have not tried any other Australian native meats for charcuterie because they are very lean and are probably not well suited to it. Kangaroo is possibly the sole exception.

Interestingly, Mrs Beeton's book ("Household Management")[56] had a section on Australian cookery including a recipe for roast wallaby as follows:

---

56   For the full title of which, see the Appendix.

"*Ingredients - Wallaby, forcemeat, milk, butter*

Mode - In winter the animal may hang for some days, as a hare, which it resembles, but in summer it must, like all other flesh, be cooked very soon after it is killed. Cut off the hind-legs at the first joints, and after skinning and paunching, let it lie in water for a little while to draw out the blood. Make a good veal force-meat, and after well washing the inside of the wallaby, stuff it and sew it up. Truss as a hare and roast before a bright clear fire from 1 ¼ to 1 ¾ hour, according to size. It must be kept some distance from the fire when first put down, or the outside will be too dry before the inside is done. Baste well, first with milk and then with butter, and when nearly done dredge with flour and baste again with butter till nicely frothed.

Time – 1¼ to 1¾ hour.

Sufficient for 6 persons.

Seasonable – Best in cold weather."

I have not been tempted to try it.

As an aside, the full title of Mrs Beeton's book is '*The Book of Household Management Comprising information for the Mistress, Housekeeper, Cook, Kitchen-Maid, Butler, Footman, Coachman, Valet, Upper and Under House-Maids, Lady's-Maid, Maid-of-all-work, Laundry-Maid, Nurse and Nurse-Maid, Monthly Wet and Sick Nurses, etc. etc. – also Sanitary, Medical & Legal Memoranda; with a History of the Origin, Properties, and Uses of all Things Connected with the Home Life and Comfort*'.

Outstanding. I wish that I could have devised such a title for this book.

BRESAOLA

Girello (eye of topside) – 1kg.

Salt – 3%.

Curing Salt No. 2 – 0.3%.

Sugar – 1%.

Pepper (black, crushed) – 0.5%.

Rosemary (dried) – 0.25%.

Juniper berry (crushed) – 0.1%.

Thyme (dried or fresh) – 0.1%.

Cinnamon (ground) – 0.05%.

*Clove (ground) – 0.025%
(a really strong spice, if in
doubt err on the side of
caution or leave it out).*

Bay leaves – 2.

*Oregano (fresh or dried) –
1tbspn.*

*Red wine (optional) –
1 cup, say.*

Remove all fat and sinew (silver skin) from the exterior.

Combine all ingredients. Place in a resealable plastic bag or a non-reactive sealed container and refrigerate for 7-9 days. Overhaul daily.

Wash, dry, weigh and record weight. Tie like a roast, to retain a pleasing shape. Use a butcher's knot. Air dry until it has lost approximately 30% of its weight.

BASTURMA

Basturma is Turkish air dried beef which is very similar to bresaola. The principal differences with basturma are the addition of fenugreek (which gives it a distinctive flavour) and a slightly different curing method. Once again, the preferable cut to use is the eye of topside or girello. Trim the meat of all fat and sinew (silver skin).

Beef (topside or girello) – 1kg.
Salt – 3%.
Curing Salt – 0.3%.
Paprika (sweet or smoked) – ¼ cup.
Fenugreek (ground) – ¼ cup.
Allspice (ground) – 1tbsp.
Salt – 1tsp.
Pepper (black, ground) – 1 ½ tsp.
Cayenne pepper (ground) – ½ tsp.
Cumin (ground) – 1tsp.
Garlic (minced) – 3tsp.
Water (use enough just to loosen and combine the paste) – 1 cup.

Remove all fat and sinew (silver skin) from the exterior of the meat.

Add ingredients to a resealable plastic bag or a non-reactive container and refrigerate for 3 days. Overhaul daily.

Thereafter remove, wash and soak for 1 hour in fresh water. Dry the meat well and air dry for 2 weeks.

Make a paste[57] from the spices.

After the initial air drying of 2 weeks, cover meat with the spice paste and place meat in a resealable or a non-reactive container and overhaul daily for 2 weeks.

Next, remove the meat from the container, do not wash the paste off but try and coat the meat evenly in the paste. Make sure no surface of the meat is exposed to air. Make a string loop through one corner of the meat or fix onto a sharp meat hook. Air dry for 2 weeks.

When complete, remove the now dried paste from the meat and slice the meat thinly. (Remove the paste as required before slicing.)

---

57 I have used imperial measurements for this because precision is not all that important for this dish. The paste coats and flavours the mixture, the precise quantity of aromatics are not really important.

BILTONG

Biltong is South African spiced air-dried beef. This is Michael's recipe. I do not know if it is also used by Boris The Blade. He does not say much.

Beef (a lean cut like silverside, or topside) – 1kg.
Salt (coarse) – 6.5%.
Curing Salt No. 2 – 0.3%.
Sugar (brown) – 5g.
Bicarbonate of soda – 5g.
Pepper (black, crushed) – 2g.
Coriander (seed, whole) – 6g.
Vinegar (white or brown) – 100ml
Worcestershire sauce – 25ml
Water (warm) – 500ml

Trim the meat of any fat.

Cut into long strips, importantly they should be cut <u>with</u> the grain, not across it.

Combine all dry ingredients and rub well into the meat.

Layer the meat in a non reactive container and sprinkle each layer with a mixture of vinegar and Worcestershire sauce.

Place in the refrigerator for 24 hours. The next day, remove and drain off the vinegar mixture. Wash the meat to remove any salt and spices.

Hang until the meat is hard, but with a little give.

LAMB AND GOAT

LAMB PROSCIUTTO

An interesting variation on prosciutto is to use a leg of lamb rather than pork. The end product is similar in appearance to prosciutto but with a somewhat gamey or *"lamb"* taste. It may be something of an acquired taste but is interesting nonetheless.

The lamb leg can either be on the bone or boned. In my view a bone-in leg is simpler and less prone to bacterial problems.

Leg of lamb[58] – 1.
Salt – 3%.
Curing Salt No. 2 – 0.3%.
Pepper (black, ground) – 1.5%.
Sugar – 3%.

Trim the leg as with pork leg for prosciutto. You will probably purchase a leg of lamb from the butcher which has been prepared for roasting, not charcuterie. If so, the leg of lamb may have been prepared by removing the *"aitchbone"* or hip bone and the end of the femur (the traditional exposed ball joint of the prosciutto). It makes no difference if this has been done.

Bury meat in remaining salt in the same manner as pork for prosciutto. Place a weight on top.

Keep in a cool, dry place for 3 days/kg. The meat needs to be in the salt cure for longer than pork because it is much smaller (probably about 1.5kg).

After the curing time has elapsed, remove the leg from the salt and brush off the excess salt. Coat the meat in sweet paprika and air dry until the weight has reduced by 30%.

The end product is a rosy colour and quite firm but with a strong lamb flavour. It is well worth a try.

---

58   The weight will vary but it will be probably at least 1.5kg in total weight.

LAMB HAM

Corned lamb or lamb ham is a very old fashioned product and one rarely seen today. The older recipes (of which there not many) sometimes refer to this as lamb ham, which in many ways it is. It is very similar to corned beef and eats very well. It is worth a try. It can be prepared with either a bone-in or boned (tied and rolled) leg. In my view it works better with a boneless leg simply because it is easier to slice thinly.

The meat is brined and then either boiled like corned beef or smoked. The smoked product has a more complex flavour but neither is excessively *"lamb"* flavoured.

As an aside, the term 'corned' derives from the process of curing the meat using coarse salt crystals, referred to as 'corns' of salt. Hence, the product was called corned beef. Quite simple really.

Leg of lamb (size does not matter for this brine) – 1kg.
Salt – 3%.
Curing Salt No. 2 – 0.3%.
Sugar (brown or white sugar will do) – 3%.
Pickling mix – 1tbsp.
Water – 3-4 litres.

Combine ingredients and prepare the brine in the usual way. Add weight to lamb and ensure it is submerged, weighing it down if needed. Keep in a sealed, non-reactive container in the refrigerator for 5-7 days. Remove meat and pat dry.

At this stage it can be treated exactly like corned beef. Simmered in a court bouillon for, say, 1 hour it will look and taste very similar to corned beef.

Alternatively it can be hot smoked, this adds more complexity to the taste. For extra flavour, the meat can be rolled in a mixture of ground fennel, ground coriander and chilli. Mix, say, 2 tbsp. of fennel and coriander with a pinch of chilli. Roll the meat in it to coat, lightly brush off excess.

Smoke at 92℃ until the internal temperature reaches at least 65℃. If the process is taking too long, increase the ambient temperature slightly.

The product is best served cold and thinly sliced, like pastrami of which it shares many similarities.

MOCETTA (GOAT HAM, ITALIAN)

Mocetta is a cured meat, usually leg of goat, or venison, hence the name goat ham. It is cured in the style of prosciutto but is quite a different product. The gamey quality of the goat gives it quite a different taste than prosciutto. It is an acquired taste. As near as I can tell, it is produced in Valle d'Aosta or Camaoire.

Goat leg (bone in, just like a prosciutto).

Salt – enough to rub into the meat and then sufficient to cover the meat whilst it cures.

Curing Salt No. 2 – 0.3%.

Sugar – ½ cup.

Garlic (powder) – 30g.

Juniper berry (crushed) 15g.

Pepper (black, ground) – 10g.

Thyme (dried) – 5g.

Rosemary (dried) – 10g.

Bay leaf (fresh or dried) 5-10 (i.e. plenty)

Combine some salt and all the Curing Salt, mix well and massage into the meat.

Take care to ensure that the cut surfaces of the meat and the hock end are well covered with the salt/Curing Salt mixture.

Combine the remaining dry ingredients and pulse in a food processor or grind in a mortar and pestle until broken down (especially the bay leaves and rosemary). Massage the spice mixture well into the meat.

Weigh and record weight.

In a non-reactive container place the meat on a layer of salt and cover with salt. Refrigerate for 3-5 days with a weight on top.

Thereafter remove and pat dry.

Hang in a cool place until the meat has lost 30% of its weight.

DUCK

DUCK PROSCIUTTO

Duck breast makes a very good cured and air dried meat not unlike prosciutto. The duck breast (off the bone) is prepared in the same way as a leg of pork for prosciutto.

Duck breast (off the bone but with fat and skin remaining) – 1.
Salt – sufficient to immerse the meat.
Curing Salt No. 2 – 0.3%.
Juniper berries (crushed) – 4.
Pepper (black, cracked) – 1tsp.

Rub the meat with the dry ingredients. Use a non-reactive container which will accommodate the duck breast. Place a layer of salt in the bottom and place the meat, skin side up, on top. Cover with salt (bury the meat), a weight may be added. The weight is not required but helps the salt to penetrate the meat and give the classic 'flat' profile of a prosciutto.

Store in a cool, dark place for 1 day/kg.

Thereafter, remove from the salt, brush off excess salt and air dry until the weight has reduced by 30%. Slice thinly, discarding the duck fat and skin.

DUCK CONFIT (CONFIT DE CANARD)

Duck confit or confit de canard is a French method of preserving duck in salt and duck fat. It is the basis of the famous French dish, cassoulet.

Cassoulet is a stew of white beans and various preserved meat including duck confit. It is quite rich and well described by Elizabeth David as follows:

> "The cassoulet is a dish which may be infinitely varied so long as it is not made into a mockery with a sausage or two heated up with tin beans, or with all sorts of bits of left-over chicken or goodness knows what thrown into it as if it were a dustbin. And the wise will heed M. Colombié's advice about eating the cassoulet at midday on a day when no great exertion is called for afterwards." [59]

Duck maryland per person – 1.[60]
Duck fat[61] *(rendered, sufficient to completely cover meat).*
Salt – 200g.
Cloves (whole) – 2.
Allspice berry (whole) – 2.
Juniper berry (crushed) – 2.
Thyme (sprig of fresh or pinch of dried) – 2.
Pepper (black, cracked) – 5g.

Place duck and dry ingredients in a resealable plastic bag or a non-reactive container. Place in the refrigerator for 12-14 hours, overhauling every few hours if possible.

Rinse and dry the duck. It will be firmer to the touch due to the water escaping from the meat. Pat dry and place in an ovenproof container and completely submerge in melted (not hot) duck fat. Use a container of sufficient size to take all the duck pieces and no more. You want to use only sufficient duck fat to cover. A large amount of duck fat is required, especially for any quantity of duck legs. Large containers of duck fat (several kilograms in weight) can be purchased from commercial duck suppliers or ordered from a butcher or poultry supplier. This can be quite expensive, but the good news is that the process creates a net increase

---

59 The ratios of ingredients to meat are not critical. This recipe, like so many, is just a guide.
60 Maryland is the cut with the duck leg and thigh attached.
61 See suppliers for details.

in duck fat because of the fat which comes out of the meat in the cooking process. After cooking, the fat can be strained, cooled, the non-fat (stock) component separated and the fat frozen for future use. It freezes well and can be re-used provided it is not heated too much. Don't you dare throw out the duck stock. Use the duck stock as a flavouring for a casserole, but that is another story.

The duck and fat mixture is cooked at a very low heat (barely a *"tremble"*, anything more will deep fry the duck).

The duck will take anywhere from 2-4 hours to cook at a low temperature. When the meat is yielding but not falling off the bone, take it off the heat.

Place the duck in a non-reactive container and pour over the duck fat to completely cover the meat. Refrigerate until needed. It will keep in the refrigerator for up to 6 months.

Confit de canard is something that, once experienced, is never forgotten.

THE CURED AND AIR
DRIED SAUSAGES

THE CURED AND AIR DRIED SAUSAGES

Once you are comfortable with whole meat charcuterie, the next step is to try air dried sausages. Air dried sausages are quite simple to make and produce good results. Salami preparation is slightly more involved than whole meat charcuterie and can go wrong a bit easier but is well worth a try. I deal with salamis later

If making your own mince, use pork shoulder or pork neck. The desirable amount of meat to fat ratio is about 80:20 or 75:25. The fat content of the pork will vary and modern commercial pork is quite lean. I think that extra fat is needed in order to get a good result. If purchasing pre-minced meat, look to see if it has a good fat content. If not, ask your butcher to mince some extra fat and add it to your mince, say 100g/kg. A good butcher will do that. The best fat for this purpose is hard back fat, minced through the course plate of the mincer.

The mixture of meat, salt and flavourings is air dried in casings until the weight has reduced by 30%.

Fermented, dried and semi dried sausages are produced with the same method. They have different names in different countries. Saucisson in France, (although fermented style is used interchangeably with dry cured sausages, as near as I can tell) salami in Italy and wurst (of various types) in Germany.

However, there is one different technique used for some (mostly Italian) forms which ferments the meat slightly. This gives the salami a characteristic sour taste.

The object is to provide conditions for lactic acid producing bacteria to grow and to produce lactic acid. It is the lactic acid conditions which inhibit the growth of other bacteria.

Some sugar, in the form of dextrose, is added to assist in the development of the lactic acid producing bacteria. Conditions for fermentation are quite warm and humid, say 25°C and 80% relative humidity (RH). The period required is about 24 hours. These conditions can probably be achieved quite easily in a warm(ish) room in your house. Hang the filled casings overnight and you will most likely achieve the desired result.

Because the technique involves hanging salami at room temperature, it is something you should approach cautiously. I do not recommend it as your first attempt. Practice with the other recipes and become confident with what you are doing before considering fermented sausages.

Nonetheless I have included some recipes for fermented sausages.

NOTE: Most commercial salamis and air dried sausages tend to be of a fairly large diameter. In my experience it is much harder to achieve success with a large diameter casing. Things just seem more likely to go wrong. The problems can either be the meat not curing properly in the centre or the links drying out unevenly resulting in air pockets within the link.

On the other hand, those made with sausage diameter casings seem to have a much higher success rate – for me anyway. The other benefit is that they cure much more quickly, 2-3 weeks for a sausage diameter link, compared to 2-3 months for a larger diameter link.

SAUCISSON SEC

Saucisson sec is a French air dried sausage which is very simple to make and gives consistent results.

"Sec" simply means "dried" in French. It is a good place to start with dried sausages.

This recipe has quite a strong garlic and pepper flavour. If you prefer a milder flavour, reduce the pepper and garlic, say by 50%.

Pork shoulder (minced but not too coarsely) – 1kg.

Back fat (minced coarsely) – 10%.

Salt – 2%.

Curing Salt No. 2 - 0.3%.

Pepper (black, cracked) – 1%.

Dextrose (caster sugar is a good alternative) – 0.75%.

Garlic (minced) – 2%.

Mix the dry ingredients with the meat and fat. Combine well. Thereafter, knead the mixture strongly for a few minutes. The meat will start to become sticky and bind together. Alternatively you can mix it with an electric mixer (not a food processor) using a dough hook or beaters. The change in texture is important. Without this step the end result will tend to be crumbly and not cohesive.

Refrigerate the mixture overnight in a resealable plastic bag or a non-reactive container. The next day mix well until sticky.

Ensure that the meat remains as cold as possible. Start with very cold meat and fat and if necessary, mix over a bowl of ice.

Fill natural casings with the mixture. The sausages will dry quickly and be less prone to spoilage if a normal sausage diameter casing is used rather than a larger salami diameter casing.

Tie and cut each sausage to the desired length – approximately 20-25 cm is about right. Weigh each link and record the weight.

Prick each link well to remove air.

Hang in a drying chamber until each link has lost 30% of its weight. This will take 15-20 days depending on the diameter of the sausages and ambient conditions. If you prefer a harder or drier sausage then let it dry for longer until it has lost at least 50% of its weight. It is a matter of preference, although I prefer it on the drier side.

CHORIZO

Chorizo is a Spanish dried sausage which is strongly flavoured with garlic and paprika (either sweet or hot). It is easy to make and works well.

It is usually made into sausage type diameters and dries quickly with little spoilage. It can be eaten as is or used in cooking as a flavouring agent for soups and casseroles. It is also very good grilled on its own or in a kebab of other meat and vegetables.

Pork (shoulder, minced) – 1kg.
Back fat (coarsely minced) – 5-10% (optional).
Salt – 2.5%.
Curing Salt No. 2 – 0.3%.
Dextrose – 0.5%.
Paprika (smoked) – 1.5%.
Paprika (sweet) – 1.5%.
Cayenne pepper – 1%.
Garlic (minced) – 3%.

Mix ingredients well until meat becomes sticky. Refrigerate the mixture overnight in a resealable plastic bag or a non-reactive container. The next day mix well until sticky. Fill sausage casings, divide, tie and cut into links. Weigh and record weight of each sausage.

Prick each link well to remove air.

Dry for 15-20 days or until weight is reduced by 30%.

The end result should be quite firm, but not too hard.

HOT SALAMI

A hot salami flavoured with hot chilli cayenne pepper and black peppercorns. It makes an excellent addition to a charcuterie plate or on a homemade pizza. Make it as hot as you like (or dare). This is an unfermented style.

Pork shoulder (minced) – 1kg.
Back fat (diced) – 500g.
Salt – 3%.
Curing Salt No. 2 – 0.3%.
Chilli (flakes dry) – 1.5%.
Cayenne or hot chilli – 1.5%.
Pepper (black, crushed) – 1%.
Fennel (seeds, crushed) – 0.5%.
Dextrose – 1%-2%.
Garlic (cloves, minced) – 4.
Red wine (dry style, cold) – 100ml.
Salami starter culture (dissolved in water) – 10g.

Combine all ingredients (save for starter culture), mix well and refrigerate overnight in a sealed non-reactive container or resealable plastic bag.

The next day, remove from refrigerator and mix until sticky.

Add starter culture dissolved in distilled water. Mix well again until sticky character is regained.

Fill into sausage sized casings (it will cure quickly) or into larger salami casings or sheep bungs.

Prick each link well to remove any air.

Weigh each salami and record weight. Place in a curing chamber until they have lost approximately 30% of their wet weight.

CALABRESE

Calabrese is a salami flavoured with chilli and hot capsicum paste. It is a standard for a charcuterie plate.

Pork shoulder (minced) – 1kg.
Back fat (diced) – 10-12%.
Salt – 3%.
Curing Salt No. 2 – 0.3%.
Pepper (black, cracked) – 0.3%.
Chilli (dried flakes) – 0.5%.
Red wine (cold, dry style) – 30ml.
Capsicum paste (hot or sweet) – 30ml.

Mix ingredients well until sticky. Refrigerate overnight in a resealable plastic bag or a sealed non-reactive container.

The next day, knead the mixture well until it is sticky.

Fill into sausage or salami casings. Prick each link all over with a pricker. Weigh and record weight for each salami. Air dry until weight loss is about 30%. This will take at least 2 weeks depending on ambient conditions and the diameter of the salami.

CRESPONE

A mild but full flavoured Italian salami with a somewhat softer texture.

Pork (shoulder, minced) – 70%.
Pork (belly, skinless, minced) – 30%.
Salt – 3%.
Curing Salt No. 2 – 0.3%.
Pepper (black, ground) – 0.2%.
Coriander (ground) – 0.15%.
Ginger (ground) – 0.15%.
Nutmeg (ground) – 0.15%.
Cloves (ground) – 0.08%.
Cinnamon (ground) – 0.04%.
Milk (powder, non fat) – 2%.
Garlic (powder) – 0.4%.
Wine (white, dry style, cold) – 3%.

Mix all ingredients well, refrigerate overnight in a re-sealable plastic bag or a sealed non-reactive container.

The next day, mix all ingredients until sticky.

Fill sausage diameter casings, or for a more traditional method use sheep bungs.

Tie each link or bung with a bubble knot. Weigh each and record weight. Incubate at room temperature for 24 hours.

Dry age until each link has lost 30% of its weight.

SOPRESSATA

Sopressata is a traditional salami flavoured with chilli and red pepper paste. Always a crowd pleaser.

Pork shoulder (minced) – 1kg.
Back fat (diced) – 22.5%.
Salt – 3%.
Curing Salt No. 2 – 0.3%.
Pepper (black, cracked) – 0.3%.
Chilli flakes (dried) – 0.3%.
Dextrose – 0.45%.
White wine (cold, dry style) – 65ml.

Optional:
Starter culture – 5g.
Distilled water (to dissolve starter culture) – 15ml.
Capsicum paste (red pepper) (sweet or hot, it is up to you) – 3%.

Mix ingredients well until mixture is sticky. Refrigerate overnight in a resealable plastic bag or a sealed non-reactive container. Fill salami casing or smaller sausage casings if preferred.

Prick each link well to remove any air.

Incubate at room temperature (27℃ and 80% humidity for 24 hours). This starts the fermentation process and gives the salami its characteristic sour background taste.

Hang in curing chamber/drying area for approximately 3 weeks or until weight has reduced by 30%.

FINOCCHIONA

This dry cured salami is flavoured with garlic and fennel seeds. A classic of the genre.

Pork shoulder (minced) – 1kg.
Back fat (diced) – 40%.
Salt – 3%.
Curing Salt No. 2 – 0.3%.
Pepper (black, cracked) – 0.3%.
Dextrose – 0.5%.
Fennel seeds (cracked) – 0.7%.
Minced garlic – 4 tsp.
Red wine (cold, dry style) – 65ml.
Starter culture – 5g.
Distilled water – 15ml.

Mix ingredients well until sticky. Refrigerate overnight in a resealable plastic bag or a sealed non-reactive container. Next day, mix until sticky. Mix culture and distilled water. Add to meat mixture. Mix well. Fill salami casing or sausage casings if preferred. Tie and cut each link. Weigh and record weight.

Prick each link well to remove any air.

Incubate at room temperature for 24 hours.

Hang in drying chamber/air dry for approximately 3 weeks until weight has reduced by 30%.

FUET

Fuet is a Spanish cured and air dried (fermented) sausage, although it is often used as a fresh sausage as well. Unusually it does not contain paprika.

Pork (shoulder, minced) – 1kg.
Back fat (diced) – 200g.
Salt – 3%.
Curing Salt No.2 – 0.3%.
Garlic (minced) – 2%.
Dextrose – 0.3%.
White wine – 50-60ml.
Pepper (white, ground) – 1%.
(optional: 1% starter culture, dissolved in distilled water, say 50-100ml).

Add all ingredients and mix well.

Keep mixture in refrigerator overnight in sealed non-reactive container or resealable plastic bag. The next day, mix well until sticky.

Fill into sausage diameter casings and link. Tie off into single lengths with a bubble knot on each end. Weigh each link and record weight. Prick well to remove air pockets.

Allow to ferment at 18-20℃ and 85% RH (if you can obtain those conditions) for 2 days.

Alternatively hang in a warmish room for 1-2 days but check them carefully each morning and night. You do not want them to spoil.

Air dry in a curing chamber until they have lost approximately 30% of their '*green*' weight.

NOTE: If you are not confident with the whole fermentation thing, then omit the dextrose and air dry the links in your curing chamber until they reach the desired weight. Do not use chlorinated tap water. The chlorine will kill the starter culture (bacteria). That is what it is supposed to do. Use rainwater or pure distilled water with no additives.

SALCHICHÓN

This is a Spanish cured and fermented, dried, sausage, very similar to an Italian style salami. Although I am sure that the Spanish would disagree with the latter bit.

Pork shoulder (minced) – 1kg.
Back fat (diced) – 200g.
Curing Salt No.2 – 0.3%.
Salt – 3%.
Garlic (minced) – 1%.
Dextrose – 0.3%.
White wine – 50-60ml.
Pepper (black, cracked) – 0.5%.
Nutmeg (ground) – 0.1%.
(optional: 1% starter culture, dissolved in distilled water, say 50-100ml).

Mix all ingredients and refrigerate overnight in a sealed non-reactive container.

The following day, mix well until sticky.

Fill into sausage diameter casings and tie each with a bubble knot at the desired length. Weigh each link and record weight.

Prick each link well to remove any air.

Allow to ferment at room temperature (18-22°C and 80+% RH) for 1-2 days or just put into curing chamber if you wish to omit fermentation (if so, omit the dextrose).

Air dry until the links have lost at least 30% weight.

HUNGARIAN SALAMI

This is a classic European dried sausage. It has very minimal ingredients.

Pork (shoulder, minced) – 1kg.
Back fat (diced) – 200g.
Salt – 3%.
Curing Salt No.2 – 0.3%.
Dextrose – 0.25%.
Paprika (smoked or sweet, but not hot) – 6%.
Pepper (white, ground) – 3%.
Garlic (powder) – 2%.

Mix ingredients well.

Refrigerate overnight in a non-reactive sealed container or in a resealable plastic bag.

The next day, mix vigorously until sticky. Fill sausage diameter casings. Link as required. Tie off each with a bubble knot. Weigh and record weight for each link.

Prick each link well to remove any air.

Hang in a curing chamber until weight has decreased by 30%.

NOTE: *This sausage smokes very well. If you intend to smoke it, dry it in the refrigerator overnight. Smoke at 85℃ until the internal temperature is at least 71° C.*

LONGANIZA

A Spanish cured and air dried sausage made with beef and pork and both sweet and hot red capsicum[62] paste.

Pork (shoulder, minced) – 30%.

Beef, lean, minced (remove as much fat as possible, fillet or sirloin (porterhouse) would be best) – 50%.

Back fat (diced finely) – 20%.

Salt – 3%.

Curing Salt No.2 – 0.3%.

Sugar (caster) – 0.3%.

Dextrose – 0.1%.

Capsicum paste (red, sweet) – 0.4%.

Capsicum paste (red, hot) – 0.2%.

Coriander (ground) – 0.2%.

Garlic (minced) – 0.2%.

Fennel seeds (cracked) – 0.2%.

Nutmeg (ground) – 0.1%.

(optional: 0.1g starter culture, dissolved in red or white wine, say 50ml).

Mix ingredients well.

Refrigerate overnight in a sealed non-reactive container.

The next day, mix again until sticky. Fill sausage diameter casings. Link as required. Tie off each with a bubble knot. Weigh and record weight for each link.

Prick each link well to remove any air.

Ferment at 18-26°C and 80% RH for 1 day. Thereafter, place links in the curing chamber until they have lost 30% of their 'green' weight.

---

62   Often referred to and sold as 'pepper' paste, but which in Australia we refer to as capsicum. We understand pepper to be a different thing.

SUCUK

Sucuk is a Middle Eastern fermented and dry cured sausage which is extremely popular in Turkish and Lebanese cuisine. The same or similar product has different names in various countries – Sudzhuk (Bulgaria), Sudschuk (Germany), Suxhuk (Albania), Sugiuc (Romania) to name a few.

Lean beef can be dry. If you do not want to add pork fat, some oil may need to be added to replace the pork fat. Add oil at a rate of, say 3-5%. Fry a small amount of the mixture to see if it has good lubrication or '*mouth feel*'.

It is not made from pork for obvious reasons.

Lean beef mince (fillet or porterhouse is good) – 70%.
Lean lamb mince (leg or loin is good) – 30%.
Back fat (diced finely) – 20%.
Salt – 3%.
Curing Salt No.2 – 0.3%.
Pepper (black, ground) – 0.5%.
Cumin (ground) – 1%.
Garlic (powder) – 1%.
Allspice (ground) – 0.3%.
Paprika (sweet) or red capsicum paste – 0.5%.

Mix all ingredients and refrigerate overnight in a sealed non-reactive container.

The next day, mix well until mixture achieves a very sticky quality.

Fill sausage diameter casings. Tie off as required with bubble knot. Weigh and record weight for each link.

Prick each link well to remove any air.

Ferment at 18-26°C and 80% RH for 1-2 days until weigh loss of 30% at least.

This dried sausage is a staple in Turkish and Middle Eastern cuisine and often seen on Turkish '*pizza*' at Turkish or Lebanese bakeries in the suburbs of Melbourne.

The fresh version is really good too, omit the Curing Salt and the fermentation step for a fresh grilling sausage.

Outstanding.

MORCÓN

A Spanish cured sausage like a chorizo but without added back fat and cured in a sheep or pig bung.

Pork (minced) – 1 kg comprising:
Cheek (glands and skin removed) – 50%.
Shoulder – 25%.
Leg or other lean cut (loin is ok) – 25%.
Salt – 3%.
Curing Salt No.2 – 0.3%.
Paprika (sweet, powder or paste) – 3%.
Garlic (minced or garlic powder) – 1.5%.
Pepper (white, ground) – 1%.
White wine (cold, dry style) – 50-60ml.
Dextrose – 0.25%.

Mix all ingredients well and refrigerate overnight in a sealed non-reactive container or resealable plastic bag.

Next day, mix again until very sticky.

Fill into sheep or pork bungs. Tie off each bung with a bubble knot.

If you do not want such a large sausage, tie each bung in the middle to create two smaller bungs. Do not cut them off. Dry them together.

Prick each link well to remove any air.

Weigh each bung and record weight. Dry until weight loss is at least 30%. With larger casings like bungs, test for firmness even when the desired weight loss is achieved. If they are still quite soft after 30% weight loss, let them dry for longer until they are firm. This may result in a weight loss of 50% or more. You must ensure that it is dried all the way through.

SAUCISSE SEC AUX HERBES DE PROVENCE[63]
(FRENCH DRIED SAUSAGE WITH MIXED HERBS)

A French dried sausage which is flavoured with a variety of dried herbs.[64]

Pork (shoulder, minced) – 1kg.
Salt – 3%.
Curing Salt No. 2 – 0.3%.
Pepper (black, cracked) – 0.25%.
Pepper (white, cracked) – 0.25%.
Fennel (seeds, cracked) – 0.25%.
Garlic (minced) – 0.75%.
White wine (cold, dry style) – 30ml.
Herbes de Provence[65] – 0.75%.

Mix ingredients well, refrigerate overnight in a non-reactive container or a resealable plastic bag. Next day, mix well until sticky.

Fill into sausage diameter casings. Tie off each link at desired length using a bubble knot at each end.

Weigh each link and record weight for each link.

Prick each saucisson well to remove air.

Dry until weight loss is at least 30%.

You will not regret this.

---

63 Forgive me, it just sounds better in French.
64 Adapted from Grigson.
65 Herbes de Provence is a French herb blend. It is commonly available in supermarkets or specialist food stores or make it yourself – see the recipe later in this book.

CERVELAT

Cervelat is a semi dry sausage from Switzerland and Alsace.

Pork – (shoulder, minced) – 70%.

Beef (lean, porterhouse or rump minced) – 30%.

Salt – 3%.

Curing Salt No.1 – 0.5%.

Dextrose – 10g.

Sugar – 10g.

Pepper (black, ground) – 5g.

Pepper (black, cracked) – 3g.

Coriander (powder) – 1.5g.

Mustard seeds (yellow or brown, whole) – 3g.

Ginger (powder) – 1g.

Mix meat and other ingredients.

Refrigerate in a re-sealable plastic bag or a non-reactive container overnight.

The following day, mix well until sticky.

Fill into sausage diameter casings or larger bungs if you wish.

Tie each link with bubble knots and prick well to remove air pockets.

Ferment at room temperature overnight.

Thereafter smoke at 85°C until an internal temperature of at least 71°C is achieved.

Chill immediately.

SAUCISSON DE MENAGE OR DE CAMPAGNE (FRENCH COUNTRY SAUSAGE)

Adapted from Grigson, this recipe is for a dried sausage which is lightly flavoured. It is close to the sausage described elsewhere as saucisson sec.

Pork (minced, shoulder or belly) – 1kg.
Back fat – 500g.
Salt – 3%.
Curing Salt No. 2 – 0.3%.
Garlic (mixed) – 2tsp.
Quatre-épice – 1tsp.
Pepper (black, ground) – 1tsp.
Sugar (white or dextrose) – 1tsp.

Mix ingredients well, place in a re-sealable plastic bag and refrigerate overnight.

The next day knead the mixture well until it becomes sticky.

Fill into sausage diameter casings.

Tie each link with string using a bubble knot. Prick each link well to remove air. Weigh each and record the weight.

Hang in a curing chamber until the links have lost 30% of their green weight.

LAP CHEONG (CHINESE DRIED AND SMOKED SAUSAGE)

Who says a charcuterie recipe cannot come from China? Not me.

Lap Cheong, I understand means 'winter stuffed intestine'. It eats better than it translates. It is the dark red cured and dried sausage that is diced and added to fried rice. You will have eaten it many times without really knowing what it is. It is quite sweet compared to other charcuterie products.

Pork (shoulder or belly, minced on medium plate) – 1kg.
Curing Salt No. 2 – 0.3%.
Salt – 3%.
Sugar – 0.5%.
Soy sauce – 30ml.
Cinnamon – 1g.
Rice wine (Shaoshing wine or if unavailable, dry sherry is a very good substitute) – 30ml.
Pepper (black, cracked) – 2g.
Garlic (minced) – 1tsp.
Cold water – 80ml.

Mix all ingredients well, refrigerate overnight in a re-sealable plastic bag or a non-reactive container.

The next day mix well until sticky.

Fill small sausage diameter casings. Tie each link with a bubble knot.

Either smoke at 85°C until internal temperature is 71°C or hang without smoking until the links lose 30% of their weight.

A spicier variation can be made with chilli and Sichuan pepper if you wish. If so, add 20 gram chilli powder, 1.5 tbsp Sichuan pepper (ground) and 1 tsp five spice powder.

Gong Xi Fa Cai (Happy New Year).

'NDUJA

'Nduja is a soft, short cured, style of salami which you will either like or not. Some may say it is an acquired taste and not for the faint hearted. Nonetheless I think that you need to know about it.

I am a river to my people.

Pork (belly, rind removed, minced) – 1kg.
Salt – 3%.
Curing Salt No. 1 – 0.3%.
Paprika (sweet or hot, smoked) – 100g.
Cayenne pepper – 10g.

Add ingredients and mix well.

Refrigerate overnight in a re-sealable plastic bag or a non-reactive container.

The next day, knead the mixture well until it becomes sticky.

Tie each link with a bubble link at each end. Prick each link well to remove any air products.

Now for the tricky bit. The 'Nuduja must be allowed to ferment for 12-24 hours in a warm room.

Conditions should be about 25°C-28°C. Allow the links to incubate overnight then they should be air dried for about one week.

Then they can be used. Traditionally it is spread on bread or toast.

ROSETTE DE LYON

This is a well known dried sausage from Lyon. It differs from the larger poaching style Rosette de Lyon in that this version is intended for longer term use.

Pork (shoulder, minced) – 700g.
Back fat (diced) – 300g.
Salt – 3%.
Curing Salt No: 2 – 0.3%.
Pepper (black, cracked) – 2g.
Sugar (caster) – 2g.
Garlic (minced) – 10g.
Nutmeg (ground) – 1g.
Ginger (ground) – 0.5%.
Cloves (ground) – 0.25%.
White wine (dry, cold) – 15ml.
Starter culture (optional) – 0.12g.

Mix meat and spices together well until sticky. Refrigerate overnight in a resealable plastic bag. In the morning, mix well until sticky. Add white wine and diced back fat together with starter culture dissolved in distilled water. Mix again to combine.

Fill sausage diameter casings, tie each link with a bubble knot, weigh and record each weight.

Prick each link well to remove any air. Ferment at 85% RH and 20°C for 48-72 hours.

Air dry until each link has lost about 30% of its green weight.

SAUCISSON D'ALSACE

An air-dried sausage from the Alsace region of France.

Pork (shoulder, minced) – 800g.
Back fat (diced) – 200g.
Salt – 3%.
Curing Salt No.2 – 0.3%.
Pepper (white, ground) – 3g.
Garlic (minced) – 2g.
Nutmeg (powder) – 0.5g.
Cloves (ground) – 0.2g.
Cinnamon (ground) – 0.5%.
Rum (dark) – 15ml.
Starter culture (optional) – 0.1g.

Mix all ingredients together well save for the starter culture and refrigerate overnight. The next day mix together well until sticky. Add the starter culture dissolved in a little distilled water (not chlorinated tap water) mix again.

Fill sausage diameter casings. Tie off each link with a bubble knot, weigh each and record weight. Prick each link well to remove any air. The links can be smoked. If so, return to the refrigerator overnight to set and develop a pellicle. Thereafter smoke at 85°C until an internal temperature of 71°C is achieved.

If not to be smoked, ferment at 20°C for 48 hours, at about 85% RH.

Air dry thereafter until each link has lost about 30% of its green weight.

SAUCISSON DE L'ARDÉCHE

A traditional sausage from the mountainous area known as the Ardéche, in the Auvergne-Rhone-Alpes region of south eastern France.

Pork (shoulder, minced) – 700g.
Pork (belly, rindless) – 200g.
Back fat (diced finely) – 100g.
Salt – 3%.
Curing Salt No. 2 – 0.3%.
Pepper (black, ground) – 2g.
Pepper (black, cracked) – 2g.
Dextrose – 3g.
Sugar (caster) – 3g.
Garlic (minced) – 10g.
Cumin (powder) – 1g.
Nutmeg (ground) – 1g.
Clove (ground) – 0.2g.
Ginger (ground) – 0.5g.
Starter culture (optional) – 1g.

Mix all ingredients, save for the starter culture, refrigerate overnight in re-sealable plastic bag or non-reactive container.

The following day, mix together well until sticky.

Add the starter culture dissolved in a small amount of distilled water (not chlorinated tap water).

Fill sausage diameter casings. Prick each link well to remove any excess air.

Ferment at 20°C for 48-72 hours at 85% RH.

Dry in curing chamber until each link has lost approximately 30% of its green weight.

LINQUICA DE PORTALEGRE

A dried sausage from the Portalegre region, in central eastern Portugal.

Pork (shoulder, minced) – 700g.
Back fat (diced) – 300g.
Salt – 3%.
Curing Salt No. 2 – 0.3%.
Pepper (black, cracked) – 2g.
Sugar (caster) – 5g.
Capsicum paste (sweet) – 30g.
Nutmeg – 0.5g.
Cumin – 1g.
Garlic (minced) – 10g.
White wine (dry, cold) – 60ml.
Water (cold) – 60ml.

Mix meat, fat, water, wine, sugar, salt and Curing Salt. Place in refrigerator overnight in re-sealable plastic bag or non reactive container.

The following day mix well until sticky.

Add capsicum paste and mix well.

Add diced back fat and mix well.

Fill sausage diameter casings. Tie off each link with a bubble knot. Weigh each link and record weight. Prick each link well to remove any air.

Either smoke at 85°C until internal temperature is 71°C (set in refrigerator overnight first to develop pellicle) or air dry in curing chamber until links have lost at least 30% weight.

CIAUSCOLO

A soft textured Italian salami from the Marche region, on the central east coast of Italy.

Pork (shoulder, skinless, minced) – 200g.

Pork (belly, skinless, minced) – 600g.

Pork (leg, skinless, minced) – 200g.

Salt - 3%.

Curing Salt No.2 – 0.3%.

Pepper (black, cracked) – 2g.

Garlic (minced) – 4g.

Dextrose – 2g.

Juniper berries – 2

Wine (red, dry, cold) – 20ml.

Combine meat and ingredients. Mix well.

Refrigerate overnight in a re-sealable plastic bag or non-reactive container. The next day, mix again well until sticky.

Fill sausage diameter casings. Tie and weigh each link. Record weights.

Dry cure until the links have lost at least 30% of their weight.

CHORIZO SORIA

A chorizo from the medieval city of Soria.

Pork (leg, minced) – 60%.
Pork (shoulder, minced) – 20%.
Back fat (diced) – 20%.
Salt – 3%.
Curing Salt No: 2 – 0.3%.
Pepper (black, cracked) – 0.15%.
Garlic (minced) – 0.15%.
Paprika (smoked) – 0.5%.
Sherry (dry – fino or similar) – 0.3%.

Mix ingredients well. Refrigerate overnight in a resealable plastic bag or non-reactive container.

The next day, mix well until sticky.

Fill sausage diameter casings. Tie and weigh each link. Record weights. Air dry until the links have lost approximately 30% weight.

SALAMI NOSTRANO

A relatively coarse textured salami from the Milan area.

Pork (shoulder, minced) – 550g.
Pork (belly, minced) – 300g.
Back fat (diced) – 150g.
Salt – 3%.
Curing Salt No. 2 – 0.3%.
Sugar – 0.5%.
Pepper (black, cracked) – 0.25%.
Garlic (minced) – 0.2%.
Wine (red, dry style, cold) – 0.5%.

Mix all ingredients well. Refrigerate overnight in a resealable plastic bag or non-reactive container.

The following day, mix well until sticky.

Fill sausage diameter casings. Tie each link and weigh. Record weight.

Air dry until each link has lost approximately 30% of green weight.

SALAMI DI CAPRA

An Italian salami made with goat and beef meat. Not all salami is made from 100% pork.

Goat (leg, minced) – 350g.
Beef (lean topside or chuck, minced) – 350g.
Pork (belly, minced) – 300g.
Salt – 3%.
Curing Salt No. 2 – 0.3%.
Pepper (black, whole) – 0.15%.
Pepper (black, cracked) – 0.15%.
Garlic (powder) – 5g.
Rosemary (dried) – 0.4%.
Cinnamon (powder) – 0.03%.
Dextrose – 0.5%.

Combine all ingredients and mix well.

Refrigerate overnight. The following day, mix well until sticky.

Fill sausage diameter casings; tie and weigh each link. Record weight.

Air dry until the links have lost 30% of their weight.

SALAMI SANT' OLCESE

A salami from Sant' Olcese made from pork and beef.

Pork (shoulder, minced) – 375g.
Beef (lean, minced – topside or chuck) – 375g.
Pork (belly, minced) – 250g.
Salt – 3%.
Curing Salt No. 2 – 0.3%.
Dextrose – 0.5%.
Pepper (black, whole) – 0.1%.
Pepper (black, ground) – 0.1%.
Garlic (powder) – 0.5%.

Mix ingredients well. Refrigerate overnight in a re-sealable plastic bag or non-reactive container.

The following day, mix well until sticky.

Fill sausage diameter casings, tie each link and weigh. Record weight. Air dry until each has lost 30% weight.

VENTRICINA TAORMINA

A salami from the Taormina region of Italy.

Pork (shoulder, minced) – 1kg.
Salt – 3%.
Curing Salt No.2 – 0.3%.
Pepper (black, cracked) – 100g.
Garlic (minced) – 20g.
Rosemary (diced) – 1tsp.
Orange (zest) – from 2 oranges.
Chilli (flakes) – 1tsp.
Fenugreek (dried) – ½tsp.
Wine (white, dry, cold) – 100ml.

Combine all ingredients and refrigerate overnight in a resealable plastic bag or a non-reactive container. The next day mix well until sticky.

Fill sausage diameter casings, tie and weigh each link. Record weight.

Air dry until each link has lost at least 30% weight.

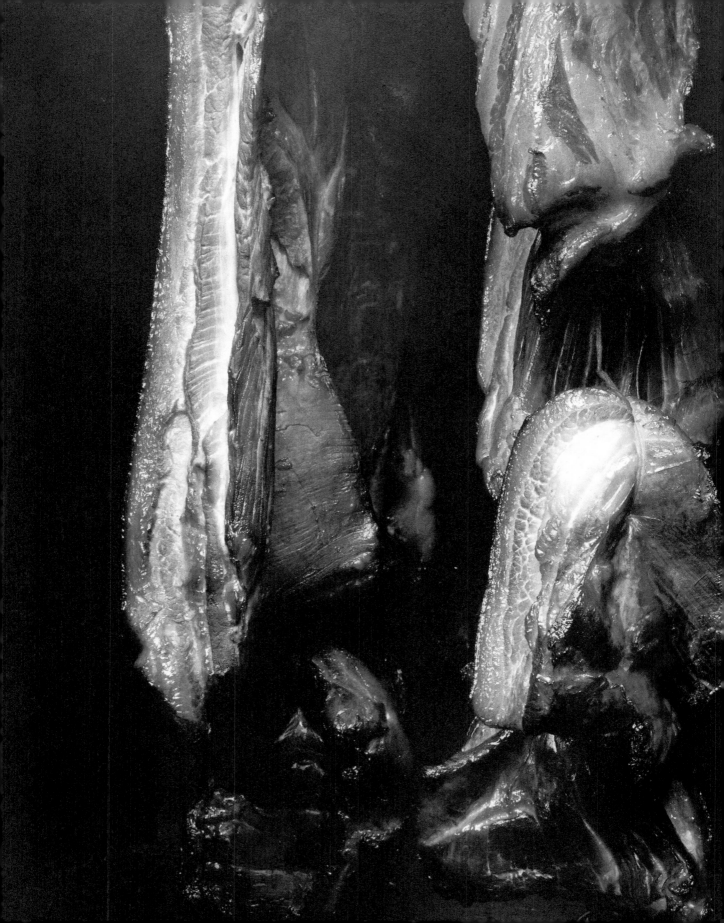

THE SMOKED
CHARCUTERIE

THE SMOKED CHARCUTERIE

Smoked charcuterie comes in all shapes and sizes. It comes from many cuts of meat and many different cultures. Smoking meat in order to preserve it for later use is as old as salting meat, maybe even older.

Smoking meat has rich cultural and historical roots. Rather than opine as to them, I am not a historian, I will share two anecdotes. The first comes from Mrs Beeton, not someone who was readily disposed to humour, it seems to me. Nonetheless Mrs Beeton recounted an anecdote in her book which I am compelled to share since it has a passing reference to charcuterie and smoked charcuterie in particular. It concerns Lord Bacon. Francis Bacon was 1st Viscount of St. Albans, from 1561 to 1626 and amongst other things Attorney General of England (1613) and subsequently Lord Chancellor (1618).

Mrs Beeton's anecdote, and I extract it in full, goes like this:

> *"As Lord Bacon on one occasion, was about to pass sentence of death upon a man of the name of Hogg, who had just been tried for a long career of crime, the prisoner suddenly claimed to be heard in arrest of judgment, saying, with an expression of arch confidence as he addressed the bench, 'I claim indulgence, my lord, on the plea of relationship; for I am convinced your lordship will never be unnatural enough to hang one of your own family.'*
>
> *'Indeed,' replied the judge, with some amazement, 'I was not aware that I had the honour of your alliance; perhaps you will be good enough to name the degree of our mutual affinity.'*
>
> *'I am sorry, my lord,' returned the impudent thief, 'I cannot trace the links of consanguinity; but the moral evidence is sufficiently pertinent. My name, my lord, is Hogg, your lordship's is Bacon; and all the world will allow that bacon and hog are very closely allied.'*
>
> *'I am sorry,' replied his lordship, 'I cannot admit the truth of your instance: hog cannot be bacon till it is hanged; and so, before I can admit your plea, or acknowledge the family compact, Hogg must be hanged tomorrow morning.'*

Forgive me, apart from anything else I think it is Mrs Beeton's only foray into humour. It is worth re-telling if only for that reason. If you have heard it before, then I apologise.

Secondly, Grigson observed that smoking is an additional but not an essential means of preserving meat which has already been brined or dried. She noted that it can be a difficult process for the amateur to attempt. Her reticence regarding smoking no doubt had a lot to do with the absence of equipment available to her. She observed that maintaining a steady smoke is extremely tricky '*... sometimes involving sleepless nights on account of visits to the fire ...*'. Her experience with smoking was by hanging meat over a smouldering fireplace in the kitchen. She considered that '*my advice is to take hams to be smoked at the nearest bacon factory, once you have pickled them in brine*'.

As discussed earlier, there is no need to do this today. There are a large range of smokers available in various sizes and using various forms of heating. You do not need to sleep in front of the open fire or make friends with the bacon producer. But, if it works for you to do so, then I will not gainsay it.

WET CURED HAM (CHRISTMAS TYPE HAM)

This is a method of curing and smoking a traditional ham such as you might have on Christmas Day. Usually a whole leg of pork is selected, however that can be particularly daunting for the beginner. A much easier method and one that I have used with success, is to cure a smaller piece of pork such as a rolled, boned leg/shoulder roast. The rolled piece of meat can be purchased from your butcher already prepared. It will be rolled and tied and have a good covering of skin (rind). You can purchase the size which you prefer to cure. The ingredients are not precise, save for the Curing Salt which should be at a rate of 0.3% by weight.

The recipe can be used for a whole ham if you prefer. In that case, keep the ham in the brine for about 1 day/kg. The longer brining time is required because the meat is much larger and the salt requires additional time to penetrate.

Pork (rolled leg or shoulder is good) – 1kg.
Salt – 350g.
Brown sugar – 350g.
Curing Salt No. 2 – 0.3%.
Juniper berries (a few).
Pepper (black, whole, several).
Bay leaves (several).

Make a brine of 3-4 litres of water, approximately 350g of salt, 350g of brown sugar and Curing Salt No. 2 (0.3%).

Dissolve the ingredients. If necessary heat the mixture to dissolve the ingredients but it must be chilled until very cold before the meat is added. Aromatics can be added to the brine as you wish – several crushed juniper berries, some cracked black pepper and fresh herbs (but not too much).

Submerge the meat in the brine, you will need a weight on top to ensure it is completely submerged. This can be a plastic bag filled with water or some other weight – make sure it does not contaminate the brine (wrap it well in plastic).

There are many views on how long to brine the meat for. The longer it is brined, the saltier it will become. I have used ½ day/500g with some success.

Place the sealed container in the fridge. Remove the meat from the brine at the end of the process, wipe dry and refrigerate for ½ - 1 day. This is important to allow the meat to develop the sticky exterior or pellicle. The pellicle enhances smoke adherence to the meat and improves the end result.

Smoke the meat at 85℃ until it reaches an internal temperature of approximately 68℃. This may take at least 6 hours, maybe up to 10 hours. If after, say 6 hours, the desired internal temperature has not been reached then increase the ambient temperature by a few degrees.[66] This will help. Once the temperature is achieved, remove the meat from the smoker. Refrigerate (covered) immediately to chill the meat and stop the cooking process.

The end result should be firm to the touch, a dark honey colour on the exterior and pink inside. It will have a smoky odour and taste.

You will be surprised how good this is.

---

66 See temperature '*stall*'.

WIEJSKA

A polish smoked sausage. Nothing more need be said.

Pork shoulder (minced) – 1kg.
Salt – 3%.
Curing Salt No. 2 – 0.3%.
Pepper (white, ground) – 3g.
Garlic (minced) – 5g.
Marjoram (dried) – 3g.
Sugar – 5g.

Mix all ingredients well and refrigerate overnight in re-sealable plastic bag or a non-reactive container.

The next day, mix well until sticky.

Fill sheep bungs or sausage casings and let dry overnight in refrigerator. This will allow a pellicle to develop.

Prick well to remove any air.

Smoke at 85℃ until the internal temperature is at least 76℃.

If you do not want such a large sausage, tie each bung in the middle to create two smaller bungs – do not cut them off. Dry them together.

Weigh each link and record weight. Dry until weight loss is at least 30%. With larger casings like bungs, test for firmness. If they are still quite soft after 30% weight loss, let them go for longer until they are firm. This may result in a weight loss of 50% or more.

HAM HOCK

Smoked pork hocks are traditionally used for pea and ham soup but can be braised with flageolet beans or other dried legumes to make great stews. The fore hock of the pig is much smaller than the rear hock but either can be used. The smoked hock which is often seen in butchers and delicatessens is usually the larger rear hock. It is a byproduct of the commercial smoked ham process.

Ham hock – 1. (I usually use a rear hock because there is more meat on the rear hock, but the recipe does not distinguish between rear and fore hocks).
Salt – 350g.
Curing Salt No. 2 – 0.3%.
Sugar (brown) – 350g.

Make a brine of 3-4 litres of water, approximately 350g of salt, 350g of brown sugar and Curing Salt No. 2 (0.3%).

Dissolve the remaining ingredients. If necessary heat the mixture to dissolve the ingredients but it must be chilled until very cold before the meat is added. Insofar as aromatics are concerned I suggest the following:

Onion (powder) – ½tsp.
Garlic (powder) – ½tsp.
Pepper (black, crushed) – 1tsp.
Bay leaves (crushed) – 2.
Garlic (cloves, whole) – 2

Submerge the meat in the brine, you will need a weight on top to ensure it is completely submerged. This can be a plastic bag filled with water or some other weight – make sure it does not contaminate the brine (wrap it well in plastic).

There are many views on how long to brine the meat. As with a wet cured ham, I use ½ day/500g with some success, overhauling each day.

Place the sealed container in the fridge. Remove the meat from the brine at the end of the process, wipe dry and refrigerate for ½-1 day. This is important to allow the meat to develop the sticky exterior or pellicle. The pellicle enhances smoke adherence to the meat and improves the end result.

Hot smoke the hock at 85°C until the internal temperature is 71°C at least.

A small fore hock will take about 6 hours, a large rear hock will take about 7 hours to achieve the desired internal temperature.

After smoking it will be a pleasing mahogany colour and firm to the touch.

Once completed, remove the hock from the smoker and refrigerate immediately (covered) until completely chilled. Vacuum packed or frozen, they will keep for at least three months in the refrigerator or six months in the freezer.

BACON

Bacon is very easy to make with excellent, reliable results. The product can be sliced and fried or cut into lardons to add flavour to soups and casseroles. In many ways, bacon is the epitome of charcuterie. It is simple to make and marvellous to eat. The process transforms a cut of meat which has little or no other use into a fantastic versatile product.

Bacon is made from pork belly, either the true belly section (the part with no rib bones) for streaky bacon or the loin section (the part with rib bones) for 'eye' bacon. I prefer the part in between, namely the section on the rib bones but not including the loin. It has, to my taste, a better ratio of fat to meat than the other sections.

Pork belly is readily available from retail butchers in pieces of whatever size is desired. About 1 kg is a convenient size to work with. It fits in a small container or large resealable plastic bag and can easily be cured in the refrigerator. The rind (skin) and rib bones can be removed at the start or not. It is a matter of preference. I leave both on and remove the bones at the end of the smoking process. The rind will be a pleasing honey/mahogany colour and the smoked ribs can be used to flavour a soup or casserole.

Bacon can be used at any time, indeed everything is better with bacon (except ice-cream). But its highest and best use, its natural habitat, is breakfast. Hunter S. Thompson got it right. He wrote that *"... breakfast is the only meal of the day that I tend to view with the same kind of traditionalized reverence that most people associate with Lunch and Dinner. I like to eat breakfast alone, and almost never before noon; anybody with a terminally jangled lifestyle needs at least one psychic anchor every twenty-four hours, and mine is breakfast. In Hong Kong, Dallas or at home – and regardless of whether or not I have been to bed – breakfast is a personal ritual that can only be properly observed alone, and in a spirit of genuine excess. The food factor should always be massive: four Bloody Marys, two grapefruits, a pot of coffee, Rangoon crepes, a half-pound of either sausage, bacon, or corned beef hash with dried chillies, a Spanish omelette or eggs Benedict, a quart of milk, a chopped lemon for random seasoning, and something like a slice of Key lime pie, two margaritas, and six lines of the best cocaine for dessert ... Right, and there should also be two or three newspapers, all mail and messages, a telephone, a notebook for planning the next twenty-four hours and at least one source of good music. All of which should be dealt with outside, in the warmth of a sun, and preferably stone naked ..."*

Except for the bits about nudity and drugs for breakfast and perhaps the quantities (although I am not at all sure as to the latter), I think Thompson was pretty much correct.

Make up your own mind.

The classic British breakfast of bacon and eggs is not so much a recipe but a reference to a way of life which has disappeared for many of us. It is easy to keep a pig and a chicken, unless you live in suburbia. The chicken is fed on kitchen scraps and forages in the garden for insects and the like. The pig is also fed on kitchen scraps. Eggs keep quite well at room temperature in the cooler climates. A chicken will lay one egg each day if you are lucky. The pig can be used to make bacon, a way to preserve the meat indefinitely. Hence, bacon and eggs, a good breakfast for the working man or woman. A way to use commonly available produce. Hundreds if not thousands of years later it is still a good dish. Charcuterie on a plate. Charcuterie is a lesson in history, if nothing else. Hence the fascination. What follows is a recipe. To the best of my knowledge it is not that of Mr Thompson.

Pork belly – 1kg.
Salt – 1tbsp.
Curing Salt No. 2 – ½tsp.
Onion (powder) – ½tsp.
Garlic (powder) – ½tsp.
Pepper (white, ground) – ½tsp.
Maple syrup – 2-3 tsp. [67]

Place all ingredients[68] and meat in a non-reactive container. A resealable plastic bag is ideal.

Refrigerate for 7 days, overhauling each day at least once.

After curing, remove and wipe dry. Leave uncovered in the refrigerator for ½-1 day until the pellicle develops.

Hot smoke at 85℃ until an internal temperature is 71℃ is achieved. Remove and allow to come to room temperature, then chill immediately.

It will keep in the fridge for about 1-2 weeks. If vacuum sealed, for at least three months or frozen, for at least six months.

---

67 If using maple syrup, use the real product, not the fake stuff. The difference is worth it.
68 The quantity of ingredients are not precise, but be careful not to overdo them.

KAISERFLEISCH (GERMAN STYLE BACON)

Cured and smoked pork belly has been a staple of many cuisines over many centuries. Bacon, to the British, pancetta to the Italians, ventréch to the French and kaiserfleisch to the Germans. Each is different but in turn, each is the same. Kaiserfleisch is cured using more aromatics than British bacon. It is outstanding nonetheless, but subtly different. Make up your own mind as to which you prefer.

Pork (belly boneless no bone in; rind on or off) – 1kg.
Salt – 3%.
Curing Salt No. 2 – 0.3%.
Sugar (brown) – 2-3tsp.
Celery (seed cracked or powder) – ½tsp.
Marjoram (dried) – 1tsp.
Mustard (powder) – ½tsp.
Caraway (ground) – ½tsp.
Garlic (powder) – 1tsp.
Onion (powder) – 1tsp.
Pepper (black, ground) – 1tsp.
Bay leaf – 1-2.

Mix all the ingredients together.

Massage well into the meat.

Place the meat and all other ingredients into a resealable plastic bag or non-reactive sealed container.

Refrigerate for 5 days, overhauling daily.

Thereafter, remove meat, rinse (lightly) and pat dry. Return the meat to the refrigerator for 12-24 hours until the meat is sticky.

Place in a smoker at 85°C until the internal temperature is at least 65°C.

Remove from the smoker and chill in the refrigerator until the meat is completely cold.

VENTRÉCH ROULÉE (FRENCH ROLLED BACON)

Ventréch is French bacon, usually rolled and always lightly smoked. The cure is light and shorter than the styles of bacon which one may be more familiar with. However, as with other styles of bacon, it is based upon a boneless pork belly. The pork belly used for this preparation is the fattier part of the belly beyond the ribs.

Pork belly (boneless, skin removed) – 1kg.
Salt (coarse or flossy salt) –2.5%.
Curing Salt No. 2 – 0.3%.
Pepper (black, cracked) – 20%.

Rub the meat well with salt and curing salt.

Place in resealable plastic bag or in a sealed non-reactive container in the refrigerator for two days.

Overhaul daily.

Remove, rinse (lightly) and pat dry.

Coat well with cracked pepper.

Roll and tie like a roast.

Place in a smoker at 85°C until the internal temperature is at least 65°C.

This will take about 4-6 hours.

KASSELER (SMOKED CURED PORK LOIN)

The Germans are famous for smoked whole muscle pork products. One of the most well known is smoked pork loin, whether boneless or bone in. With the bone in it is often described as the kasseler 'chop'. Either way it is an outstanding product.

Clever chaps, these Germans.

Pork loin (skin removed, either bone in or boneless) – 1kg.
Brine:
3-4 litre of water.
Salt – 350g.
Sugar (brown) – 350g.
Curing Salt No. 2 – 0.3%.
Sage (dried or fresh) – 3-4 leaves.
Thyme (dried) – 1tsp.
Juniper berry – 3-4 (crushed).
Coriander (dried) – 1tsp.

Mix all ingredients to make the brine.

Add meat to brine.

Place in the refrigerator in a sealed non-reactive container, weighed down if necessary.

After 2 days remove, rinse (sparingly) and pat dry.

Refrigerate overnight or for 1 day until meat is sticky.

Smoke at 85°C until an internal temperature of at least 65°C is achieved.

This is good eaten cold but best if fried slightly in a pan until warm, and eaten with sauerkraut and boiled potatoes.

SPECK (GERMAN SMOKED PORK SHOULDER OR LOIN)

Speck is a German variety of smoked pork shoulder or loin. It differs from more familiar bacon in that loin or shoulder is used rather than belly but also the cure is heavily spiced. Speck can be made from loin, shoulder or belly. It is probably more traditional to use boned shoulder but it works well with other cuts. It is the spice mix which makes it different. Also, it is quite heavily smoked. It is a very good product and worth trying.

Pork (loin, bone in or boneless, this works well with pork shoulder also) – 1kg.
Salt – 3%.
Curing Salt No. 2 – 0.3%.
Pepper (white, ground) – 0.5%.
Juniper berry (crushed) – 0.015%.
Garlic (powder) – 0.1%.
Basil (dried) – 0.05%.
Sugar (brown) – 0.2%.
Bay leaf (fresh or dried) – 1.

Rub the meat with a mixture of salt and Curing Salt.

Add the other ingredients.

Place the meat and curing mix in a resealable plastic bag or a sealed non-reactive container in the refrigerator.

Overhaul daily for 7 days.

Remove, wash (sparingly) and pat dry.

Replace in the refrigerator for 1 day or overnight, until the meat becomes sticky.

Smoke at 85°C until the internal temperature is at least 65°C.

Cool in the refrigerator and vacuum seal.

Achtung baby.

SCHINKENSPECK (GERMAN BACON)

Schinkenspeck, or 'ham bacon', is a German bacon which is cured with aromatics and then smoked. It is very good, as German smoked meat is want to be.

Pork belly (boneless) – 1kg.
Salt – 3%.
Curing Salt No.2 – 0.3%.
Brandy – 1.5 tbsp.
Sugar (brown) – ¼cup.
Celery seed (cracked) – ½tsp.
Marjoram (dried) – 1tsp.
Mustard (powder) – 1tsp.
Caraway (ground) – 1tsp.
Garlic (powder) – 2tsp.
Pepper (black, ground) – 2tsp.

Rub the meat with the ingredients and place in a resealable plastic bag or a non-reactive container.

Place in the refrigerator for 7 days, overhauling daily.

Thereafter remove from the refrigerator. Wash off the cure, sparingly.

Pat the meat dry and replace in the refrigerator on a plate or rack for a few hours, overnight is better. This allows a pellicle to develop. Smoke at 85°C until an internal temperature of 70°C is achieved. Refrigerate immediately.

GAMMON

Gammon is a traditional British cured pork which can be boiled or roasted. The cut of meat usually used is boneless pork from the upper leg, the chump end, or rump of the animal. However a boneless piece of shoulder would work just as well. The meat is brined and then either boiled or roasted.

Pork – (shoulder or leg – boned, rolled and tied) – 1kg.
Curing Salt No.1 – 0.3%.
Salt – 350g.
Sugar – 200g.
Juniper berries – (crushed) – 3.
Bay leaf – 2.

Make a brine from the ingredients, submerge meat in the brine in a sealed non-reactive container.

Refrigerate the meat/brine for 2 day/kg; not more than 7 days, but not less than 4 days.

Remove the meat from the brine solution, discard the brine solution. Rinse the meat well in fresh water.

Refrigerate uncovered for 2 days.

Simmer the gammon in a court bouillon for one hour per kg. Remove and allow to cool. Then glaze with any glaze recipe you prefer. Roast in a 180°C oven until the glaze has caramelized. A variation on this method is to hot smoke the gammon and omit the simmering step. If so, smoke at 85°C until an internal temperature of at least 70°C is achieved.

MOLASSES CURED HAM

An old British method of curing a ham involved brining with molasses and stout. Thereafter the ham can be baked or hot smoked. I think the latter is better. The end result is a dark caramel coloured exterior and a succulent sweet ham interior. In either method of cooking the rind should be left on the meat.

Pork leg (either boneless or bone in, but keep the rind on. If the leg has been boned you will need to tie it tightly like a roast).

Brine:

Water – 2 litres.

Stout – 1 litre.

Molasses – 300g.

Salt – 300g.

Bay leaves – 6-8.

Cloves (whole) – 6.

Cinnamon stick – 1.

Pepper (whole, black) – 10.

Juniper berries (crushed) – a few.

Curing Salt No: 2 – 0.3%.

Mix ingredients to make the brine, warm if needed to obtain a solution. Submerge the meat in the cool brine using a weight if necessary.

Place the meat/brine into the refrigerator in a sealed container.

Keep the meat in the brine for 1 day/kg of meat.

Thereafter remove the meat from the brine. Discard the brine and pat the meat dry.

Return the meat to the refrigerator on a plate for 1 day to allow the pellicle to develop.

Smoke at 85°C until an internal temperature of 68°C – 71°C is achieved.

JAMBON DE BAYONNE (BAYONNE HAM OR FRENCH HAM)

Grigson described this as a ham which is '*...to be attempted after the hay harvest in a dry summer.*' The recipe subsequently explained the significance of hay to the process. Further she recommended that if the ham is from a '*...newly killed pig...*' it should be beaten with "*a butter pat*". The reason being, apparently, that it brings out a certain amount of blood but also to '*... smooth out the wrinkles in the skin*'. At all events it is a lightly cured and flavoured ham. Whilst usually made with a bone-in leg of pork there is no reason why it would not work with a bone-less rolled piece of pork meat, say leg or shoulder. Keep the rind on. It is up to you.

This recipe is based upon Grigson, but with significant variations as you will observe.

Pork leg (boned or boneless but with skin on. Grigson uses a boneless piece. I do not think that it matters).
Salt – 3% (Grigson does not give precise quantities).
Curing Salt No.2 – 0.3% (Grigson refers to '1 scant ounce of saltpetre'. If you can obtain saltpetre, then you are welcome to try it).
Sugar – 500g.
Brine:
Red wine – 2 litres.
Water – 2 litres.
Salt – 500g.
Sugar – 50g.
Rosemary – 6 fresh sprigs.

Grigson's method is a little unusual, First combine salt, Curing Salt and sugar.

Rub well into the surface of the meat especially into any exposed meat and at the hock end. If deboned make sure the salt cure is worked into the cavity left by the bone.

Leave the ham overnight on the salt cure in the refrigerator.

Thereafter wipe off the salt cure and submerge the meat into the cool brine, weighing it if need be. Return the meat in brine to the refrigerator.

Grigson used an earthenware crock, a plastic container will do nicely if you do not have a salt crock.

After 1 day/kg (Grigson says 12 days, I prefer to have less time for this period and 1 day/kg is not a bad ratio).

After the brining process remove the ham and pat dry. Return to the refrigerator for 1 day to allow the pellicle to develop.

Grigson suggested that during this period that '... *you go searching for newly dried hay and suitable wood for the smoking fire*'. The reason being that the next step in her recipe is to wrap the ham in hay and to smoke it until it '... *is deep golden brown*'.

For my part I think it is somewhat easier to smoke it in 85°C until an internal temperature of 70°C is achieved.

NOTE: This recipe illustrates the problems confronting one when referring to some of the older books in this area. There is nothing wrong with them and they are a great source of inspiration. Sadly, they are not very user friendly.

KOLBÁSZ (HUNGARIAN SMOKED SAUSAGE)

A basic smoked cured sausage from Hungary.

Pork (shoulder, diced, skin removed) – 1kg.
Back fat (diced into small cubes) – 25%.
Salt – 2%.
Curing Salt No. 2 – 0.3%.
Pepper (black, ground) – 2%.
Paprika (sweet, smoked if possible) – 1.5%.
Garlic (minced) – 0.6%.
Caraway (ground) – 0.1%.
Sugar – 2%.
Paprika (hot) – 2%.

Mince approximately 25% of the pork shoulder using the fine plate on the mincer. Mince the remaining pork using the coarse plate. Mince the back fat on the coarse plate of the mincer or chop as finely as you can with a knife.

Combine meat, fat and spices.

Mix well and place in the refrigerator overnight in a sealed plastic bag or a non-reactive plastic container overnight.

The next day, mix well by hand or with an electric mixer until it becomes quite sticky.

Fill sausage diameter casings, tie off each link, weigh and record weights.

Replace in the refrigerator overnight.

Thereafter smoke at 85°C until an internal temperature of 71°C is achieved.

Chill immediately in the refrigerator.

SAUCISSE DE MORTEAU (MORTEAU SAUSAGE)

A traditional French dry smoked sausage which has a good place on a charcuterie board.

Pork (shoulder, minced) – 400g.
Pork (belly, rind-off, minced) – 300g.
Back fat (diced) – 200g.
Pepper (black coarse ground) – 0.25%.
Salt – 3%.
Curing Salt No. 2 – 0.3%.
Garlic – 1g.
Quatre épicés – 2.5g.
Cumin – 10g.
Shallots (minced) – 3g.

Combine all ingredients (except for back fat) and mix well.

Refrigerate overnight in a re-sealable plastic bag or a sealed non-reactive container.

The following day, mix well until sticky.

Mince back fat or dice very finely. Add to mixture and combine.

Fill large sausage diameter casings. Tie each link with a bubble knot at each end.

Return to refrigerator on a rack overnight to set and allow pellicle to develop.

Smoke at 85°C until an internal temperature of 71° C is achieved.

Chill immediately.

PFEFFERBEIßER

Pfefferbeißer is a German pepper sausage which is smoked and dried. I do not know how to pronounce it.

Pork (shoulder, minced) – 700g.
Back fat (minced or finely diced) – 300g.
Salt – 3.0%.
Curing Salt No.2 – 0.3%.
Pepper (black, whole) – 0.25%.
Pepper (black, ground) – 0.25%.
Marjoram (dried) – 0.03%.
Paprika (sweet, smoked) – 0.25%.
Dextrose – 0.5%.
Milk powder (low fat) – 0.05%.

Mix all ingredients well.

Refrigerate overnight in a re-useable plastic bag or non-reactive container.

The next day mix well until sticky.

Fill into sausage diameter casings.

Allow to ferment at 20°C and 80-85% RH for 48 hours.

Hot smoke at 85°C until an internal temperature of at least 71°C is achieved.

Chill immediately.

Air dry until they have lost 30% of their weight.

TROUT[69]

Farmed freshwater trout are readily available in fishmongers and are very economical to purchase. They are usually rainbow trout (*Oncorhynchus mykiss*) but there is little difference in eating quality between farmed rainbow or brown trout (*Salmo trutta*). Trout is a medium oily fish with a subtle taste but benefits greatly from hot smoking. Commercially available trout are usually about 500g in weight but maybe up to about 900g. The size makes little difference to this recipe, although larger fish tend not to dry out compared to small fish.

The fish may be filleted if you prefer but in my view, the fillets tend to dry excessively during the curing and smoking process. The end product is superior if left whole. The head is an added touch of reality which I quite like. On no account should the skin be removed. The scales, however, should be removed (which is easily done). This improves smoke penetration.

Freshwater trout are very good for smoking and more economical than ocean trout or Atlantic salmon. However I note that Elizabeth David[70] was less than complementary: *'It is the most unfortunate fish on earth. If an atomic bomb destroyed the world tomorrow, the human race would vanish without ever having known the taste of a trout. Of course, I am no more talking of tank-bred trout than I would give a recipe for cooking a dog or a cat.'* Whilst she does appear to be confining her comments to 'tank-bred' or farmed trout, I do not agree. Indeed commercially available trout is almost universally a farmed product, and a very good product it is too.

Farmed ocean trout or ocean salmon are also very good products and most affordable. They are farmed in salt water but are the same species as found in freshwater. They are often marketed as Atlantic salmon or Atlantic trout. All that means is that they are farmed in pens in salt water, usually in the open ocean.

The fish tend to be quite large (often in excess of 5kg). They have a stronger taste and a firmer flesh. The whole fish can be cured and smoked in exactly the same way as a smaller freshwater trout.

---

69   Once again, this is a recipe for which precision, in the form of ingredients calculated by reference to weight of meat, is unnecessary.

70   In *"French Provincial Cooking"*.

If this is too much fish to deal with then a whole side (filleted) or a smaller piece will work just as well. Insofar as a whole large fish is used, I cure it for slightly longer, maybe ½-1 day in order for the cure to penetrate. Insofar as a fillet of fish is used or smaller pieces, I cure for the same time as a whole fish.

Use the same amounts of salt and other ingredients as with freshwater trout (see above). They will keep, vacuum sealed in the refrigerator for say 2 months. I do not recommend freezing.

Fish – 500g.
Salt – ½tbsp.
Brown sugar or maple syrup – ½tbsp.
Garlic (powder) – ½tsp.
Onion (powder) – ½tsp.

Wash the fish well and remove as much slime and blood as possible. Check inside the abdominal cavity and remove, if necessary, any blood along the spine. For each kilogram of fish (approximately) add 1 tablespoon of salt and 1 tablespoon of brown sugar. Put fish and dry ingredients into a resealable plastic bag or other non-reactive container.

Refrigerate and overhaul for about one hour or two but not more than half a day. Any longer will result in a product which is too salty. Thereafter, wash and dry well.

Return the fish to the refrigerator uncovered for several hours to develop the pellicle. Sometimes it does not develop on fish, I do not know why. If it does not develop in a few hours, then proceed without it. Do not let it dry out in the fridge waiting for the pellicle to develop.

Hot smoke at about 70℃ until an internal temperature of 65℃ is achieved. Remove and allow to cool at room temperature then chill and vacuum pack. The fish will keep in the refrigerator for at least two months (vacuumed packed). I do not recommend freezing.

MACKEREL

Mackerel is an oily fish which is greatly assisted by salting and hot smoking. A good species for this is the small fish which is commonly caught in colder southern waters of Australia often called blue mackerel (*scomber scombrus or scomber australasicus.*). It is an attractive fish of about 10cm in length with silver and turquoise colouring and vertical black bands. It has a pink or red flesh which is very oily, not quite as oily as a sardine but close. The other species of mackerel caught in warmer waters (for example, Spanish mackerel) may smoke well but I think they are not quite oily enough for the process. In any event I have not tried them.

Mackerel are usually sold whole and ungutted. Clean (gut) the fish, remove the head and scales. The latter are small and will wash off under water, there is no need to use a harsh scaler. The flesh is extremely soft and will damage easily. Treat them quite gently. They are a naturally *"bloody"* fish. You will find this out when you clean (gut) them. Wash them well to remove the blood.

The flesh has a robust flavour, like a sardine, but somewhat milder, therefore it can accommodate strong aromatics like chilli if you prefer. I do not use sugar with the cure, only a modest amount of salt.

[71]*Fish (gutted and head removed) – 500g.*

Salt – 2tbsp.

Garlic (clove, crushed) – 1.

Chilli (dried, optional) – 1tsp.

Lemon (zest) – 1tsp.

Combine fish and ingredients. Place in a non-reactive container and keep in the refrigerator for 1 hour. The fish are very small and will over cure reasonably easily. Accordingly, do not be tempted to leave them in the salt for too long as they will become over salty (to my taste at least). Remove and pat dry. Chill in refrigerator for at least 1 hour to allow the pellicle to develop.

Hot smoke at 75℃ until firm to the touch. They should be firm but not hard. It is important to ensure that the flesh is cooked and not raw.

The fish are generally too small for a temperature probe but you can try. If so, 65℃ internally is about right.

One way to assist in the process is to split or butterfly the fish. This opens out the fish and assists in curing and cooking. This can be done by cutting through the head and pressing down gently on the fish to open it out. Alternately, the incision can be made (prior to opening the abdominal cavity and gutting) through the back bone and head but not through the belly. The guts can then be removed. This is the method of preparing herring for smoking, they are thereafter referred to as kippers. Hence the technique is often called kippering. It is not essential but looks quite appealing and is good knife practice.

Use immediately but they will keep vacuum sealed in the refrigerator for up to two months.

71　This fish is strong flavoured and forgiving. The quantities are a guide only.

EEL

Freshwater eel[72] is very good eating, although not partaken of so much in this country. Curiously, although there are a number of eel producers in Australia, eel is rarely (sadly) available in retail fishmongers. Fishmongers supplying Asian communities sometimes have supplies, although they will normally be sold alive. In the event that you are fortunate enough to possess a live eel, remember *"Larousse"*,[73] *"...To kill an eel, seize it with a cloth and bang its head violently against a hard surface."* For my part, I would add, immediate decapitation of the now stunned animal is only polite.

I further add that eels are quite hard to kill, indeed Mrs Beeton observed as much:

> *"Tenacity of Life in the Eel – There is no fish so tenacious of life as this.*
> *After it is skinned and cut in pieces, the parts will continue to move for*
> *a considerable time, and no fish will live so long out of water."*

Eel is a white fleshed oily fish which is ideal for smoking. The end result is sweet and almost bacon-like in flavour. However it is in the nature of an eel to be slimy. Do not hold that against them. The method, set out below, describes how to deal with that.

Preparation:

Clean (gut) and remove the head. Leave the skin intact. Eels are extremely slimy critters and the slime must be removed before the process of curing is started.

Put the eel in a plastic bag with a few handfuls of salt. Mix well and refrigerate for 1 hour.

Remove the eel and wash to try and remove as much slime as possible. (If necessary, repeat the process).

Next, make a brine to remove any further slime and blood.

---

72 Either Short Finned Eel (*Anguilla australis*) or Long Finned Eel (*Anguilla reinhardtii*).
73 Larousse Gastronomique: *'Fish and Seafood'*.

Brine:
Water – 3-4 litres.
Brown sugar – 200g.
Salt – 400g.
Juniper berries (crushed) – 2.
Pepper (black, crushed) – 1tsp.
Thyme (dried or fresh) – 1tsp.
Chilli (ground or fresh) (to your taste, say 1tsp.).

Add the eel to the brine mixture, refrigerate overnight in a resealable plastic bag or non-reactive container. Weight the eel such that it is completely submerged in the brine. Refrigerate for at least one hour.

Thereafter, remove the eel from the brine and wash well to get rid of slime and blood. Wipe and pat dry.

Rub with mixture of 1 teaspoon of paprika and 1 teaspoon of hot chilli.

Hot smoke at 75℃ until the internal temperature is approximately 65℃. Remove once the temperature is reached. Chill immediately.

Once cooled, use immediately or vacuum seal. If vacuum sealed it will last in the refrigerator for say two months.

SMOKED OYSTERS

As I have observed earlier, raw oysters are nasty slimy suckers. I add that in their natural state, they are not fit for human consumption. Those of you who think that you like them are just wrong. Smoked oysters, however, are an entirely different matter. They are very good and, in any view, are a special delicacy. You will be familiar with the tinned variety. They are excellent and still a favourite of mine; after all these years. However, smoking fresh oysters is a whole lot better. Much better. They are a labour of love, but well worth the modest effort. Don't you worry about that. This recipe brines, blanches and smokes the oysters. It leaves very little to chance. Other recipes may omit the brining step or the blanching step. The reason that I have included blanching is because oysters are filter feeders which may accumulate undesirable things in their feeding process. Secondly you are consuming the whole animal, guts and all (sorry but it is true). You need to be sure that they are properly cured, cooked and smoked. Do not take any chances with these little suckers. You will regret it if you do.

Oysters (raw, shelled) – As many as you dare.
Basic brine –
3-4 litre water.
Salt - 350g.
Sugar (brown) – 350g.
Aromatics to taste say:
Pepper (black, crushed) – 1tbsp.
Bay leaf – 2.
Garlic (powder) – 1tsp.

Mix all ingredients to make the brine.

Add shelled oysters.

Refrigerate for 2 hours.

Remove and dry oysters.

Retain brine, heat until boiling. Boil it for 5 minutes.

Blanch oysters for 30 seconds in boiled brine. Do not boil the oysters.

Remove, place the oysters in ice water immediately to cool.

Remove, dry and place in refrigerator to cool and dry.

After 30 minutes remove the oysters and smoke in 75°C for 30 minutes.

Place the oysters on a rack in the smoker.

NOTE: Do not overcook/smoke the oysters.

They should be darker in colour, plump, firm in texture but not dry or hard and certainly not black. Remember that they are very delicate.

Remove and dress with olive oil, lemon juice, salt and pepper.

Use immediately, or put in sterilized glass jar under oil.

This recipe will work just as well with mussels.

Also, if you just do not have the patience for this. Put unopened mussels and oysters on the barbeque. When they are open, they are poached. Perfect.

NOTE: There are many variations to this process – for example:

Add fresh or dried chillies for extra zing. Be very careful not to add too many;

Add lemongrass, soy sauce, ginger and star anise. Again not too much. You will lose the oyster flavor; lemon zest, orange zest, garlic. But be careful.

JAGERWURST (HUNTER SAUSAGE)

Jagerwurst is a hot smoked sausage which has a somewhat drier consistency than traditional Italian salami. It was made in small hard links to be carried by hunters in their pockets, hence the name Hunter sausage. It is an excellent sausage, very similar to commercially available Polish sausage or Strasburg types. I have made this, if I may say with all modesty,[74] to considerable critical (family) acclaim.

Pork (shoulder, minced) (50:50 coarse and finer mince) – 1kg.
Salt – 2%.
Curing Salt No. 2 – 0.3%.
Pepper (black, cracked) – 0.3%.
Coriander (ground) – 0.1%.
Garlic (crushed) – 0.6%.
Mustard seed (yellow or brown) – 0.8%.
Nutmeg (ground) – 0.2%.
Ginger (ground) – 0.1%.
Milk powder[75] – 35g.

Jagerwurst has a characteristic profile of larger meat mixed in with finer mince. Also it has no large pieces of diced fat added. The result is a more homogenous product which is less prone to spoilage. The meat is half coarse ground and half finer ground. Simply purchase the meat and ask the butcher to mince it accordingly.

Alternately pass all the meat through the coarse plate of the mincer. Take one half of the coarse mince and mince it again through the finer plate.

Combine the two different minced meats (coarse and fine) and other ingredients. Mix well until sticky. Refrigerate overnight. The next day fill into sausage diameter casings. Prick each link well.

Place the links in the refrigerator to dry for 1-2 hours. Thereafter, hot smoke at 85℃ until an internal temperature of 65℃ is achieved.

An outstanding smoked dry sausage.

---

74 A relative term.
75 Non-fat, if possible.

ANDOUILLE

Andouille is a hot smoked sausage which does not have added fat (such as back fat). It is similar to jagerwurst but with a slightly different texture and flavour.

Pork (shoulder, minced) – 1kg.
Salt – 25%.
Curing Salt No. 1 – 0.2%.
Cayenne pepper – 0.2%.
Thyme (dried) – 0.05%.
Mace (ground) – 0.01%.
Clove (ground) – 0.01%.
Onion (powder) – 3.5%.
Garlic (minced) – 0.5%.
Pepper (white, ground) – 0.5%.

Mix ingredients well until a sticky texture is achieved. Refrigerate overnight. The next day, fill sausage sized casings. Tie each length individually for hanging in the smoker. Prick each to remove air pockets.

Hot smoke at 85°C until an internal temperature of 65°C, at least, is achieved.

This is somewhat easier to make than jagerwurst (if you are mincing the meat yourself) but just about as good.

KABANOSY (POLISH SAUSAGE)

This is a caraway flavoured cured sausage which is usually smoked, but not necessarily so.

Pork (shoulder, minced) – 1kg.
Back fat (diced) – 100g.
Salt – 3%.
Curing Salt No. 2 – 0.3%.
Pepper (white, ground)[76] – 0.5%.
Dextrose sugar (caster sugar is a substitute if you have no dextrose) – 0.1%.
Nutmeg (ground) – 0.1%.
Caraway (ground) – 0.1%.

Mix all ingredients and refrigerate overnight. The next day, mix well until sticky.

Fill sausage diameter casings to desired length. Tie each link with a bubble knot at each end.

Weigh each and record weight.

Prick each link well to remove air.

If they are to be smoked, allow to dry in refrigerator overnight so they are sticky to touch (a pellicle has developed). They then should be placed in the smoker at 85°C until an internal temperature of 76°C is reached.

If they are to be air dried, then place them into the curing chamber until a weight loss of or at least 30% is achieved.

---

76 Cracked black pepper can be used for a bit more 'kick'.

PETIT JAMBON FUMÉ (SMALL SMOKED HAM)

This is a French version of a smoked pork loin. It eats very well and is not difficult to make at home.

Pork loin (select the size that suit you. A full pork loin can be 3kg. Try it first with a piece of about 1kg).

Brine:

Water – 3-4 litres.

Pepper (black, whole) – say, 6.

Salt – 75g.

Curing Salt No.2– 25g.

Bay leaves (crushed) – several.

Juniper berries (crushed lightly) – several.

Garlic (minced) – 5g.

Sugar (brown) – 20g.

Dissolve salts and sugar in water. Add other ingredients.

Trim meat of all fat and sinew (silverskin). Place meat in brine, ensuring it is completely submerged (weighing it down if necessary).

Place in refrigerator for 3 days/kg. Remove and pat dry.

Leave uncovered in refrigerator for 1 day to encourage a pellicle to develop. Remove and smoke at 85℃ until the internal temperature is at least 65℃.

SAUCISSE DE MONTBELIARD (MONTBELIARD SAUSAGE)

A smoked French sausage from the town of Montbeliard (or so I am lead to believe).

Pork loin (select the size that suit you. A full pork loin can be 3kg. Try it first with a piece of about 1kg).

Brine:

Pork (shoulder, minced) – 1kg.

Back fat (diced or coarsely minced) – 30%.

Salt – 3%.

Curing Salt No.2– 0.3%.

Sugar (caster or dextrose) – 0.3%.

Pepper (white, ground) – 0.3%.

Garlic (minced) – 0.9%.

White wine (cold, dry style) – 30ml.

Combine all ingredients and mix well. Refrigerate overnight in resealable plastic bag or non-reactive container.

Next day, mix well until sticky. Fill sausage diameter casings.

Weigh and record the weight of each link. Prick each link well to remove air. Hang in refrigerator overnight until a pellicle develops. Hot smoke at 85°C until internal temperature is at least 65°C.

Alternatively, the sausage mix can be filled into a larger diameter casing (like a pork or sheep bung) and poached until an internal temperature of 65°C is reached.

THE POACHING SAUSAGES

THE POACHING SAUSAGES

French cuisine includes both fresh and dried sausages. The latter are in the style of salami and often simply referred to a saucisson sec ('*sec*' meaning dried in French).

However, the French also make a variety of large sausages, similar to, say, cotechino but which are poached rather than grilled. They are really excellent. They are referred to as saucisson or saucisse, seemingly interchangeably. Nonetheless, they are well worth a try.

A family Christmas in Paris several years ago included lunch cooked in the apartment by Moi, the French do not open their restaurants for Christmas Day lunch, preferring to indulge on Christmas Eve, like so many Europeans. One of the dishes which I prepared was a large saucisson flavoured with truffles, purchased from a butcher on Christmas Eve. It was outstanding, as were the oysters, prawns, magret de canard and bûche de Noël, but I digress.

These sausages are easy to make and should be stuffed into a sheep bung.

I have never met a sausage that I did not like.

NOTE: The recipes call for 2% salt and 0.3% Curing Salt No.1, you may add more salt if you wish. The Curing Salt is added for colour and pre-servative value. Although if the sausage is to be smoked (see below), it is essential. All of these sausages can be lightly smoked before poaching. If so, let them dry in the refrigerator overnight to develop a pellicle. Then smoke lightly, say for 2 hours or about 85ºC. The temperature is not so important if you intend to poach for 1-1.5 hours. If you do not, then smoke until an internal temperature of at least 75ºC is achieved. Then poach gently to warm only.

SAUCISSON L'AIL (FRENCH GARLIC SAUSAGE)

This is a basic garlic sausage for poaching. Variations on the saucisson include adding unsalted pistachios or black truffles. This recipe uses pistachios but they can be omitted if unavailable, alternatively truffles can be added or substituted for the pistachios.

Pork (shoulder, minced) – 1kg.
Salt – 2%.
Curing Salt No.1 – 0.3%.
White wine – 60ml.
Garlic (chopped) – 0.5%.
Pepper (black, cracked) – 0.5%.
Coriander (ground) – 0.1%.
Water (cold) – 60g.
Pistachios (shelled, unsalted, skin removed and roughly chopped)[77] – 11%.
Quatre épicés[78] – 0.5% (optional).

Mix ingredients well. Refrigerate overnight in non-reactive sealed container.

Next day, mix well until sticky. Fill sheep bungs. Prick each saucisson to remove any air bubbles.

If not using the saucisson in a few days, the completed saucisson can be frozen (vacuum sealed is best). It will keep for months.

To cook:

Poach gently in a court bouillon until the sausage is cooked through. This will take at least 1.5 hours.

If using a digital thermometer, aim for an internal temperature of about 75°C. Remove from the poaching liquid and allow to cool slightly.

Slice thickly and serve with lentils (lentil de puy go well with this), a green salad and Pinot Noir are crucial. (Omit the greens if one does not make friends with salad.)

---

77   Substitute finely chopped black truffle for a fantastic variation. Truffles are strongly flavoured (and very expensive) so I would use about 50g only.

78   Quatre epicés is a French spice mixture consisting of ground pepper (white or black), cloves, nutmeg and ginger. It can be difficult to source in Australia. If using quatre epicés, omit the ground black pepper and coriander from this recipe.

BOCHWURST

Bochwurst is a German sausage made from pork and veal. It is poached before eating.

Is Bochwurst. Is good.

Veal (shoulder, minced) – 1kg.
Pork (shoulder, minced) – 85%.
Back fat (finely diced) – 35%.
Pepper (white, cracked) – 0.5%.
Cloves (ground) – 3.
Mace or nutmeg (ground) – 0.1%.
Allspice berries (ground) – 2.
Salt – 3%.
Curing Salt No.1 – 0.3%.
Ginger (ground) – 0.1%.
Onion (minced) – 10%.
Chives (chopped) – 0.1%.
Parsley (chopped) – 0.1%.
Milk – 475ml.
Eggs (beaten) – 4.

Grind all spices in a mortar and pestle or, even better, into a spice grinder. Add dry ingredients to meat. Refrigerate overnight in a sealed non-reactive container or resealable plastic bag.

The following day, add 'wet' ingredients (onion, chives, parsley, milk and eggs), mix well until sticky. You will need to use an electric mixer or hand beater.

Fill sausage size casings. Link at lengths required with bubble knot at each end.

Gently poach each link in simmering water until the internal temperature is at least 75℃. Once at desired temperature, remove and place in ice/water bath to cool quickly. Dry and place in refrigerator.

The sausage can be used immediately, either cold or grilled slightly.

Eat with a cold beer like '*ze Germans – Wunderbar!*'

ROSETTE DE LYON (LYON SAUSAGE).

A large fresh garlic sausage for poaching from France.

Pork (shoulder, minced) – 1kg.
Bacon (fatty smoked, rind removed) – 25%.
Salt – 2.5%.
Curing Salt No.2– 0.3%.
Sugar – 0.15%.
Garlic cloves (chopped finely) – 4.
Quatre épicés.[79] – 0.5%.
Chilli (ground) – 2%.

Mix all ingredients well and let stand in refrigerator overnight in a sealed non-reactive container.

The next day, mix thoroughly until mixture is sticky.

Fill into sheep bung and dry overnight in the refrigerator.

Poach in a court bouillon for 1 hour until cooked through (you should aim for an internal temperature of at about 72℃ - 76℃).

---

79 Quatre epicés means four spices. It is a French spice blend usually comprising pepper, clove, nutmeg, cinnamon and ginger. See later in this book for a recipe; or you can purchase it at specialty retailers.

SAUCISSE PAYSANNE (FRENCH COUNTRY SAUSAGE)

French 'country' sausage with fresh parsley and thyme.

Pork (shoulder, minced) – 1kg.
Pork (belly, minced, rind removed) – 35%.
Salt – 2.5%.
Curing Salt No.1 – 0.3%.
Thyme (roughly chopped) – 1%.
Parsley (flat leaf, roughly chopped) – 2%.
Pepper (black, cracked) – 0.75%.
Garlic (minced) – 2%.

Combine and mix all ingredients well. Refrigerate overnight in a sealed non-reactive container or resealable plastic bag.

The following day, mix well until sticky, fill into sheep bungs.

Poach gently in a court bouillon. Ensure it is cooked well, it will take 1-1.5 hours, or until an internal temperature of 75°C is achieved.

SAUCISSON CERVELAS

A poaching sausage made from pork and beef.

Pork (shoulder, minced) – 1kg.
Beef (lean, fillet is good, minced) – 50%.
Back fat (finely diced) – 50%.
Salt (2%) – 2%.
Curing Salt No.1 (0.3%) – 0.3%.
Pepper (black, ground)– 0.5%.
Garlic (crushed) – 0.5%.
Shallots (finely chopped) – 2.

Mix well, refrigerate overnight in non-reactive sealed container.

Next day, mix well until sticky. Fill sheep bungs. Poach gently in court bouillon. Cook for 1-1.5 hours or until an internal temperature of at about 76°C.

Allow to cool somewhat. Slice thickly and serve with lentils or mashed potato.

SAUCISSON DE LYON

A French poaching sausage from Lyon. Elizabeth David, wrote of *"Saucisson Chaud A'La Lyonnaise', a dish of hot poached Lyon sausage with boiled potatoes".* **She noted (correctly) that it was** *'an exceedingly simple, almost primitive dish'.* **After describing how to make it, she observed:** *'Given a good sausage and well-seasoned potatoes, it is a most delicious dish, which will not be despised by the most fastidious. Francis Amunategui, a distinguished French gastronome and journalist, writes of this Lyonnaise sausage in deeply emotional terms: 'The appearance,' he says, 'of a hot sausage with its salad of potatoes in oil can leave nobody indifferent ... it is pure, it precludes all sentimentality, it is the Truth.'.*

She well knew her stuff.

Pork (shoulder, minced) – 1kg.
Back fat (finely diced) – 50%.
Salt – 2%
Curing Salt No.1 – 0.3%.
Pepper (white, ground) – 0.5%.
Quatre épicés (or 1g each of ginger, coriander, nutmeg and cloves) – 0.5%.
Sugar – 1%.

Mix well, refrigerate overnight in non-reactive sealed container.

On the next day, mix well until sticky. Fill sheep bungs. Tie each with a bubble knot. Poach gently in a court bouillon until an internal temperature is about 75°C (approximately 1-1.5 hours) is achieved.

If not using immediately, vacuum seal and freeze.

COTECHINO

Cotechino is an Italian pork sausage made with pork shoulder, skin and fat. It is traditionally made from pigs head but it is easier to use shoulder. It is poached gently to cook and becomes very rich and gelatinous. Thereafter it can be sliced and eaten with lentils or mash. Alternatively it is left to cool and the sliced sausage is fried quickly to crisp the outside just a little.

It is a robust, rich sausage which eats very well with mashed potato or polenta and red wine (a lot).

It is usually cased in a sheep bung or a salami sized casing.

This sounds like an offal dish and therefore you may be put off but do not be. I do not want you to think that I am a fan of offal, I am not, (recall The Rule Against Offal) but sometimes some offal type things can be good. This is one of those (rare) times. I defer again to Roald Dahl: *"The little pig began to pray but Wolfie blew his house away. He shouted, "Bacon, Pork, and Ham! Oh what a lucky wolf I am!" And though he ate the pig quite fast, He carefully kept the tail till last".*

Give it a try.

Pork (shoulder, minced)[80] *– 1kg.*
Pork skin – 25%.
Back fat (diced) – 15%.
Curing Salt No. 1 – 0.7%.
Salt – 2.5%.
Pepper (black, ground) – 0.6%.
Cayenne pepper – 0.1%.
Cinnamon (ground) – 0.1%.
Bay leaf (ground) – 1tsp.
Nutmeg (ground) – 0.1%.
Garlic (minced) – 3tsp.
White wine (optional) – 125ml.

The skin and back fat are minced (separately) using the coarse plate or cut finely. Dicing the skin by hand is reasonably difficult. If you are lucky the butcher may mince it with the meat all together. If you are going to mince it then first cut the skin by hand (it is best to almost freeze it first to make it easier to dice). If using a mincer, cut the skin into smallish pieces (not more than 2.5cm wide) and place in the freezer until almost frozen. This will make it easier to mince, even so, the skin can be quite a challenge for a domestic mincer.

Combine ingredients and mix well, until sticky.

Fill casings with the mixture. You can use a salami size casing although often cotechino is made using much larger ox or sheep bung (a large diameter casing). It is a matter of preference. Prick well to remove any air pockets.

The sausage needs to set, preferably overnight in the refrigerator. Thereafter it can be vacuum sealed and/or frozen or used immediately. However, it must be cooked prior to eating.

Poach the cotechino gently in a court bouillon[81] for about 1 hour. If you are using a thermometer, poach until an internal temperature of 70-75℃ is achieved. Be careful not to boil or the sausage will split and fall apart. Slice and serve immediately or cool somewhat and fry slices.

---

80   Shoulder is best, but add belly if you need to get about a 80:20 ratio of
        meat and fat.
81   A court bouillon consists of water to cover, one carrot, one onion (halved),
        one celery stick, several black peppercorns and a few bay leaves.

SAUCISSE DE STRASBOURG

Either referred to as cervelas de Strasbourg or saucisse de Strasbourg, this is a sausage made with two different grades of minced pork. This gives it a distinct texture, a mixture of fine and coarse minced meat. It is poached and served either hot or cold. It is quite mildly flavoured.

Pork (shoulder, minced) – 1kg.
Back fat (diced) – 600g.
Salt – 2.5%.
Curing Salt No. 1 – 0.25%.
Pepper (white, ground) – 0.3%.
Nutmeg (ground) – 0.1%.
Cayenne pepper (ground) – 0.1%.
Cumin (ground) – pinch.
Garlic (powder) – 0.5%.
Milk powder – 300g.

Combine the minced meat and the dry ingredients. Mix well and refrigerate overnight in a re-sealable plastic bag or a non reactive container.

Blanch the half of the back fat in boiling water for 1 minute. Remove and refresh immediately.

Mince the remaining back fat using a 3mm plate (the small one).

Using a food processor process the meat/spice mixture, minced back fat and milk powder.

Work in batches if need be.

Do not let the food processor heat up the meat mixture beyond 10-12°C. Return to freezer. Combine the now emulsified meat and fat with the blanched back fat. Add the remaining minced pork to the emulsified meat and diced back fat.

Fill large diameter sausage casings. Tie each link with bubble knots. Allow to dry and set in the refrigerator for a few hours.

Bring a large pot of water to a simmer. Add the sausages and poach gently until an internal temperature of 71°C is reached. Serve immediately or remove and refresh immediately in ice water.

SABODET

Sabodet is a French sausage flavoured with pork skin and pork fat. It is very like cotechino except that the skin is scraped of fat and the de-fatted skin is boiled before being added to the mixture. The result has the flavour of cotechino but lacks the unctuous gelatinous qualities of cotechino, to its detriment in my view. It is cooked and served the same way as cotechino.

If you do not like the very fatty consistency of cotechino (although I cannot understand why that would be so), then you should try this.

Pork (shoulder, minced) – 2kg.
Back fat (diced) – 450g.
Pork skin ('de-fatted') – 1.5kg.
Salt – 8g.
Curing Salt No. 1 – 7g.
Pepper (black, ground) – 9g.
Garlic (minced) – 1g.
Cayenne pepper (ground) – 1g.
Cinnamon (ground) – 1g.
Dextrose – 18g.
Mace (grated or ground) – 0.5g.
Nutmeg (grated or ground) – 0.5g.

Mince the back fat coarsely or dice into small cubes. Cut the skin into 2.5cm squares and boil for 40-60 mins. Remove and allow to cool slightly. Scrape away the fat from the skin. Discard the fat. Put the skin into the freezer until it is almost frozen. This will make mincing or dicing easier. Mince the fat coarsely or dice by hand.

Add the fat and skin to meat with all ingredients. Mix well until sticky. Fill salami casings or beef/sheep bungs or middles.

Cook as with cotechino, very gently.

Eat as with cotechino.

THE OTHER
RECIPES

THE OTHER RECIPES

The following recipes are neither air dried sausages nor whole muscles. However they are products of which I am very fond and which work well for a charcutier (of which you are almost certainly one).

There are two sections in this chapter. The classic recipes and the recipes for the brave.

As for the classics, these are an eclectic mix of recipes but all have some relationship with, or relevance to, charcuterie. Gravlax, tuna in oil, bottarga and salted fish all use methods of preservation which are appropriate for fish. However each recipe is quite different.

Corned beef, pastrami and petite salè each use salt preservation but to quite different ends. Corned beef is a long salt cured beef, petite salè is a very short cure. Pastrami adds several other techniques, normally smoking, to achieve a unique product.

Ham baked in salt dough is included for reasons of nostalgia. Parfait, paté, rillettes, brawn, lardo and terrines are methods of using every last bit of the animal which in my view is just polite.

Pickled eggs are included because I like eggs.

As for the brave recipes, they perhaps are unusual, or require some more techniques. Approach them with interest, if not caution, you may be surprised. Be brave.

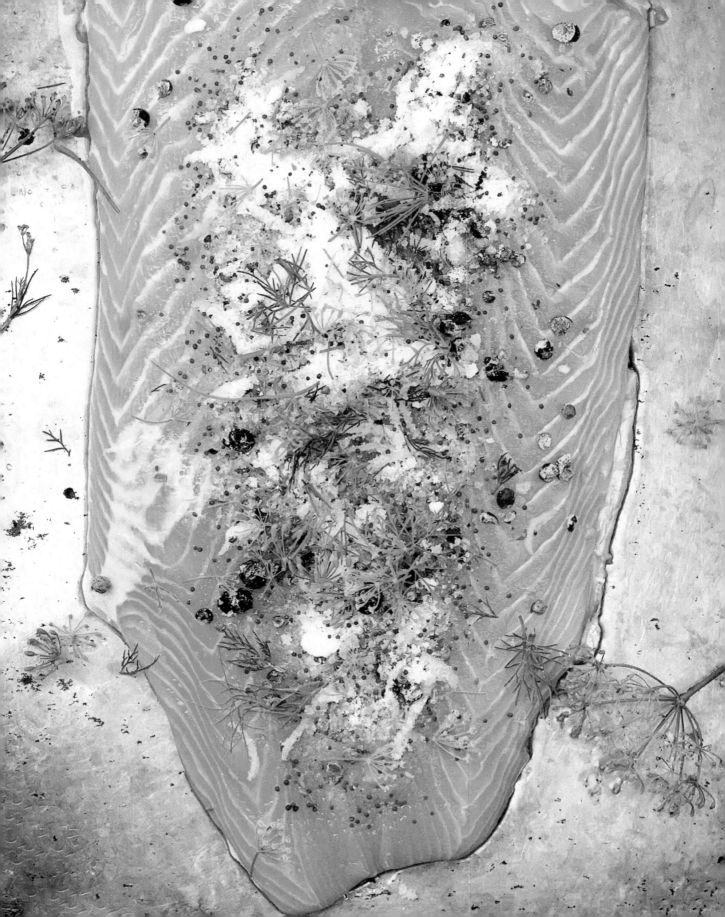

THE CLASSIC
RECIPES

GRAVLAX

Gravlax is salt and sugar cured salmon common in northern Europe. It is easy to prepare and, to my taste, just as good as smoked salmon. Atlantic salmon *(Salmo salar)* **works best for this.**[82]

It is usually prepared with fillets rather than whole fish. However, it can be prepared with a whole side of fish or with smaller pieces. A whole fish would not work.

[83]*Salmon*
Salt
Sugar (brown)
Aromatics to taste.

Fillet the salmon, leaving the skin on (de-scaled) but removing the pin bones (fish tweezers make short work of this).

Rinse and dry the fish fillet. Place a layer of salt and sugar (50:50) in a non-reactive container of sufficient size to accommodate the fillet.

Lay the fish (skin side down) on the salt. Flavourings can be added at this point, say a few crushed juniper berries to remaining salt and sugar (50:50). This is then lightly covered over the fish. Use sufficient salt and sugar mixture so that the flesh is just covered.

Traditionally, chopped fresh dill is then layered over the fish.

Place a weight on top of the fish and refrigerate for 1-2 days in a seated non-reactive container. Thereafter, remove the fish, rinse off the salt and pat dry. Slice thinly so as to leave skin behind or skin the fillet before slicing.

If this is too salty for your taste, then leave the fish in the cure for a shorter time. An interesting variation is to cover the fish with raw grated beetroot. The colour from the beetroot penetrates the outer layer of flesh resulting in a rosy colour which contrasts with the deep orange interior.

---

82 I am not a fan of chinook or king salmon (Oncorhynchus tshawytscha)
83 The quantities are not important, save that a salt: sugar ratio of 50:50 is about right.

CORNED BEEF

Corned beef is easy to make and surprisingly good. Use eye of topside (girello) or any piece of topside. The important thing is to have as little fat as possible. Remove external fat and sinew (silver skin). A childhood favourite of mine and now, happily, that of my children.

[84]*Beef (topside trimmed of fat and sinew) – 1kg.*

Brine:
Water – 3-4 litres.
Salt – 450g.
White sugar – 100g.
Garlic (minced) – 3tsp.
Bay leaves – 2.
Pepper (black, whole or cracked) – 1tsp.
Coriander seeds (cracked) – 1tsp.
Fennel seeds (cracked) – ½tsp.

Make a brine with all ingredients, ensuring that the salt and sugar are well dissolved. It may be necessary to warm the liquid to dissolve the salt and sugar. If so, allow it to cool completely before adding the meat. Add meat and ensure it is completely submerged in a sealed non-reactive container (weight it if needed). Refrigerate for 5 days.

Remove the meat from the brine and simmer reasonably vigorously for 3 hours or until yielding. The poaching liquid can be flavoured with 2 whole carrots, 2 small whole onions, 2 bay leaves and 1 tsp. of black pepper (a court bouillon).

When the meat is cooked, remove the meat and all the vegetables. Strain the poaching liquid if necessary. Bring it back to the boil and in the poaching liquid cook some vegetables (potato, cabbage, carrot and celery).

Serve meat with vegetables and some of the poaching liquid spooned over the dish to make it glossy.

---

84 I have used imperial measurements because the precise amounts are not necessary for this dish.

PASTRAMI

Pastrami is cured, smoked and steamed beef brisket. It is usually heavily spiced. The process is somewhat arduous for the home producer but does give one a sense of achievement once completed.

Beef (brisket, boneless. The thickest part of the brisket is best. It needs to be a reasonably large piece due to the process of curing and cooking) – 2kg.

Brine:

Water – 3-4 litres.

Salt – 350g.

Sugar (white) – 250g.

Curing Salt No. 1 – 40g.

Pickling mix – 1tsp.[85]

Sugar (brown) – 90g.

Honey/maple syrup – 60ml.

Garlic cloves (minced) – 5tsp.

Remove as much external fat from the brisket as possible. Trim the meat to remove loose bits. Make the brine with all the ingredients. Ensure the ingredients are well dissolved. Heat the brine if necessary to achieve a solution. If it has been heated, refrigerate it until completely chilled before adding the meat. Place meat in a sealed non-reactive container with the cool brine (ensure that it is completely submerged).

Brine for 3 days in a refrigerator. Thereafter, remove the meat from brine and pat dry. Coat the meat liberally in a 50:50 mix of ground black pepper and ground coriander.

Hot smoke until the internal temperature is at least 65°C. Remove the meat from the smoker.

Place the meat on a rack over water in an oven tray. Cover with aluminium foil. Cook at 120-150°C until yielding. This may take some hours.

Remove, cool and slice. It will keep for quite a long time.

Quite a lot of work, but a product that is well worth it.

---

85   *"Pickling mix"* is a mixture of dried spices (usually whole) which is added to a brine to flavour the product, whether vegetables, fish or meat). It can contain whole pepper, coriander, fennel, mustard and other aromatics. It is available from supermarkets, specialty suppliers, or online.

PETIT SALÉ

Petit salé is a lightly salted pork belly which is poached and served with puy lentils. "Petit salé" means lightly salted; referring to the short time the meat is cured before cooking. Recipes for the dish[86] usually do not use a Curing Salt. I think the dish benefits from a small amount of Curing Salt No. 1 if for no other reason that it gives a pleasing pink colour to the finished dish. Without the Curing Salt it is not so attractive to the eye.

If you like corned beef, then you will like this.

If you do not like corned beef, then there is something wrong with you.

This is one of my all time favourite dishes. If you make nothing else from this book, you should make this. If you do not make this dish, I will find you. There will be nowhere to hide.

[87]Pork (belly, skin on, bones removed) – 1kg.
Salt – 45g.
Brown sugar – 15g.
Curing Salt No. 1 – 2g.
Bay leaves (crushed) – 2.
Juniper berries (crushed) – 4.
Thyme (fresh) – 1 sprig or if using dried thyme, 1 tsp.

Place the pork in a resealable plastic bag together with all the other ingredients for 2 hours in the refrigerator. Thereafter remove and rinse the meat well.

Gently poach the meat in a court bouillon (water with 1 carrot, 1 celery stick, ½ onion, 1 bay leaf, 4 pepper corns) until well-cooked but not falling apart (treat it like corned beef but a bit more gently, it is not as robust). Slice thickly and serve with puy lentils which have been cooked in the poaching liquid from which the petit salè has been removed.

If you do not like this then I cannot help you.

---

86   For example Elizabeth David in *"French Provincial Cooking"* or Rick Stein in *"French Odyssey"*.
87   The quantities are a guide only, this is a quick cure so the precise measurements really do not matter. Go wild. But not too wild.

SAUERKRAUT

Sauerkraut is pickled and fermented cabbage. It may not sound too good but it eats very well. It is really good with rich meats like smoked pork hock. Millions of Germans cannot be wrong.

[88]Fresh green cabbage, any green cabbage will do but sauerkraut is traditionally made using savoy cabbage[89].

Salt – 0.5%.

Pepper (black, whole - maybe half a handful).

Bay leaf – 1-2.

Slice the cabbage thinly. Add 0.5% of salt by weight of cabbage. Mix cabbage and salt really well by hand. Add a few black peppercorns and a bay leaf or two.

Add this to a container with a well sealing lid. A glass preserving jar (also called a mason jar) is a good way to keep the mixture because you can clearly see what is happening inside. Pack the cabbage into the container as tightly as you can. Seal the container. Leave in a cool dark place.

Check it every few days. Release any gas which has come out of the cabbage. Smell and taste it regularly. If it does not look, smell or taste good, then throw it out.

It will start to taste like pickled cabbage after a while. The time will depend on the size of the jar and ambient conditions but may be 1 week to 2 months.

---

88   The quantities of ingredients, save for salt are not really important. Go wild, if you wish but not too much.

89   Red cabbage can be used also if you like but it is not so traditional.

CHICKEN LIVER PARFAIT

Parfait is like pâté but it is passed through a sieve to remove any larger pieces which gives it a much softer, silky texture. The French word "parfait" means "perfect". I assume this to be a reference to the product being free from any lumps unlike pâté which may contain a few.

[90]*Chicken livers – 500g.*
Milk – 500ml.
Butter (unsalted) – 225g.
Large shallot (or a smallish brown onion) – 1.
Garlic clove (crushed) – 1.
Thyme (fresh is best but dried will do) – 1 sprig/½tsp.
Bay leaf – 1.
Olive oil – 2tbsp.
Brandy (cognac if you have it) – 25ml.
Cream – 100ml.
Salt – 1tsp.
Black pepper (fresh ground) – to taste.

Wash and trim livers to remove any sinew and nasty bits. Take your time with this, chicken livers have a surprising amount of nasty bits. Chop the livers into small pieces.

Soak the livers (with the bay leaf and thyme) in milk overnight in the refrigerator. Clarify the butter (melt gently in a saucepan). It will separate into solids and a clear yellow oil. Discard the solids, the remaining yellow oil is clarified butter.

Drain the livers, discard the milk, bay leaf and thyme. Add the livers to a hot frying pan with a little olive oil. Cook fast and hot, but do not overcook. Try and keep them a little pink in the middle. Cook for no more than 30 seconds. Cook in batches so they do not crowd the pan and stew.

Remove the livers and dry them on kitchen paper. Into the same pan add 25g of butter (not the clarified butter) together with chopped shallot (or onion) and garlic. Sweat the onions and garlic until translucent, being careful not to burn the shallot (or onion) and garlic. Add the livers to the pan with shallot (or onion) and garlic. Add brandy and flame off the alcohol.

---

90   This is a traditional recipe and I have not used percentage weights of ingredients. It is a matter of taste and touch, like most cookery.

Allow to cool somewhat.

Add the crushed liver/onion/garlic to a blender or food processor together with the cream and clarified butter. Blend until smooth. Pass the mixture through a fine sieve using the back of a spoon or ladle. Repeat the process (discarding any tough bits in the sieve each time).

Put the parfait into a small ramekin and cover with melted clarified butter.

Eat on dry toast.

Outstanding.

If you do not like this, then I cannot help you.

This does not breach The Rule Against Offal because I like it.

CHOUCROUTE GARNIE

Choucroute garnie is a great winter dish from Alsace consisting of sauerkraut, boiled potatoes, white wine and several different types of charcuterie. This is one of my all time favourite winter meals. A great way to feed a large number with very little effort on your part. It is a crowd pleaser, just don't say how easy it is. It is our secret. If you tell anyone, I will find you.

[91]*Sauerkraut – 1kg.*

Riesling (one bottle, less one glass, that is for you whilst you do this) – 750ml.

Small new potatoes (the golf ball sized white skinned ones called chats) – 12.

Whatever charcuterie you would like, say, 1 smoked pork hock, 1 good length of smoked sausage (jagerwurst, andouille or Polish to name a few), several boudin blanc (white pudding sausages), and 1 piece of smoked bacon or speck (say 500g-1kg). The quantities will depend upon how many you intend to feed with this dish.

Bay leaves – 2.

Juniper berries (crushed) – 2.

Chopped parsley (a lot).

Warm the sauerkraut in a large pot together with the bay leaves and juniper berries. Add the riesling (it may only need about 500ml, if so there is another glass for you).[92]

Try and boil off the alcohol without burning the sauerkraut. In this regard, you will need to stir the sauerkraut mixture constantly.

Add the charcuterie, it only has to warm through, it does not need to be cooked.

Add the just boiled potatoes (you have already steamed or boiled them separately. Do not overcook them, they need to remain whole).

Gently spoon through a good amount of chopped parsley. Serve immediately with a good Riesling or Gewurztraminer (from Alsace if you can), mustard and horseradish. It needs nothing else.

Outstanding, just don't tell anyone how easy it is.

---

91 A traditional recipe. Precise measurements are not required.
92 I am a river to my people.

TÊTE DE PORC FARCI

Tête de porc farci is French for deboned, rolled, stuffed pig head. I hasten to say that it eats better than the English translation. It is also a very good way to practice basic knife skills. Before you say that you couldn't possibly eat this, remember Marjorie Kinnan Rawlings' writing in 1942:

> *"Rattlesnake meat is canned commercially in Florida and served as a delicate hors-d'oeuvre. I have never tried it and do not intend to. ... Steak from the tail of an alligator is another matter..."*

This is a good dish, try it once. You never know, you just might like it. (The pork dish, not the rattlesnake.)

[93]*Pig head – 1.*
Pork (shoulder, minced) – 500g.
Parsley (chopped finely) – handful.
Garlic (chopped) – 3tsp.
Salt and pepper to taste.

First, debone the pigs head. Start from the back or neck side. Carefully peel away the meat (and skin) from the bones. Try not to cut through the skin. Leave the snout on the peeled away face.

Keep the skull/bones for stock, but discard them for present purposes.

Lay the pig face on a board, skin side down.

If necessary, do the "Texas Chainsaw Massacre" thing now and scare the kids. Get it out of the way.

Cut away any glands (they are strange looking and a paler colour) and other nasty bits that do not look good to eat. There are a lot of nasty bits in a pigs head. Remove the ears.

Place the pig face on a board skin side down. Season the meat side generously with salt, pepper and a handful of chopped garlic and parsley.

---

93   A traditional recipe. Precise measurements are not required.

Make a *"sausage"* of seasoned pork mince along the middle of the pig face from snout to neck on the flesh side. The ears can be finely sliced and added if you wish (you should).

Roll the pig face tightly such that the mince filling is in the centre and the snout is visible at one end. Tie it tightly like a roast. It will look like a long sausage with a nose at one end. Quite attractive really. Wrap it in muslin or a clean tea towel.

Poach in a court bouillon for 1-1.5 hours until very soft. Remove and let cool in the refrigerator in a loaf tin or a terrine mold (depending on the size). Put a weight on top. It is best if left overnight.[94]

The next day remove the sausage from the tin or terrine mold. It now resembles a terrine more than a sausage. Remove the string.

Slice and serve with green salad, cornichons and hot mustard or sauce gribiche.

A pinot noir or a merlot would be good with this.

This is an exception to The Rule Against Offal.

---

94 Don't you dare discard the poaching liquid. Strained and reduced, it will be outstanding pork stock.

FROMAGE DE TÊTE (BRAWN)

Fromage de tête (head cheese)[95] coppa di tessa[96] or brawn[97] is a terrine made from a pigs head. It might sound a bit off-putting but the result is like a very good terrine. It is also a way to use every last bit of the pig. This not only makes sense but is polite, to paraphrase Fergus Henderson.

[98]*Pig's head (halved or quartered by your butcher if your stockpot will not fit a whole head) – 1.*
Celery sticks (roughly chopped) – 2.
Carrots (roughly chopped) – 2.
Onion (large brown, halved, skin on) – 1.
Pepper (black, whole) – 4.
Bay leaves – 2.
Parsley (flat leaf, finely chopped) – a lot

Place the pig's head into a large stockpot of sufficient size to cover the pig's head with water. Add the other ingredients.

Simmer until the meat is falling off the bone (this will take several hours and the liquid will need to be replenished from time to time). Do not let the pot boil dry and do not let it go past a good simmer. If you boil it too hard the meat will fall apart.

Cook the head until the meat is falling off the bone, but not completely boiled into a soup.

Remove the head and allow to it cool sufficiently to handle.

Keep the poaching liquid. This is very important.

Reheat the strained liquid to a vigorous boil and reduce it by about ½ - ⅔ in volume.

Remove meat and skin from the head. Do not forget the ears. Discard the eyes and any other nasty bits (a pig head has quite a few glands beneath the surface which do not eat at all well). Discard the bones, they have done their work.

95   A literal translation from the French.
96   To use the Italian.
97   As described by British and Australians, including my late mother, although she did not use the head of the pig to make it (sadly).
98   A traditional recipe. Precise measurements are not required.

Separate meat from fat and skin. Chop the head meat into a rough dice, do not mince or cut too finely. Discard fat, skin and nasty bits. Mix through salt and pepper to taste and a good quantity of chopped parsley. If the pig's head came complete with its tongue, then remove the tongue and skin it (the skin is very tough). Chop the tongue or use it whole. If using it whole, place a layer of chopped head meat in the bottom of the mold, then the tongue, cover with the remaining chopped meat. If using chopped tongue, simply add it to the other chopped head meat.

Add to a terrine mold lined with several layers of plastic film (easier to turn it out later). Press the mixture quite well to remove air pockets. Carefully add the cooled reduced cooking liquid, weigh the mold and refrigerate. The cooking liquid is rich in gelatine from the bones and skin. It will set to a jelly which will hold the brawn together.

Turn it out and slice about 2.5cm thick. Eat with dry toast or fresh bread and a green salad. Cornichons[99] are essential as are Riesling or Pinot Noir.

If it is too large for a terrine mold, use a loaf tin or similar. All that is important is that you can contain all the mixture together with a good amount of cooking liquid, weigh it down and allow to set.

Again, a well known exception to The Rule Against Offal.

---

99 Cornichons are the small pickled gherkins that the French do so well. There is no substitute.

RILLETTES

Rillettes are made from pork which is slowly cooked in pork fat, like confit de canard, for example. To the British, it is called potted meat. It is a very good thing with bread and wine (Pinot noir probably, perhaps shiraz).

Pork (shoulder, diced) – 1kg.
Pork (belly, diced) – 200g.
Lard or other rendered pork fat – 300g.
Onion (finely diced) – 2.
Rosemary (fresh or dried) – If dried, say 1 tsp, if fresh say a sprig 6cm long.
Bay leaves (fresh if you have them but dried will do just as well) – 1 or 2.
White wine (cold, dry style) – 400-500ml.

In a heavy based saucepan (an enamelled casserole dish with a lid is good), add lard, onions, white wine, rosemary, bay leaves, wine and add meat.

If the quantity of wine is insufficient to cover the meat, then add more wine or water.

Cook very gently until the meat breaks down (maybe 3-4 hours). Do not let the fat boil, you will get deep fried pork. It should be a tremble, not even a simmer. The French term is '*mijoter*', which means (roughly) a very low simmer. If it takes more than 3 hours to cook, then so be it. It is a dish which cannot be rushed.

Once complete, remove the meat from the rendered fat and strain the remaining rendered fat through a sieve or open weave kitchen cloth. Shred the meat with two forks. Season well with salt and pepper. Place the shredded meat in a sterilised jar or ramekin.

Cover the meat with the lard. Allow to cool. This will keep in a sealed jar for several weeks in the refrigerator.

JAMBON PERSILLE[100] (HAM HOCK AND PARSLEY TERRINE)

A classic terrine from the south of France, using smoked ham hock and fresh parsley.

Ham hock (large, smoked) – 1. Parsley (one large bunch, finely chopped) (either flat leaf parsley or curly parsley, although I prefer the former).

Make a court bouillon with 2 litres of water, 350ml of good white wine, a few peppercorns, one celery stick, 2 bay leaves, 1 head of garlic, one onion (with skin on) and two carrots.

Poach the ham hock gently until it is falling off the bone. This may take several hours. Remove the hock from the liquid and allow to cool. **Keep the poaching liquid** (this is very important).

Separate the meat from the bones, skin, fat and nasty bits. Chop the meat roughly. Discard the bones, skin, fat and nasty bits.

Strain and remove the aromatics from the poaching liquid and reduce it by ¾ in volume. Set it aside to cool. Season the chopped meat with pepper (it probably does not need salt but check it).

Combine the meat and parsley and mix well. Pack into a terrine mold which has been lined with several layers of cling film (it makes it easier to turn it out once set).

Pour in tepid reduced poaching liquid to cover the meat. Cover and refrigerate overnight. A weight on top is a good idea. Slice thickly and eat with bread and salad. Riesling is essential.

NOTE: If you are worried that the liquid will not set into a jelly, add some gelatine powder to the liquid. Alternatively, add a pork trotter or two to the poaching liquid at the start. They contain lots of gelatine.

---

100   Sounds better in French, n'est pas?

TUNA IN OIL

Preserving tuna in oil is a very old technique which gives excellent results. The home-made product is much better than the most expensive tinned tuna, in my view.

Tuna is available from fishmongers. Sashimi quality tuna is available all year round but is very expensive. Cheaper species of tuna (usually Southern Bluefin)[101] are seen in some fishmongers usually in winter. Yellowfin Tuna[102] would be excellent but is hard to find and quite expensive, Bonito[103] or Skipjack Tuna[104] are cheap and not a bad substitute. Consider also using Spanish Mackerel[105] which is quite cheap and readily available.

You probably do not want to purchase a whole tuna (a small one would be about 20kg) but often cutlets or steaks are available. These are ideal to use for this recipe. If you have access to a whole tuna, so much the better, use the same principles but you will need a lot more glass jars. An awful lot more.

Tuna (cut into cutlets, skin and bones left on).
Salt (sufficient to make a 10% brine solution)
Bay leaves – several.
Pepper (black, whole) – several.
Pepper (black, cracked) – 2tsp.
Water to cover.
Chilli (fresh or dried) – 2tsp.
Lemon rind – say 3 good pieces
Garlic – 2 cloves, whole

In a large stockpot make a brine using salt and cold water (about 10% solution, i.e. 100g salt to 1 litre of water).

Add aromatics and tuna steaks/cutlets.

Bring the pot up to a boil and turn down to a low simmer (not a fast or 'rolling' boil, the fish will disintegrate).

Make sure that you use the extraction fan, this can smell very strongly of boiled fish. If you are worried about smells, do this on an outside barbecue. Give the neighbours the benefits of a charcutier in motion.

---

101 *Thunnus maccoyii.*
102 *Thunnus albacares.*
103 *Sarda australis.*
104 *Katsuwonus pelamis.*
105 *Scomberomorus commerson.*

Cook for at least 1 hour until the fish is cooked through.

Allow the fish to cool in the liquid. When cool, remove skin and bones. Discard any dark flesh or bloodlines. They are unattractive and do not eat well.

Pack tightly into sterilised glass jars (old jam jars will work but some specialised preserving jars – 'Mason' jars are a good investment).

Pour in sufficient oil to cover the fish, tapping the jar firmly to get out any air bubbles. Any oil will do (vegetable or canola are good). You do not need to use olive oil but can if you would like.

Add a few bay leaves, peppercorns and a chilli if you like. I do and I think they make a difference.

Seal the jars with sterilised lids (not too tightly).

Pack the jars into a single layer in a large stockpot, add water to just below the level of the jar lid. (A tea towel on the bottom of the pot stops the jars from moving and breaking or cracking).

Heat to a low boil for about ½ hour. Allow to cool in the water.

The preserved tuna will keep for at least one year, unrefrigerated.

Once completed, the result is good firm flakes of meat with a pale, almost, white colour, just like the finest tinned tuna but better.

SALT CURED WHITE FISH

Salt cured white fish, mainly cod, has been a worldwide staple for centuries.

It is sufficiently important that Kurlansky has written one book about cod, and another book about salt. Salt and salt cod have been major reasons for the establishment of trade routes, empires, wars and more recipes than you can poke a stick at. Salt fish is also a really easy thing to make and the end result is quite a different product. The ingredients and method are really easy and embedded in history. The problem is that cod, the subject of the books and all the other stuff, is not a fish available to me. Mr Cod does not live anywhere near me or any fishmonger whom I may care to visit – at least not in a fresh form. Mr Cod lives in the Northern Hemisphere. The question is what to use as an alternative? The answer is that the recipe requires a firm white fish, which is reasonably plentiful but also a fish which will cope with the curing and smoking process well. It needs to be thick and it needs to be readily available.

There are at least, several contenders available to me as follows. Snapper or schnapper (*Pagrus auratus*), **rockling** or **pink ling** (*Genypterus tigerinus, blacodes*), gurnard (red gurnard – *Chelidonichthys kumu)*; **painted latchet** – (*Pterygotrigla andertoni)*; latchet – *Pterygotrigla polyommata*); **stargazer**[106] (*Kathetostoma laeve*), or flathead (dusky flathead – *Platycephalus fuscus*; **rock flathead** – *Platycephalus laevigatus* or tiger flathead – *Platycephalus richardson*).[107]

These are all good fish, having white, sweet firm flesh. Stargazer and gurnards being the firmest. Firm fleshed fish is important to this dish. Soft fleshed fish just will not work.

---

106   Recently called monkfish in my local markets because of its European cousin, but stargazer it is to me. A fish familiar to scuba divers before anyone else knew of it and one only its mother could love. As far as I can tell, monkfish (*Lophius pissatorius*) is not related to stargazer (*uronoscopidac*) but looks very similar.

107   These fish have several common names each. I have tried to give scientific names for precision.

White fish fillet (skin on but deboned).

Salt (fine salt is best) – a lot, sufficient to coat the fish.

Sugar (brown) – the same quantity as the salt.

Rub the fillets well with the salt and sugar mixture.

Place in a sealed non-reactive container or in a resealable plastic bag.

Place the fish in the refrigerator.

Leave for 24 hours.

Overhaul every few hours if you can.

Remove the fish, wash (sparingly) and pat dry.

Refrigerate for 7 days to allow the fish to dry out. A muslin cover will help the fish not dry out too quickly.

Thereafter wash the fish or vacuum seal.

In order to use the now salted and dried fish, rehydrate by soaking in water for 12-24 hours, changing the water every few hours.

The now rehydrated fish will be good as a mixture with mashed potato to make salt cod fritters or in a casserole with tomatoes and potato. It is a really good product and quite different from the fresh fish with which you started. A really, really good variation is to smoke the fish after the first salting stage. Smoke at 70°C until an internal temperature of at least 65°C is achieved. Use quite a lot of wood to get a good smoky flavor.

PICKLED EGGS

Maybe this recipe does not qualify for inclusion in a charcuterie book, but I make no admissions nor do I care. I told you this was an idiosyncratic book and I like eggs, so I included this recipe. If you do not like eggs or think that it upsets the purity of a charcuterie book then do not read it. If you do not then you will miss out. It is a good recipe. Older eggs work better for this, really fresh eggs are harder to peel once boiled. McGee, explained why older eggs are easier to peel than really fresh eggs. Difficult peeling is characteristic of fresh eggs with a relatively low albumen pH, which somehow causes the albumen to adhere to the inner shell membrane more strongly than it adheres to itself. The shell will peel away easily after a few days of refrigeration. The pH will typically be at around 9.2.

Clever chap, that McGee.

Eggs – hard boiled.
Vinegar (white) – ¾cup.
Sugar (white) – ½cup.
Water – ¾cup.
Mustard seeds – 1tsp.
Herbes de provence – 1tsp.
Tarragon – fresh or dried – 1tsp.
Onion – (sliced) small.
Beetroot – (fresh) – 2 medium sized (optional).

Add eggs, cold from the refrigerator, into boiling water. Allow 10 minutes for hard boiled egg yolks. Neither more nor less. Add the eggs gently into the boiling water. Pause when they are half way into the water. Observe the bubbles fizzing from the pointy end of the egg. This is the air from the air sac expanding rapidly through the porous shell. Add the eggs too quickly and the shell will shatter. This is the air escaping too quickly. Any scuba diver will understand the problem and live in fear of it. Allow the air fizzing to subside, this will only take a few seconds. There is not much air in the air sac.

Boil the eggs for 10 minutes.

Do not put the lid on the saucepan, the temperature gets too hot for the eggs and they will invariably burst from the shell.

After 10 minutes, neither more nor less, cool the eggs in running cold water and allow to sit in colder water. Replace the water if needed – it will get hot very quickly.

If you allow the eggs to cool in hot water they will develop the characteristic grey ring between the yolk and the white. Just like mum used to make. It is not altogether pleasing to the eye and easy to avoid. Just cool correctly and you will not get grey rings in your boiled eggs. Why does this happen, I hear you ask? Once again McGee comes to the rescue[108]. The occasional green-gray discoloration on the surface of hard-cooked yolks is a harmless compound of iron and sulfur, ferrous sulfide. It forms at the interface of white and yolk because that is where reactive sulfur from the former comes into contact with the iron from the latter. The alkaline conditions in the white favor the stripping of sulfur atoms from the albumen proteins when heat unfolds them, and the sulfur reacts with iron in the surface layer of yolk to form ferrous sulfide. The older the egg, the more alkaline and white, and the more rapidly this reaction occurs. High temperatures and prolonged cooking produce more ferrous sulfide. Yolk "greening" can be minimized by using fresh eggs, by cooking them as briefly as possible, and by cooling them rapidly after cooking.

Boil the peeled beetroot separately for 20 minutes and allow to cool. Boil all remaining ingredients until the onion is soft. Strain and retain liquid. Drain beetroot and retain liquid and the cooked beetroot. Add peeled boiled eggs to a sterilized glass jar. Add some cooked beetroot pieces (this helps fix the colour). Add the cooled vinegar solution and enough cooled beetroot liquid to give a good dark beetroot colour. Refrigerate for a few days. The eggs will have a sweet pickled flavor and a pleasant beetroot colour into the white for a few millimeters. The longer the eggs are in the cure, the stronger they will taste and the further the colour will penetrate. Pickled eggs are good in a salad, on a charcuterie plate or on their own.

If you do not like the idea of adding beetroot, then omit that step.

An old fashioned dish but a dish which has stood the test of time for a good reason.

---

108 Clever chap, that McGee

CULLEN SKINK (SMOKED FISH SOUP)

A soup with a name like Cullen Skink cannot be overlooked, especially in a charcuterie book. It is a velvety soup made with potatoes and smoked white fish. It comes from Scotland where one needs food like this.

Smoked white fish – (haddock, cod, or that which you have made, however it must be undyed) – 500g.
Milk – full cream – 500ml.
Potato – (white floury variety) – 2 large (about 250-300g).
Shallots – diced – 4.
Butter – about 1tbsp.
White wine – 100ml.
Bay leaf – (fresh or dry) – 1.
Cream – 90ml.
Chicken stock – 500ml.
Mustard powder – 1tsp.
Salt and pepper to taste.
Parsley – chopped (quite a lot).
Chives - chopped (quite a lot).

It is important to use an undyed smoked fish; otherwise you will end up with orange soup. The brightly coloured, orange 'smoked cod', which is widely available has a dye added to give the yellow colour. Make your own or buy a non dyed smoked white fish. Add the fish to a saucepan with milk and 1 bay leaf.

Poach the fish gently until it is opaque and firm, this will take about 10 minutes.

Remove the fish and allow to cool. Strain and reserve the milk.

Peel and cut the potato into small cubes. Fry lightly in a pan with butter and shallots. Do not brown the potato or shallots, merely soften somewhat.

Into the same fry pan, add chicken stock, white wine, cream and reserved milk. Simmer until potatoes are very soft and falling apart. Add salt and pepper to taste. Blend the mixture until smooth. Flake the fish into large chunks, removing skin and bone.

Add the fish to the blended soup, stir through gently with chopped herbs. Add lemon juice to taste. Check the seasoning at this point, if necessary add more salt and pepper.

Clever people these Scottish.

A nice variation is to reserve some cubes of cooked potato, added to the finished soup gives some interesting texture.

SMOKED PORK HOCK AND WHITE BEAN TERRINE

A really simple terrine made with smoked pork hock (which, of course, you have made yourself) and soft white beans cooked in the same liquid as the pork hock.

It makes a delicate summer lunch or an addition to a charcuterie plate. It is a good way to use your home-made smoked hocks.

Smoked pork hock – (large) – about 1kg.
White beans (dried haricot, or similar) – 250g. (soaked overnight).
Carrot – 1 large (peeled).
Onion (brown) – 1 large.
Garlic – ½ head.
Bay leaf (fresh) – 2.
Celery – 2 sticks.
Juniper berries – 3 or 4.
Nutmeg (ground) – about ½tsp.
Salt and pepper to taste.

Place onion, garlic, carrot, celery, juniper berries and bay leaves in a large stock pot. Slash the pork hock to the bone, to speed up cooking. Add pork hock to the pot, cover with cold water.

Simmer quite hard (but not a boil) until meat is falling from the bone. This may take a few hours. Remove the carrot when it is yielding. I will explain why later.

Skim off any scum regularly. Top up the liquid if necessary. Once cooked remove the hock and allow to cool.

Strain the cooking liquid and return to the pot. Drain and rinse the beans.

Add beans to the cooking liquid and simmer until the beans are soft but not falling apart. They need to keep their shape for this dish. They will take 30-60 minutes to cook. Once cooked remove the beans and refresh under cold water to stop the cooking process. Strain the cooking liquid again and reserve.

Returning to the hock, separate meat from bone, skin, fat and nasty bits. Discard skin, fat and nasty bits. Chop or shred the meat into chunks, do not turn it into mince or finely dice. It needs to keep texture, and a mix of smaller and larger pieces. This is both for visual and textural reasons.

Combine (gently), meat, beans and salt and pepper to taste. Go easy on the salt, the meat will be quite salty and so too the beans.

At this point you can make the mixture look more appealing by adding some finely chopped parsley.

Recall the carrot? Now here is why it was removed. Chop it into quite small pieces. Add to the terrine and carefully combine. It gives a good splash of orange to the finished dish.

Line a terrine mold with several layers of cling film, overlapping the edges. This is to assist in removing the terrine once set.

Add the meat and bean mixture to the mold, pressing down firmly to remove air pockets. Add some of the reserved cooking liquid, this will help set the mixture together, it being replete with gelatin from the ham bock.

Cover the mold, and allow to set in the refrigerator.

THE RECIPES FOR
THE BRAVE

PAUPIETTES (PORK PARCELS WRAPPED IN BACON)

Paupiettes are meat mince parcels rolled in a thinly sliced meat and sealed (rolled) with bacon. Sometimes called '*Alouettes sans tête*' or '*Larks without heads*'. I do not know why they are called this. I think that I do not want to know, nor, I suspect, do you. The British equivalent, using beef, would be beef olives. These are equally as good.

This recipe uses pork mince and thinly sliced pork loin. It is worth a try.

Pork (loin, trimmed of fat and sliver skin) – 1kg.
Pork (shoulder, medium mince) – 400g.
Salt – 1.4%.
Bacon (cured and smoked, streaky or belly bacon is best) – sufficient slices to roll the paupiettes.
Parsley – 1tbsp or as much as you would like.
Onion (white, finely chopped) – 1tbsp.
Garlic – ¼tsp finely chopped.
Pepper (black, ground) – 0.2%.

Mix the pork mince with the salt, onion and herbs, knead well.

Slice the pork loin thinly.

Using the back of a knife smash out the pork loin until very thin.

Do not break the meat slice.

Onto the pork loin, place about one tablespoon of minced pork and meat mixture.

Roll the pork loin around the mince to make a small parcel.

Roll the loin and mince parcel in bacon.

Tie the bacon/loin and mince parcel with string.

Return to refrigerator for at least 1 hour to set.

Seal briefly on a high heat to give the bacon some colour.

Poach gently in a court bouillon with some chicken stock.

Serve with mash potato or lentils and a reduction of the poaching liquid.

NOTE: If you are worried about the meat mixture holding together, add some breadcrumbs, say 2tbsp, and perhaps one beaten egg. The breadcrumbs give a softer texture to the mince. The egg binds it all together.

PÂTÉ DE PAQUES (PATE WITH HARDBOILED EGGS WRAPPED IN PASTRY)

Pâté de Paques is a coarse pâté or terrine with hardboiled eggs which is then wrapped in pastry. It is in the vein of many classic French charcuterie dishes which are wrapped in pastry, called encroute. Somewhat unusually, it is a pork and beef pâté, not pure pork.

Beef (minced, coarse) – 500g.
Pork (shoulder, minced, fine) – 250g.
Salt – 2.5%.
Espelette pepper – 1tbsp.
Nutmeg – ½tbsp.
Crème fraiche – ½ cup.
Eggs – 5 whole eggs and one extra egg yolk.
Eggs – hardboiled (5).
Rosemary – ½tsp.
Parsley – ½tsp.
Thyme – ½tsp.
Pepper (black, cracked) – ½tsp.
Puff pastry – sufficient to cover (maybe two packets of prepared pastry).

Mix beef and pork mince well, together with dry ingredients. Refrigerate meat mixture overnight.

Separately, mix crème fraiche and eggs. Add to the meat mixture and mix well.

Grease a loaf tin or terrine mold and line with baking paper. Lay pastry in the bottom of the tin such that it comes up the sides and over with a good excess.

Fill the tin with 1/3 of the mixture. Lay the whole peeled hardboiled eggs lengthwise in the mold. Cover the eggs with the meat mixture, pressing down hard to remove any air pockets.

Cover with pastry, pinch and seal the edges of the bottom sheet with the top sheet. Glaze with egg wash, make a hole to release steam. Cook for 15-25 minutes at 200°C until golden brown.

Serve cold with a green salad and really cold white wine.

NOTE: Espellette pepper is mild chilli powder from Espelette in the Basque region of France. Substitute any mild chilli powder or chilli flakes. It is important not to overpower the dish with chilli heat. It is a mild background flavor only. If you are in doubt, omit the chilli powder completely.

HAM IN SALT DOUGH

Hot baked ham is a fantastic dish. There are many recipes for glazed hams, with the glaze becoming the centre piece of the dish, rather than the ham. They are great dishes and I have cooked them many times for Christmas lunch. This dish, however, is different. It is one of my strongest childhood memories, even though it was only cooked once. The cured ham is wrapped in a salt dough before baking. The smell is fantastic and fills the house. The cooked dough, rich in ham fat is not bad to eat, especially if you are 5 or 6 years old. I am sure the salt police will not like it but I did.

This dish, although never forgotten, was not in the foreground for this book. Re-reading Grigson I found a recipe for "*Jambon á l'Anglaise or en Chausson*". Literally translated this means English ham or ham in a shoe. The latter I understand to be a reference to the covering of dough.

This recipe is for a cured ham baked in salt dough. This is adapted from Grigson. I just had to include it. Does it belong in a charcuterie book? I do not care.

Pork leg (boned or bone in but with rind intact).
Brine:
Salt – 3%.
Curing Salt – 0.3%.
Sugar (Brown) – 3%.
Juniper berries – a few, crushed.
Bay leaf – 2.
Water – 3-4 litres.
Dough:
White flour – 1kg.
Salt – 650g.

Mix ingredients for the brine, submerge the meat completely in the brine.

Place meat/brine into the refrigerator in a sealed non reactive container.

Grigson overlooks any instruction about the starting point, she refers to a 'ham' which is then '3/4 cooked'. Not terribly helpful in my view. I think that one should start with a cured unsmoked ham. Hence the brine step described above. Keep the meat in the brine for 1 day/kg.

Thereafter remove the meat and pat dry. Allow to come to room temperature.

The dough is just flour, salt and water. Grigson adds butter and lard. I do not think either is required. Make as much dough as you need to wrap the meat, probably 1.5–2kg of flour will be required. Roll out the dough so it is approximately 2cm thick at least. Place the ham, cut side down in the centre, gather up the pastry and seal with an egg wash. Patch any holes with pastry and seal with egg wash. Place the now dough encased ham in an oven preheated to 180°C.

Cook for approximately 40 min/kg. Once cooked, remove from the oven, crack off the now cooked dough and serve immediately.

Childhood.

BRANDADE (SALT FISH PATÉ)

Salted white fish has a variety of uses, one of the most common is to make a type of pâté. It is common in Mediterranean countries although it has a variety of names brandade or brandade de morue (France), a brandada de bacalo (Spain). Brandade is an emulsion of salt fish and olive oil which is beaten or whipped to a puree.

Outstanding.

Salted white fish (cod or any which you have already made from species available to you) – 500g.

Potato – use a floury potato, not a waxy type potato – one large potato of about 250g.

Milk – full cream, sufficient to cover the fish.

Bay leaf (fresh or diced) – 1.

Garlic (minced) – 3tsp.

Shallots (finely chopped) – 3 small shallots.

Cream – 200ml.

Lemon juice – ½ one lemon, juiced.

Pepper (black, ground) – to taste.

Soak the salt fish for 24 hours, changing the water every few hours; at least 4 times in total. Cook the potato (unpeeled) and allow to cool. Once the potato is cool, remove the skin and chop into small pieces (say ½ cm dice). The ratio of potato to fish should be about 1:2, otherwise you end up with bland brandade. This is no good and something to be avoided.

Flake the salt fish, discarding any bones and skin. Add to a saucepan and cover with milk. Add a bay leaf and bring to a simmer. Do not allow it to boil. Cook until soft but not falling apart.

In a separate sauce pan, add olive oil, chopped shallots and garlic. Sweat until translucent, do not allow the shallots and garlic to brown. Add cream and warm through before adding the drained salt fish and potato. Using a stick blender or food processor, blend the mixture until silky smooth. Use some of the poaching milk to get a good consistency if need be. Add lemon juice and pepper, blend to integrate and emulsify the mixture. Add salt now if needed, it probably will be sufficiently salted but test it.

Excellent on a dry biscuit or toast, just like chicken liver paté.

HOT SMOKED EGGS

Eggs can be preserved in a variety of ways including pickled, salted (which I do not care for) or smoked. Smoking of eggs is simple and results in a very good product.

Eggs, fresh and free range of course.

Boil the eggs for 10 minutes. If the eggs are cold from the refrigerator, 10 minutes should be sufficient. If they are already at room temperature then perhaps 6 minutes would be enough.

When cooked, immediately refresh in plenty of cold running water.

Peel the eggs and place on a rack in the smoker at about 85°C for 10 minutes. Do not smoke them at a high temperature or for very long. If you do then the whites will become very tough and rubbery.

TONNE DI MAIALE (TUNA PORK)

Tonne di maiale is pork leg meat cured and preserved in the style of tuna. It has a soft, mild texture and flavour not unlike preserved tuna. Hence the name. It is very good.

Pork (leg deboned, skinned and trimmed of all fat and sinew) – 1kg.
Salt – sufficient to bury the meat.
Wine (cold, dry style, white) – 500ml.
Bay leaf – fresh or dried – 10.
Oil (olive) – 1 litre.

Cut the pork leg meat into small pieces, say 1cm dice.

Immerse the meat in salt making sure it is well covered. Place in the refrigerator in a non-reactive sealed container for 36 hours.

Remove and rinse excess salt (sparingly), pat dry.

Add to a pot with white wine, bay leaves and water to cover.

Bring to boil and then return to a simmer.

Simmer for 2 hours.

Remove from heat and allow to cook.

Place meat in sterilized glass jars, cover with oil, tap each jar well to remove air bubbles, add one bay leaf. Seal the jar.

Place in the refrigerator. It will keep for 4-6 weeks.

LEBERWURST (LIVERWURST)

Leberwurst is a German spreadable paté or terrine made from pig liver and pork shoulder.

The addition of pork shoulder rescues what would, for me, be an altogether too much liver experience. Accordingly it does not breach The Rule Against Offal (but only just).

Pork (lean shoulder or leg; minced) – 800g.
Liver (pig, fresh) – 200g.
Onion (brown, finely chopped) – 300g.
Paprika (sweet) – ½tsp.
Pepper (white, ground) – ½tsp.
Marjoram (dried) – ¼tsp.
Nutmeg (ground) – ¼tsp.
Cloves (ground) – pinch.
Coriander (ground – ½tsp.
Lard – 1 tbsp (olive oil if you cannot get lard).

Add lard and onion to a pan and cook until onion soft and translucent but not brown. Add chopped liver and cook through. Then add sugar, salt and spices and mix well.

Allow to cool and add minced pork.

Transfer the mixture to a food processor and puree until smooth.

Fill sausage casings and tie each link with a bubble knot. Do not overfill, they will expand during the next phase (cooking).

Add to simmering water and poach for about 45 minutes. Refresh immediately in cold water.

The mixture can also be cooked like a terrine. Add to a terrine mold. Place in a baking dish such that water can be added up to about 2/3 of the height of the terrine mold.

Place in the oven (covered) for 2 hours at 150°C until an internal temperature of about 80°C.

PIG HEAD AND POTATO PIE

What can I say? This is a Fergus Henderson recipe, slightly adapted, and it has to be included. The process is simple, first, persuade a pig to part with its head. The rest is quite easy really.

Pig head (halved) – 1.
Onion (brown) – 1, cut in half unpeeled.
Celery (sticks uncut) – 2, each cut in half.
Carrot (unpeeled) – 2.
Leek (washed) – 1.
Garlic (whole head) – 1.
Pepper (black, whole).
White wine (dry) – 500ml.
Chicken stock (sufficient to cover the pig head) – say 1 litre.
Potato (waxy, yellow flesh) – 1.5kg.
Sage (fresh, chopped) – 6-8 leaves.
Garlic (minced) – 12tsp.
Salt and pepper – to taste.
Puff pastry – store bought, one packet.

In your largest stock pot, place pig head, stock, vegetables (except potato, chopped sage and minced garlic). You are making a court bouillon to cook the pigs head.

Boil until yielding, about 3 1/2 hours. Once the meat is falling from the bone, remove the head, from the stock. Separate the meat from bone, skin and nasty bits. Discard bone, skin and nasty bits.

Chop the meat into ½ cm dice.

Strain and reserve cooking liquid.

Assembly:

Grease a 20 cm round springform tin with butter and then lightly flour the surface. Cut a round of baking paper to fit the bottom of the springform tin.

Roll pastry such that a circle is used to line the base. Cut a strip(s) such that the sides are covered with pastry and a 2 cm 'collar' is left over the top edge. Seal and crimp the joins between bottom and side and with any side joins. Use milk or egg wash to seal the joins.

Next make alternate layers of sliced potato, and chopped pork meat. Start with potato, season each layer well. Some fresh or dried thyme and parsley added to each layer together with the chopped garlic and sage would be a good idea.

Press each layer down firmly. Add some finely sliced onion if you wish (I think it is a good idea). When the top has been reached, make a pastry lid, seal and crimp it to the pastry sides.

Paint the top with milk or egg wash. Sprinkle crushed pepper and salt, sesame or nigella seeds if you have them.

Make a hole for the steam to escape.

Place in a medium oven (say 180°C) for two hours. Ensure that the potatoes are cooked, use a skewer to test the resistance.

Serve at once.

For my part, I think this dish would benefit from some chopped spinach (squeezed of all moisture) and maybe some finely sliced mushroom added to the meat or potato mixture, or perhaps a separate layer.

FRICANDEAU DE AVIGNON

Fricandeau is a traditional terrine wrapped in caul fat and, somewhat unusually for a terrine, served hot. It is similar to British faggots. The liver melts into the dish and there is not much of it, accordingly it does not conflict with The Rule Against Offal. If you disagree, add less liver or omit it entirely.

Pork (shoulder, minced) – 350g.
Pork (belly, skin removed, minced) – 250g.
Liver (pig, finely chopped) – 35g.
Caul fat – sufficient to wrap the fricandeau.
Egg (whole, beaten) – 1-2.
Garlic (minced) – 1-2tsp.
Parsley (flat leaf, finely chopped) – 1tbsp.
Cognac or brandy – 1tbsp.
Breadcrumb (dried) – ½ cup.
Bay leaf – one for each fricandeau.

Mix all ingredients except caul fat and bay leaf.

Refrigerate overnight in resealable plastic bag or non-reactive container.

The next day, mix well until sticky.

Shape into balls about the size of a medium onion. Place a bay leaf on top, wrap in caul fat.

Bake in oven at 200°C for 40-50 minutes. Serve warm or cold.

Faggots are essentially the same although often have finely diced bacon and onion added to the mix. I think that is a good idea.

ZAMPONE (STUFFED PIGS TROTTER)

Before you get too excited, let me say this is an exception to The Rule Against Offal and therefore does not fall within the definition of offal. It is a classic Italian dish and you need to learn about it. Some versions of this recipe include sweatbreads. "Sweatbread" is a euphemism for pancreas, usually that of the pig or calf. I do not do pancreas or sweatbreads or whatever you care to call them. Remember The Rule Against Offal; it will never let you down.

Pig trotter – (as many as you wish but this recipe has quantities sufficient for one stuffed trotter.
Pork (minced, shoulder or belly) – 45g.
Olive oil – sufficient to fry onion and garlic.
Porcini mushroom (dried - soaked in warm water, drained and chopped) – 1tbsp.
Onion (chopped) – 1tsp.
Parsley (chopped) – 1tbsp.
Garlic (minced) – ½tsp.
Pine nuts (toasted and crushed or chopped) – 1tbsp.
Egg (beaten) – 1.
Salt and pepper to taste.
Bay leaf – 1.
Pickling spice – 1tbsp.

Fry onion and garlic in a little oil until softened. Allow to cool in the refrigerator. You must debone the trotter. It is not that hard, but care needs to be taken to avoid piercing the skin (save for the first incision).

Cut lengthways along the underside of the trotter. With the knife around the bones, remove the bones, but keep the hoof part intact. Be careful not to make holes in the skin.

Combine sautéd onion, garlic, beaten egg, meat and herbs. Soften the porcini in hot water, chop and add to mixture. Add some mushroom liquid if need be.

Fill the boned out trotter with the mixture of sautéed onion and garlic, pork mince, herbs, and the like. Roll into a long cylinder and tie with buttered string.

To cook the zampone, place the stuffed trotter in an oven dish, add 1 litre of chicken or beef stock, 1 cup of red wine, several juniper berries, the bay leaf and 1tbsp of pickling spice.

Bring the container up to a boil, on the cook top. Add to an oven at, say 200°C, and cook for about 2 - 3 hours. If the liquid is reducing too much, add some water and cover the dish with foil (if it does not have a lid).

Once the trotter is completely cooked and the skin gelatinous, remove and keep warm. Add lentils to the remaining liquid and cook until tender (about 20 minutes). Slice the trotter and serve with the lentils.

LARDO

One of the more unusual charcuterie products is cured pork fat. Nothing else. The most famous lardo is Lardo di Colonnata, made in Colonnata in Italy. The lardo from Colonnata is cured in containers made from the local marble. I do not have an Italian marble container to cure the lardo, sadly. I prepare it the same way as the other recipes. The key however is to use back fat. It needs to be as thick as possible. The other important point is that care must be taken to keep the fat in a cool dark place whilst curing. If not, the chances are that it will go rancid. You will regret it if it does.

Back fat – 1 kg (as thick as possible, cleaned of all meat, skin intact).
Salt – 250g.
Curing Salt No.2 – 3%.
Peppercorns (black, crushed) – 20g.
Garlic (minced) – 10tsp.
Rosemary (fresh) – 3-4 sprigs.
Bay leaves – 5-6.
Juniper berries (crushed) – 25g.

Combine all ingredients and rub well into surface of the back fat.

Place a layer of the cure in a non reactive container. Place fat on salt layer and pack remaining mixture around sides and on top.

Place a weight on top of the fat. Seal the container.

Wrap the container in black plastic or put in a black plastic bag.

Refrigerate for at least 3 months, preferably 6 months.

Thereafter brush off the cure mixture, do not rinse the lardo.

Remove the skin and slice the lardo as needed but always as thinly as possible. It should be translucent.

The skin can be added to a soup for extra flavor, do not mince it.

BLUTWURST (GERMAN BLOOD SAUSAGE)

This is another of the limited and rare exceptions to The Rule Against Offal. Accordingly, by definition it is not offal and therefore allowed to be included in this book.

There are many variations of this theme of making a sausage using cured pigs blood. Morcilla di cebulla uses only onions as the binding agent, black pudding uses barley and oatmeal as binding agents, other recipes use cooked rice.

Blood (pig, fresh) – 100g.
Milk (full cream) – 400ml.
Onions (brown, chopped) – 150g.
Garlic (fresh, minced) – 1 tbsp.
Apples (any kind, peeled, cored and chopped) – 2.
Paprika (sweet, smoked) – 1tsp.
Cinnamon (ground) – 1tsp.
Coriander (ground) – 1tsp.
Back fat (finely diced) – 150g.
Oats (rolled or cut) – 30g.
Breadcrumbs – (white, dried not fresh) – 30g.
Salt and pepper to taste.
Duck fat – a little.

Pass the blood through a sieve to remove any solids. This may need to be done more than once.

Add blood to milk, stir to incorporate. Cook onions and garlic gently in some duck fat until translucent, do not let them brown.

Remove the onion and garlic. In the same pan cook the apples in some duck fat until they soften, but do not let them brown.

Combine onions, garlic, apples, spices, diced back fat, oats and breadcrumbs, mix well. Add milk and blood mixture, salt and pepper. Mix together well.

The next part can be difficult. The mixture is either cooked in a loaf tin or filled into casings. The latter is more traditional, the former is easier.

Assuming that you are a traditionalist, a charcutier after all is nothing if not a traditionalist, then here is how to do it. Wash and soak pork bungs (the large casings with one opening). Using a funnel pour the mixture into the bungs. You will need two people to do this. Tie off each bung with a bubble knot. Be careful with this process, the bungs are resilient but the process is a bit tricky and apt to burst if you are not careful. There is no recovering from a burst bung and a liquid filling. Let the pudding sit while you bring a stockpot of water to a bare simmer.

Add the puddings carefully and simmer, nothing more, for, say 30 minutes.

Immediately refresh in cold water.

They are a part of a breakfast of bacon and eggs. Slice and fry the puddings. They are really good and, as stated above, an exception to The Rule Against Offal.

NOTE: As discussed above, there are many variations. Grigson has several, namely Boudin Nois in l'Ail (add an egg, use ½ flair fat and ½ back fat), Boudin de Saint – Quentin (add quatre epics, cayenne pepper and brown sugar), Boudin de Poitan (aux Épinards) (add spinach, vodka and 'orange fleur water') to name a few (in fact, she refers to 13 in total).

Pig's blood can be ordered from your butcher in advance. Some Asian butchers carry it regularly. I told you that you had to be brave.

BOUDIN BLANC

Boudin blanc is a mild white sausage with a soft mousse like interior. It is made with milk, eggs and quatre épices. The meat component can be either lean pork, chicken or rabbit. Grigson described several variation Boudins Blanc di Paris (pork, chicken and onion), Boudins Blanc du Mans (pork leg, back fat, onion and parsley), Boudins Blancs (pork loin, chicken, egg whites and ground rice) and Boudins de Lapin or de Liévre (with rabbit or hare, back fat, pork loin, fresh herbs, rabbit blood and rabbit liver). This version uses lean pork and chicken.

Pork (loin, trimmed of fat and sinews) – 500g.
Chicken (breast, skinless, minced) – 500g.
Salt – 2%.
Pepper (white, ground) – 0.2%.
Quatre épices – 3g.
Eggs – 4.
Onion (brown, finely diced) – ½ small onion.
Breadcrumbs (soaked in a little milk) – 100g.
Milk – 600ml.

Combine mixed meat, spices, onion and salt.

Blend in a food processor until a soft smooth texture is achieved. Do not let the mixture get above 10-12°C.

With the motor running, add eggs one at a time, followed by breadcrumbs and milk.

Fill sheep bungs and tie with a bubble knot. Chill in the refrigerator overnight to set.

Poach gently in a pan or barely a simmer until an internal temperature of 71°C is achieved.

To serve, lightly grill.

MORTADELLA

Mortadella is the soft silky textured sausage studded with cubes of fat and green olives. It is a very different type of charcuterie due to the emulsification of meat and fat. A little more work than a salami but well worth it.

Man up and give it a try. You can do it.

Pork (shoulder, minced) – 1kg.
Back fat (minced) – 125g.
Salt – 2.5%.
Curing Salt No.1 - 0.25%.
Pepper (black, ground) – 2g.
Pepper (white, ground) – 1g.
Nutmeg (ground) – ½ tsp.
Coriander (ground) – ½ tsp.
Cloves (ground) – ¼ tsp.
Garlic (minced) – 5g.
Pistachio (whole, shelled, blanched) – 60g.
Milk powder (nonfat) – 35g.
Water (very cold).

Mix all spices together and ensure that they are ground as finely as possible. If necessary use a spice grinder or mortar and pestle.

Mince the meat and the back fat as finely as your mincer will allow.

Combine mixed meat and mixed fat, garlic, salt, Curing Salt, milk powder and spices.

Make sure that the bowl and blade of the food processor are really cold.

Add the meat mixture to a food processor with some ice water to lubricate. Blend in small batches, be careful because the food processor will heat the meat as it blends it. The mix needs to stay below 10-12°C to avoid ruining the emulsion.

Return the processed batches to the freezer once completed so they stay really cold. The end result should be soft, pink mush that no longer resembles minced meat. It is a paste, not dissimilar in appearance to true sausage mince (the type used to make sausage rolls).

Add all processed meat to a mixer (ensure the bowl is ice cold) and add the chopped olives, mix until combined. Make sure that it does not heat up too much.

Fill sheep bungs. Tie each with a bubble knot.

Chill the sausages overnight in the refrigerator to help them set. The next day, poach the sausages in barely simmering water until they reach an internal temperature of 65°C.

Refresh immediately in cold water.

BOTTARGA (SALTED FISH ROE)

Bottarga is salted cured fish roe, usually freshwater or salt water mullet, which is much favoured by Italians. The Italians make bottarga from either grey mullet (bottarga di muggine) or tuna (bottarga di tonno). It has other names in other countries – Butarga (Croatia), Poutargue (France) or Avgotaraho (Greece), but is essentially the same thing.

Mullet has a fine small egg but the egg sac is very large. Mullet roe is rarely seen in fishmongers but you may be able to order it if the fishmonger also deals in mullet regularly. Bottarga is very easy to make, the only hard part is procuring the fish roe. What is important is a large quantity of eggs in a large egg sac but that the eggs are very small. The large eggs of species like trout or salmon are unsuitable for this dish because they are very large. Other species which can be used include flathead, tuna, trevally and swordfish, each of which have large egg sacs with very small roe.

There are many species of Mullet in Australian waters. The best for this recipe is the thin-lipped sea mullet (Mugil cephalus). It is used as a condiment for pasta or sliced thinly and eaten with bread and oil.

Fish roe (an intact egg sac is desirable) – 1.
Salt – sufficient to cover the roe.

Trim the egg sac of excess connective tissue and massage any blood from the veins which surround the egg sac.

Make a brine with salt and cold water, to about 20% strength. Add the roe to the brine and refrigerate overnight.

Next day, remove the roe and pat dry. Place a light layer of salt in the bottom of a sealed non-reactive container and place the roe on top. Cover the roe lightly with salt.

Place the sealed container in the refrigerator. Each day drain the liquid, add new salt. A layer of absorbent kitchen paper on the bottom of the container (one that will not disintegrate) will help keep the roe out of the liquid.

After the first 24 hours, there will be a lot of water in the container; the amount of water is not so great thereafter. However, you must drain it off.

Each time the salt is refreshed, turn the roe.

Air dry in a cool place for 7-14 days until the roe is quite hard. It will keep vacuum sealed for a very long time.

It adds a depth of flavour to pasta while lightly grated on top, in much the same way as a salted anchovy.[109]

---

109 See for example, spaghetti alla chitarra con bottarga.

BATH CHAPS (THERE IS NO TRANSLATION OF WHICH I AM AWARE)

A dish for the seriously committed and not at all for the faint hearted. Nonetheless it deserves a place in a book on charcuterie. Such is our way, charcuterie is a broad church after all.

Mrs Beeton has a recipe for Bath chaps, starting with a pig head which is then salted and smoked before boiling.

Traditionally, Bath chaps are cured pork cheeks which are boiled, set in a cone shape mold and then rolled in breadcrumbs. They were usually sliced and served cold, like ham. The term 'chap' I understand is derived from 'chop' which was a reference to the jowls of a pig. Apparently they originated in the town of Bath.

Pork cheek (skin left on) – 1.
Sugar (brown) – 350g.
Salt – 350g.
Juniper berries (crushed) – 3-4.
Curing Salt No: 2 – 0.3%.
Coriander (dried) – 1tsp.
Sage (dried or fresh) – 1tsp.

Combine ingredients to make the brine. Add the cheek to the brine.

Refrigerate for 3-4 days in a non-reactive container, making sure the meat is completely submerged.

Remove the meat from the brine, discard the brine.

In your largest stockpot add meat, water to cover and make a court bouillon with 2 carrots, 2 celery sticks, 2 bay leaves, a handful of peppercorns, one head of garlic, and one onion.

Bring it to the boil and then simmer until meat is tender. This may take 2 hours.

Remove the meat and when cool enough to handle, remove the skin but leave as much fat on as possible.

Using double clingfilm roll the meat into a tapered roll shape (ie slightly larger diameter at one end).

Allow to set and cool overnight in the refrigerator. Thereafter slice, crumb lightly and fry to give the meat some colour.

NOTE: Fergus Henderson gives an interesting variation using a whole pig head, thereafter it is boned and rolled with the muzzle at one end. Not for the squeamish.

THE ACCOUTREMENTS[110]

---

110 French for a variety of other things which are really good and which you should know about.

THE ACCOUTREMENTS

Charcuterie in all its forms, whether hot or cold usually benefits from some accompaniments. These accompaniments, or accoutrements, can be sauces, pickles, or spice blends. I have included a variety of such accoutrements for the sake of completeness if nothing else.

I am a river to my people.

THE SAUCES

Dishes like cotechino, petit salé and choucroute are quite rich and not for the faint hearted. They are complimented by sharp sauces to cut the fatty richness. Here are a few good classic sauces which go really well with these types of dishes. (They are also very good with grilled meat or fish).

Each of the sauces are characterised by their freshness, strong flavours and acidity. They are best made fresh when required. They do not keep at all well in the refrigerator, with the exceptions of remoulade which may keep for a few days, and Cumberland sauce which would keep for a few days longer.

Make them fresh and use straight away.

SAUCE GRIBICHE

Gribiche is a classic French herb sauce or dressing. It is like the Italian salsa verdè but sharper and with the addition of chopped boiled egg. It is really good with petit salè.[111]

Egg yolk – 1.

White wine vinegar – 1tsp.

Oil – 250ml (olive or vegetable it does not matter, although olive can sometimes be a bit strong – I think vegetable oil is OK, but try 50:50 olive and vegetable oils as an alternative if you wish).

Mustard – 1tsp.

Egg (hardboiled, finely chopped) – 1.

Capers (finely chopped) – 1tsp.

Shallot (finely chopped) – 1.

Chives (finely chopped) – 6.

Lemon juice – 1tsp.

Salt and pepper to taste.

Whisk the egg yolk, vinegar and salt. Gradually add the oil, whisking constantly. Add mustard and season with salt and pepper (you can use a blender or food processor for this but do not allow it to become too thick).

Add the chopped herbs, capers, chives and egg. Stir gently and add lemon juice.

It will keep in the refrigerator for 1-2 days, but best used immediately.

---

111   A traditional recipe. Precise measurements are not required.

SAUCE VIERGE

Another fresh, sharp French sauce which goes well with rich dishes like cotechino or choucroute.[112]

Lemon – 1.
Tomatoes (peeled, seeded and diced) – 3.
Shallots (finely chopped) – 3.
Chives (fresh, finely chopped) – 6.
Olive oil – 500ml.
Salt and pepper to taste.

Grate some lemon rind into a fine zest, say ½ of the lemon skin. Peel the lemon. Cut the lemon into its segments but avoid the membranes in between each segment. Dice the lemon flesh finely but not into a mush.

Mix diced lemon and zest with all other ingredients. Add salt and pepper to taste.

Keep in the refrigerator for 1-2 days but best used immediately.

---

112   A traditional recipe. Precise measurements are not required.

SALSA VERDE

An Italian sauce made with fresh herbs, mostly basil, which is very good with rich meat or fish.[113]

Flat leaf parsley (finely chopped) – 1 cup.
Basil (finely chopped) – 1 cup.
Garlic (finely chopped) – 2 cloves.
Olive oil – ½ cup.
Capers (finely chopped) – 2tsp.
Lemon juice - the juice of one lemon.
Salt and pepper to taste.

Add parsley, basil, garlic and capers to a food processor and process until quite finely minced (a mortar and pestle will do the same job but it is much harder work).

While the motor is still running, add the oil and lemon juice gradually.

It will keep in the refrigerator for 1-2 days, but best used immediately.

CHARCUTIÉRE (THE CHARCUTIÉRE'S WIFE'S SAUCE)

This recipe comes from Grigson's book. I have not altered it (much) to suit modern sensibilities or tastes. It can best be described as a hot vinaigrette. The sauce is somewhat astringent, but think of it like hot mint sauce. It is very similar. Maybe a grown up version of the childhood staple. Try it with roast lamb. It goes very well with hot baked ham, choucroute, or a terrine.

Be brave.

---

113 Precise measurements are not required.

CHARCUTIÉRE (THE CHARCUTIÉRE'S WIFE'S SAUCE)

"1 tablespoon butter.

4 shallots, or 1 medium mild onion, chopped.

1 tablespoon flour.

4 tablespoons white wine.

4 tablespoons white wine vinegar.

Stock to about a pint.

½ lb. tomatoes.

1 teaspoon sugar.

Gherkins, and fines herbes to finish.

Salt and pepper.[114]"

Melt the shallots or onion to a *"golden hash"*[115] in the butter, sprinkle with the flour and cook until it is a pale coffee colour. Stir in the wine and vinegar, then the stock, until everything is smoothly amalgamated.

Leave the sauce to cook down on a low heat, until it is the desired consistency.

Meanwhile cook the tomatoes and sugar to a puree, and sieve into the onion and wine sauce towards the end of their cooking time. Taste and season. Just before serving add the gherkins sliced, and the *fines herbes*.

NOTE: Grigson refers to 'stock', I assume she meant chicken stock. At least that is what I use. It would have been useful if she had written as to what type of 'stock'.

'Fines herbs' is complicated; try this - a mixture of fresh chopped herbs, whatever you have but all green, together with chopped shallot, all in equal amounts. Sweat in the some white wine and chicken stock. Reduce to half the volume. This is a modern equivalent of 'fines herbs'

Maybe now you might understand how offputting these old recipes can be. At the very least they assume a significant familiarity with the ingredients and techniques. I assume nothing of the kind.

I am a river to my people.

---

114 This is her recipe, just like I said. It is exactly as she wrote in her book. So too, the method.

115 Grigson's term, not mine.

SALSA VERDE AL RAFANO

This is a variation of the classic Italian salsa verde, with horseradish for extra depth. It goes well with cold meat like ham or corned beef.

Parsley – (flat leaf variety works best) – 1 large bunch.
Mint – 2 sprigs.
Horseradish (peeled and grated) – 1tbsp.
Breadcrumbs – 1 ½tbsp.
Olive oil – sufficient to mix the ingredients.
Tomato – 2 medium size.

Blanch the tomatoes in boiling water for 20 seconds, peel, deseed and dice finely.

Finely chop the green herbs.

Mix tomatoes, herbs, horseradish and sufficient oil to make a sauce.

Salt and pepper to taste.

Lemon juice or sherry vinegar can be added for extra panache.

HORSERADISH CREAM

To some, horseradish may be an acquired taste. In my view it is an essential part of the garde manger, the cold larder of French cookery or charcuterie.

It can be as pungent and as nostril clearing as you would like, or not, as the case may be.

Certainly, a little can go a long way.

Horseradish (fresh, ground) – As much as you want, or dare. (Stand back when you grate it, it can be quite an experience).

Lemon – fresh juice – say, from ½ of one lemon.

Lemon zest – say from ½ of one lemon.

Créme fraîche – 1 ½ cup.

Salt – to taste.

Pepper (black, ground) – to taste.

Grate horseradish, mix well with all ingredients.

Serve now.

It will not keep.

MUSTARD SAUCE

A white (béchamel) sauce with whole grain mustard and parsley, a classic accompaniment to corned beef.

Butter – 20g.
Flour (plain) – 1tsp.
Milk (hot) – 300ml.
Mustard (Dijon, whole grain) – 1 ½tbsp.

Melt the butter in a saucepan. Add the flour. Cook for around one minute, stirring briskly. Do not let it go dark in colour or burn.

Add the hot milk a little at a time, stirring constantly. The mixture will thicken to a creamy thick white sauce. Add mustard to taste, salt and pepper. At the last, add chopped parsley (a lot).

A variation is to add only softened chopped white onions (with or without parsley, but definitely without the mustard).

REMOULADE

This is a classic French mayonnaise based sauce which is very similar to tartaré sauce but with anchovies and conichon.

Egg yolks (hard boiled) – 2.
Egg yolk (raw) – 1.
Mustard (French, mild) – 1tsp.
Sugar – ½tsp.
Vinegar (white wine vinegar) – 1tsp. (or to taste).
Oil (vegetable or mild tasting, not olive oil) – 450ml.
Salt and pepper to taste.
Green herbs (whatever you have, say, parsley, chives, oregano, thyme, finely chopped) – a lot.

In a mortar and pestle (or food processor) blend the hardboiled egg yolks with the raw egg yolk and other ingredients (except the oil).

Add oil a little at a time as if making a mayonnaise. Add the chopped green herbs, not too much, the sauce should be more like mayonnaise with some herbs than herbs with some mayonnaise.

Finely chopped coriander can be added.

Add salt and pepper to taste, perhaps extra vinegar or lemon juice.

CUMBERLAND SAUCE

Cumberland sauce is a classic British sauce which uses fruit. It goes very well with rich dishes like terrines.

Lemon – medium size.
Orange – medium size.
Red currant jelly (store bought, or homemade, a good quantity) – 4tbsp.
Port – 4tbsp.
Mustard powder (any commercial variety is satisfactory) – 1tsp.
Ginger (powder) – 1tsp.

Zest the lemon and orange skin.

Add the zest to boiling water, boil for a few minutes.

Drain and refresh in iced water (not for too long). Drain the zest well.

Melt red currant jelly with the port and whisk until combined.

In a separate bowl, mix ginger powder, mustard and sufficient lemon juice to combine.

Combine all ingredients.

Add some finely chopped green onion tops (not too much) at the end for some colour.

SAINTE – MÉNÉHOULD SAUCE

A fresh, tart sauce which goes very well with dishes like pig trotters or cotechino.

Onion – lightly chopped – 2tbsp.

Butter – 1tbsp.

White wine vinegar – 2tbsp.

White wine – 150ml.

Beef stock – 250ml.

Mustard (Dijion, <u>not</u> whole grain) – 1tsp.

Green herbs (chopped) – parsley, tarragon, dill, chervil) – 2-3tbsp.

Gerkins (chopped) – 2tbsp.

Flour (plain) – 1tbsp.

Bouquet garni – 1 (whatever you have, say a parsley, oregano, bay leaf).

Salt and pepper to taste.

Soften onion in melted butter. Add wine and vinegar. Cook down until almost all liquid has gone. Add the beef stock and bouquet garni. Simmer until reduced in half.

Make a beurre marnié with one tablespoon each of flour and butter. (A buerre marnié is simply well mixed together flour and butter). Add to the liquid a little at a time, stirring constantly. This will thicken the sauce quickly.

Finish by adding chopped herbs, mustard, gerkins, salt and pepper.

PESTO ALLA GENOVESE (PESTO)

The fresh flavor of basil is what makes this sauce unique. It has many variations but the original came from Genoa, hence the name. It is very similar to the French pistou which emanates from Provence. However pistou does not include pine nuts.

Basil (green basil, not one of the coloured varieties) – 1 large bunch.
Pine nuts (lightly toasted in a pan) – 50g.
Parmesan cheese (grated) – 50g.
Garlic (minced) – 2tsp.
Olive oil – sufficient to make a sauce.
Salt and pepper to taste.

Remove the basil from the stalks, pound the leaves in a mortar and pestle, add pine nuts and garlic.

Continue pounding in the mortar, adding a little oil at a time until a sauce like consistency is achieved (not too fine). Add in cheese and mix well.

Season with salt and pepper.

The cheese is naturally quite salty so tread carefully when adding salt.

Clearly this can be done in a food processor, however you should be deprived of the simple pleasure of making this sauce the way it has been made for centuries. Charcuterie and the accoutrements thereto are all about tradition.

PIRI PIRI SAUCE

Piri piri is a traditional sauce from Portugal. It can be quite hot and is a very good accompaniment to grilled meat or fish. In this context, it goes well with a hot poached sausage like sabodet or cotechino.

Olive oil – 250ml.
Tomato (very ripe) – 100g.
Butter – 50g.
Sugar – ½tsp.
Salt and pepper to taste.
Chillies (dried or fresh) – say 4-6.
Garlic (minced) 4-5tsp.

Chop tomato roughly, add to a saucepan with garlic and some butter.

Simmer for 5 minutes. Add sugar and chillies. Simmer until cooked to a paste.

Remove and add to food processor and process until smooth, adding the oil a little at a time. Add salt and pepper to taste. Allow to cool.

Fill sterilized jars and refrigerate.

PARSLEY, GARLIC AND CAPER SAUCE

This is an extremely simple sauce and easy to make. It is reminiscent of salsa verde but is thinner and served as a hot sauce rather than a cold sauce.

Good with, say, pig head and potato pie, if you happen to have one to hand.

Olive oil – 4-5tbspn.
Garlic (minced) – 3-4tbspn.
Parsley (flat leaf, finely chopped) – 3-4tbspn.
Capers (small, finely chopped) – 1tbspn.
Butter – 1tbspn.
White wine – 1-2 cups.

Warm the oil in a pan, add garlic and parsley until softened.

Add white wine, bring to boil.

Boil for a few minutes to remove the alcohol. Reduce to a simmer until the volume of liquid has reduced by about ⅓ to ½.

Add capers and warm through.

Add butter to give a glossy finish.

NOTE: If using bottled capers, rinse well before adding. If using salted capers soak in water for a few hours before use, changing the water frequently.

THE PICKLES

THE PICKLES

No charcuterie board is complete without a sharp pickle of some variety or a sweet relish. This classic accompaniment is cornichon, the tiny pickled cucumber from France.

Equally acceptable are pickled vegetables of different types, such as beetroot, onion or carrot. Pickled eggs are not to be overlooked.

Relishes and chutneys may not be as common place as they once were, but they are a very, very good addition to a plate of charcuterie. Usually vegetable based, such as tomato or onion but apple chutney is very good also.

PICKLED CUCUMBER (BREAD AND BUTTER PICKLES)

A charcuterie board must have cornichon, the small pickled cucumbers from France. Cucumbers of that size are not readily available unless homegrown. A good alternative is to pickle larger, more easily available, cucumbers. The result is the same but you can adapt the pickling mix to your own tastes.

Cucumbers (smallish size, green cucumber, the variety sold as 'Lebanese' cucumber are a good size) – 1kg.

Cider vinegar – 600ml.

Sugar (dark brown) – 350g.

Salt (fine sea salt) – 35g.

Mustard seeds (yellow or brown) – 1tbsp.

Allspice berries – ¼tsp.

Celery (seeds, cracked) – ½tsp.

Turmeric (ground) – ¼tsp.

Onion (brown) – ½ minced.

Capsicum (red) – 1 medium size, deseeded and chopped.

Garlic (cloves) – 3-4, lightly crushed.

Chillies (dried) – one or two, depending on how hot you like.

Add cucumbers to cold water and leave for 3 minutes. Drain and trim any stalks or blemishes.

Make a brine with the ingredients, heating until all dissolved. Simmer for a few minutes.

Allow to cool.

PICCALILLI

Piccalilli is a classic accompaniment to a British pork pie. It is hot and sweet and can be made with a variety of vegetables. Use whatever vegetables are available but green bean, cauliflower, carrot and onion are a good start.

Green beans (chopped into 1 cm dice, topped and tailed) – 150g.

Shallots (small, finely diced) – 4-5.

Cucumber (1 cm dice) – 150g.

Cauliflower (cut into florets, discard the central stalk) – 150g.

Salt – 3tbsp.

Vinegar (white wine vinegar) – 300ml.

Vinegar (malt) – 150ml.

Chilli (fresh or dried) – ½tsp (or more if you prefer).

Mustard seeds – 2tbsp.

Sugar (caster) – 350g.

Mustard powder (hot or mild, depending on your preference) – 2tbsp.

Corn flour – 1tbsp.

Turmeric (ground) – 2tbsp.

Combine vegetables and salt in a resealable plastic bag or non-reactive container. Place in the refrigerator overnight or up to 24 hours. Combine vinegars and chilli in a saucepan and bring to boil, allow to cool.

Return to the vegetables, rinse them well to remove excess salt and allow to drain.

Combine sugar, mustard, mustard seeds, turmeric, cumin and corn flour. Mix with some cooled vinegar solution to make a paste.

Add the paste to the vinegar solution. Bring the mixture up to the boil until it thickens slightly.

Add vegetables to sterilized glass jars, pour over spice/vinegar solution to cover.

Seal and refrigerate immediately.

PICKLED BEETROOT

Sweet pickled beetroot in a salad is quintessentially Australian to me. The tinned varieties are very good and well familiar to all. However making your own is very easy and, in my view results in a superior product.

Any colour beetroot can be used but if golden or paler beets are used together with red beetroot, the paler colour will be subsumed by the red colour released during the process. As in life, it is with beetroots, one must make a choice.

Grigson, in her book on vegetables, wrote:

> "We do not seem to have had much success with the beetroot in this country. Perhaps this is partly the beetroot's fault. It is not an inspiring vegetable, unless you have a medieval passion for highly coloured food. With all that purple juice bleeding out at the tiniest opportunity, a cook may reasonably feel that beetroot has taken over the kitchen and is far too bossy a vegetable.'

I am conscious that not everyone likes beetroot. To me that is a great shame. It is a versatile and flavorsome vegetable. It can be roasted or boiled. It can be pickled and eaten cold. It can be made into a puree as a dip . It can be finely sliced and deep fried , eaten hot or cold as with a potato chip. Available in winter when not much else is being productive. It is reliable and importantly reminds me of summer days. No salad is complete without it.

As for the colour I think it is just perfect. Why is the beetroot not held in higher esteem?

Use it wisely and it can be your friend. Over use it and you will regret it.

Beetroot (large) – 4-6.
Cloves (whole) – 2.
Salt – 1tbsp.
Sugar (caster) – ¾ cup.
Pepper (black, whole) – 1tsp.
Mustard seed (brown) – 1tsp.
Bay leaf (fresh if possible) – 2.
Vinegar (white wine) – 1 ½ cup.
Water – ¾ cup.
Cinnamon (stick) – ½.
Balsamic vinegar – 2tbsp.
Salt and pepper to taste.

The beetroot must be trimmed to remove the top and the root. Wash well to remove any soil. The beetroot needs to be cooked until it is soft but not falling apart. To this end it can either be boiled or roasted. In my view roasting is better because the flavor does not end up in the cooking water.

Line an oven tray with foil, add the whole, trimmed, but unpeeled, beetroot. Season well with salt and pepper, add a splash of vegetable oil (not olive oil) and a good splash (say 2 tbsp) of balsamic vinegar. The vinegar adds a sweet flavor to the beetroot as it roasts. If available add some fresh rosemary sprigs, a few bay leaves and some lemon peel. Cover the tray with foil. Cook in a hot oven (say 200°C) until the beetroot is easily pierced with a sharp knife. This may take several hours , depending on the size of the beetroot.

Remove and allow to cool. When cool enough to handle, peel the skin from the beetroot. Disposable gloves are a good idea unless you do not mind purple stained hands for a few days.

Cut beetroot into slices, chunks or julienne strips (not too thin) as you prefer. I prefer slices, just like in the canned variety. Although for a charcuterie plate, perhaps lean toward chunks.

Combine all other ingredients and bring to a boil. Allow to boil for 5 minutes and set aside to cool.

Pack beetroot into sterilized jars and cover with vinegar mixture, add a fresh bay leaf also. Finely sliced onion can be added at this stage. Seal the jars and refrigerate.

PICKLED CHILLIES

Chillies can either be sweet, mild or very hot. Use whatever you prefer but I think a sweet or mild chilli is what you want for a charcuterie board. A hot chilli will overpower the subtle flavours of charcuterie like prosciutto or ham. Also, the milder chillies are usually the large long ones which look very good.

Chillies (long, red, green or yellow, mild or sweet) – 350g.
Salt – 30g.
Sugar – 15g.
Vinegar (white wine or cider vinegar) – 400ml.
Pickling spices (use a commercial variety, or make your own) – 1-2tsp.

Wash chillies, trim stalks and remove any blemishes. The white seeds and white membranes inside the chilli contains most of the capsaicin, the active chemical which makes them hot to eat. You can slice the chillies lengthways and remove seeds and white membrane if you are concerned about the heat of the chillies. I think it is a good idea for a different reason, the white seeds and membrane are not much good to eat so I discard them at this stage.

Blanch the chillies in boiling water for 1 minute, refresh immediately in ice water. This softens the chilli slightly and helps set the colours.

Combine all other ingredients in a saucepan and bring to the boil for 5 minutes. Set aside and allow to cool.

Pack chillies in a sterilized jar, adding a bay leaf, flavor with the pickling liquid.

Seal and refrigerate immediately.

PICKLED EGGPLANT (AUBERGINE)

Eggplant or aubergine takes to pickling very well although it is not a common dish in this country. It is very common in Spain and often seen in tapas.

The large black eggplant does not lend itself readily to the pickling process. However there are many different types and shapes of eggplants. The small round shaped variety are preferred. The purple and white, golf ball sized eggplants seen in Asian grocers, sometimes called Thai eggplant are ideal. The small pea sized green ones are not so good. They tend to be somewhat bitter.

Eggplant (small Thai eggplant) – 1kg.
Vinegar (red wine vinegar) – 500ml.
Oil (olive oil or vegetable oil) – 120ml.
Paprika (smoked, sweet) – 2tbsp.
Sugar (caster) – 3tbsp.
Garlic (whole peeled cloves crushed lightly) – 20-25 cloves.
Cumin (ground) – 2tsp.
Oregano (dried) – ½tsp.
Water – 300ml.
Salt – 1tbsp.

Wash eggplants well, trim stalk but do not remove the stalk completely. The stalk is used to hold the eggplant for eating.

Bring a pot of salted water up to a boil. Add the eggplants and simmer for a few minutes until yielding but still having a crunch. To avoid the eggplants bursting, make a small cut through the skin lengthwise.

Once cooked, refresh immediately in ice water.

Combine all remaining ingredients in a pan, bring to boil and cook for 5 minutes.

Add eggplants to a sterilized jar, cover with pickling liquid.

Seal and refrigerate.

PICKLED ARTICHOKES

Globe Artichokes (*Cynara carenculus var scolynus*) are a form of giant thistle. They are tough and prickly but eat very well once the outer leaves are removed. The whole flesh of the artichoke 'heart' is what is desired. The flesh oxidizes and turns brown extremely quickly. Once the outer leaves are removed, immerse the heart in acidulated water to prevent oxidization. Once trimmed of leaves and the fibrous 'choke' in the centre of the heart, immerse the artichoke in acidulated water. Acidulated water is simply cold water with the juice of a few lemons squeezed into it. Add the lemons, once squeezed, to the water also.

Artichokes – 15 large.
Salt – 2tsp.
Lemon (juice) – 2 lemons.
Vinegar (white) – 2 cups.
Olive oil – 1 cup.
Garlic (whole peeled cloves, lightly crushed) – 5 cloves.
Chillies (dried or fresh) – 4 medium size.
Bay leaf (fresh) – 2.

Trim the artichokes – cut about 1/3 of the flower, remove the remaining tough outer leaves, cut the flower in half lengthways, peel the tough skirts from the stalk, remove the fibrous 'choke' in the centre of the heart. You will be left with not much compared to what you started with but this the only edible part for this recipe. This is the heart of the artichoke. Rub well with a cut lemon. Immerse in acidulated water immediately. Combine all other ingredients in a saucepan and bring it to boil.

Allow to cool.

In a separate saucepan of boiling salted water, add artichokes and cook until tender. This will not take long.

Remove and refresh in iced water immediately. Add to sterilized glass jar and cover with pickling liquid. Seal and refrigerate.

TOMATO RELISH

Tomato relish is a childhood memory for me. Sadly I do not have my late mother's recipe. However this recipe is an adaptation of a recipe from the Country Women's Association (CWA) cookbook which she gave me 25 years ago. I think it is very similar to hers. The tomato need not be pristine, in fact the recipe works best if they are somewhat overripe.

Tomatoes (very ripe finely chopped) – 3kg.
Onion (brown, finely chopped) – 1kg.
Celery – six large stalks.
Curry powder (mild) – 1tbsp.
Flour (plain) – 2tbsp.
Mustard (powder) – 1tsp.
Vinegar (malt) – 5 cups.
Sugar (caster) – 3 cups.
Salt – a handful.

Blanch the tomatoes in boiling water and remove the skins. Peel, chop and de-seed the tomatoes. (If you do not feel like de-seeding, that is OK).

Peel and chop the onion finely. Chop the celery finely.

Place all vegetables in a resealable plastic bag or non-reactive container and add a 'good handful' of salt.

Place in the refrigerator and leave overnight.

Mix curry powder, mustard, flour and sufficient vinegar to make a paste.

Rinse the vegetables. Put vegetables into a pot of boiling water for 5 minutes or until just tender. (They must retain some crunch).

Dissolve the sugar in the remaining vinegar. Add the sugar/vinegar solution to the curry/mustard paste to the vegetables, simmer for 30 minutes. Add the flour and cook for a further 3 minutes.

Place in sterilized jars and seal.

PICKLED ROASTED CAPSICUM

Large red capsicum (peppers) are ideal for this dish. They are sweet and flavoursome, not hot like their smaller cousins. These are a staple in a Spanish or Portuguese kitchens and there is no reason why they should not be on your charcuterie board.

Capsicum (pepper) – (large red bell capsicum) – 6-8.
Vinegar (malt) – 40ml.
Salt – 20g.
Olive oil.

Drizzle whole capsicum with oil, season with salt and pepper.

Roast the whole capsicum in an oven at 200ºC for 40-45 minutes until the skin is blackened.

Remove from the oven, place in a bowl and cover with clingfilm.

Allow to cool. When cool enough to handle, de-seed and peel the capsicums, discarding as much black skin as possible.

Mix vinegar, oil and salt together.

Place capsicum in a sterilized jar, cover with salt/oil/vinegar mixture.

Seal and refrigerate immediately.

THE SPICE BLENDS

THE SPICE BLENDS

Some of these recipes refer to spice blends with which you may not be familiar. Herbes de Provence and quatre épicés to name a few. I have included them because they are part of the traditional recipe. They are not difficult to make. You should try them.

There are many other traditional spice blends which I have not included, say, ras el hanout, dukkah, berbere or harissa.

I will deal with them on another occasion (maybe).

HERBES DE PROVENCE

A popular blend of dried herbs from southern France. The mix will not keep if you use fresh herbs.

Bay leaves (dried) – 6-7.
Rosemary (dried) – 30g.
Thyme (dried) – 30g.
Oregano (dried) – 30g.

Crush bay leaves well (use a mortar and pestle or a spice grinder).

Combine all ingredients. Store in airtight container.

It will keep indefinitely but best used within a few months.

QUATRE ÉPICÉS

This is a French spice blend used in many sausage recipes from France. It literally means '*four spices*'. Sadly there are at least 5 ingredients, therefore I do not know why it is called four spices. It is easy to make as follows:

White peppercorns
(ground) – 30g.
Nutmeg (ground) – 2g.
Cloves (whole) – 2g.
Cinnamon (ground) – 2g.
Ginger (ground) – 2g.

Blend all in a spice mill or food processor and place in an airtight container. It will last for a long time.

Adjust the ratio of ingredients to suit your taste.

FIVE SPICE

As with quatre épicés, the name five spice is quite misleading. The spice blend known as five spice consists of at least six spices and goes well with Asian style food. Insofar as charcuterie is concerned, it is a good spice mixture to use when curing corned beef or pastrami. Give it a run.

Star anise – 8
Sichuan pepper – 2tsp
Cinnamon – 1 stick
Fennel seed (cracked) – 1tbsp
Cloves (whole) – ½tsp (barely)
Chilli (flakes) – 1tsp.

In a frypan toast all ingredients until aromatic, but take care not to burn.

Allow to cool to room temperature.

In a spice grinder, grind all ingredients to a medium/fine powder.

Place in an airtight container.

The spice mixture will keep for 3-6 months.

PICKLING SPICES

Pickling spices or pickling mix is a blend of whole spices which are used as a quick way of adding to a pickling cure. It is easy to make and very useful to have on hand.

Cinnamon stick – 1
Bay leaf (diced) – 4
Cloves – 2
Mustard seeds (yellow or brown) – 20g.
Coriander seeds (whole) – 20g.
Pepper corns (black or a mixture of black, white and pink) – 10g.
Allspice (whole) – 1
Dill seeds – 10g.
Chilli flakes (dried) – 5g.

Crumble bay leaves, break up cinnamon stick into small pieces, lightly crack ½ the remaining whole spices.

Combine all ingredients, mix well and keep in an airtight container.

FINES HERBS

A French mixture of dried herbs which can be added to curing or pickling preparation. It is also very good as a seasoning with grilled meat or fish.

Basil (dried) – 25g.
Chervil (dried) – 10g.
Marjoram (dried) – 5g.
Thyme (dried) – 5g.
Tarragon (dried) – 15g.
Parsley (dried) – 25g.

Combine all ingredients, put in a food processor and process until very fine. Store in an airtight container.

ÉPICES COMPOSÉS

A traditional French herb blend with black pepper. It is good for rubbing on meat before cooking, for example a jambonneau.

Thyme (dried) – 20g.
Bay leaf (dried) – 20g.
Basil (dried) – 20g.
Sage (dried) – 20g.
Coriander (dried) – 10g.
Mace (dried) – 5g.
Pepper (black, ground) – 30g.

Add all ingredients to a processor to process completely into a fine powder. It will keep, in a sealed container, for quite awhile.

SEL EPICE

Another traditional French dried herb composition but blended with salt. Good for rubbing on a dish like Jambonneau or adding to a brine.

Nutmeg (ground) – 10g.
Cloves (ground) – 5g.
Bay leaf (dried) – 5
Cinnamon (ground) – 10g.
Pepper (black, ground) – 10g.
Coriander (ground) – 5g.
Salt – 250g.

Add all ingredients to a food processor, process until it is a fine powder.

THE SALT BLENDS

THE SALT BLENDS

What follows are the recipes for *'Dad & Son Salt'*. In each case, the production team[116] aimed for a strongly flavoured product, with a ratio of about 50:50 salt/spices. However depending upon your taste this can be varied. We only used dried spices, never fresh herbs. Fresh herbs will become mouldy and no good. We also made them very strong. The reason being that only a small amount of salt is used on food, it needs to be really quite strong if it is to be tasted at all. Accordingly, the recipes call for quite bold flavours which we found to be good. However, you can adjust the flavours to your taste. The other aspect we were concerned about was the visual appeal. We wanted the salt to look good. We adjusted the seasonings to assist in that regard. Adding a lot of dried parsley gives a pleasing green colour. Similarly, lots of paprika gives a good reddish colour.

Make a reasonable quantity and give away what you do not need. It makes a great Christmas gift and keeps indefinitely.

The salt which we used was a fine sea salt, although a flossy salt (medium grain) would be good also. Coarse rock salt would not work very well.

Expensive, flaky sea salt would work very well, but for our purpose because of its expense, it would have rendered the exercise wholly unprofitable. You may have different views.

Stored in an airtight container (or frozen), the salts will last a very long time.

I have followed No.1 Son's original names for each blend. Furthermore, I have remained true to the original recipe for each, which No.1 Son and I devised. These are the original, and the best.

These recipes are secrets.

Do not tell anyone about them.

Ever.

There will be nowhere to hide if you do. I will find you.

---

116   No. 1 Son and Moi, mostly Moi.

TANGY HERB

For every 1kg of salt, you will need:

Garlic (powder) – 175g.

Pepper (black, ground) – 70g.

Onion (powder) – 175g.

Oregano (dried, ground oregano would be ok) – 50g.

Thyme (dried) – 50g.

Rosemary (dried) – 50g.

Celery salt – 50g.

Saffron – a small pinch.

Parsley (dried) (this gives it a good green colour) – approximately 300g (or as much as you want to get the colour you like).

The dried herbs can be somewhat coarse and woody. They are not very nice to eat in that form. To overcome this problem, we put all ingredients (except the salt) into a food processor and blended until it was a fine powder. This also enables you to see what colour the mixture is and add more ingredients if you choose to adjust colour and taste. A good colour is very important. Adjust the seasoning to give a nice appealing colour.

This spice blend was then added to the salt and mixed through. Taste it and adjust as necessary.

LAMB'S BEST FRIEND

For each 1kg of salt, you will need:

Garlic (powder) – 175g.

Pepper (black, ground) – 70g.

Bay leaf (ground) – 25g.

Paprika (sweet) – 100g.

Rosemary (dried) – 50g.

Marjoram (dried) – 50g.

Proceed in the manner described in '*Tangy Herb*'.

BRAIN BUSTER

For each 1kg of salt, you will need:

Garlic (powder) – 150g.

Cumin – 150g.

Pepper (black, ground or cracked) – 70g.

Onion (powder) – 100g.

Paprika (sweet) – 100g.

Sumac – 50g.

Hot paprika (ground) – 50g.

Chilli (powder) – 50g.

Ginger (ground) – 50g.

Fennel (ground) – 20g.

Caraway (ground) – 20g.

Proceed in the manner described in '*Tangy Herb*'.

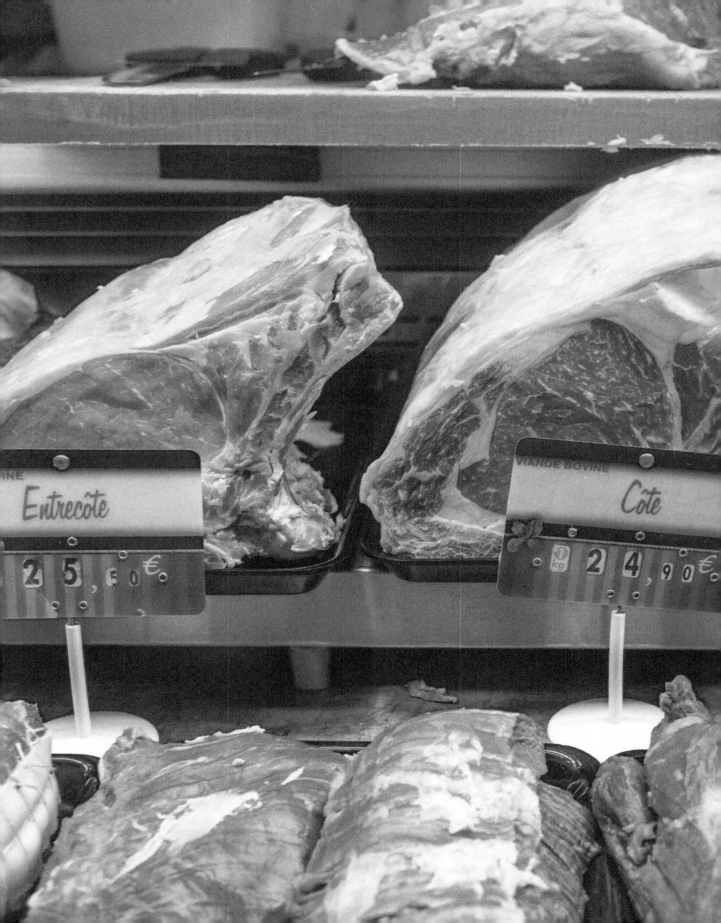

THE DRY
AGED BEEF

THE DRY AGED BEEF

Finally, even though this topic does not strictly qualify for inclusion in a charcuterie book, let me provide you with an introduction to dry ageing beef. Dry ageing is a technique to enhance flavour and texture in beef.

There are many who say that this cannot be done in a domestic environment. To those nay sayers I say, I have done it several times in a domestic refrigerator and lived to tell the tale.

The process of dry ageing meat has had something of a resurgence. At one time all beef was hung (dry aged) by butchers. That does not occur so much today. During the hanging process, the meat becomes more tender and flavoured partly as a result of enzymes breaking down the meat fibres and partly due to the dehydration of the meat and therefore a concentration of its flavour.

McGee explained the chemical basis of the changes which occur when hanging meat. Carcasses are hung up in such a way that most of their muscles are stretched by gravity, so that the protein filaments cannot contract and overlap very much; otherwise the filaments bunch up and bond very tightly and the meat becomes exceptionally tough. Eventually, protein-digesting enzymes within the muscle fibres begin to eat away the frame work that holds the actin and myosin filaments in place. The filaments are still locked together, and the muscles cannot be stretched, but the overall muscle structure weakens, and the meat texture softens. This is the beginning of the ageing process.

What is actually going on at a molecular level is a little more complex, as described by McGee. The ageing of meat is mainly the work of the muscle enzymes. Once the animal is slaughtered and the control systems in its cells stop functioning, the enzymes begin attacking other cell molecules indiscriminately, turning large flavourless molecules into smaller, flavourful fragments. They break proteins into savoury amino acids; glycogen into sweet glucose; the energy currency APT into savoury IMP (inosine monophosphate); fats and fat-like membrane molecules into aromatic fatty acids. All of these breakdown products contribute to the intensely meaty, nutty flavour of aged meat. During cooking, the same products also react with each other to form new molecules that enrich the aroma further.

Further, the meat is tenderised by the enzymes. Uncontrolled enzyme activity also tenderizes meat. Enzymes called calpains mainly weaken the supporting proteins that hold the contracting filaments in place. Others called cathepsins break apart a variety of proteins, including the contracting filaments and the supporting molecules. The cathepsins also weaken the collagen in connective tissue, by breaking some of the strong cross-links between mature collagen fibres. This has two important effects; it causes more collagen to dissolve into gelatin during cooking, thus making the meat more tender and succulent; and it reduces the squeezing pressure that the connective tissue exerts during heating, which means that the meat loses less moisture during cooking. Clever chap, that McGee.

Hanging, or dry ageing was overtaken by wet ageing in which the meat is sealed in a vacuum plastic bag and aged in a refrigerator for some time. The resultant product is not to everyone's tastes. The meat is dark, it has been immersed in juices which have now become dark and thick. When first released from the plastic bag, it has an unpleasant odour. Wiped and allowed to breathe for an hour or so, it revives its composure. But, in my view, it is not a natural thing for a piece of meat to do, and it shows.

Dry ageing, however, is another matter.

You can experiment with dry ageing at home in a domestic refrigerator. There are only a few rules:
- Do not use a steak sized piece of meat. It will only spoil, there is too much surface area for air and bacteria.
- Use a cut of beef which has very little intramuscular fat. Porterhouse, also called sirloin or ribeye, is best.
- Use porterhouse on the bone. This is usually sold as ribeye. It is the beef roast with the rib bones still attached.
- Do not use the piece which has been trimmed of fat for roasting. What you need is a piece of porterhouse on the bone, but with the full chine bone intact and the fat cap still on. The fat cap and full chine bones (spine) protect the meat from drying out too quickly. The only meat part which is exposed is at either end of the piece. Ask your butcher, he will know what you want. Select as large a piece

as you want, say a 4 rib section (a butcher calls this a 4 point porterhouse or ribeye). This will have four rib bones attached and will be about 25cm long (at least).

- Do not trim the fat. Do not remove the chine bones. Make sure that the meat is covered with fat on all sides except the ends. Ideally you want the thickest part of the porterhouse. It will work much better than a thin section of the same cut of meat.
- Place the meat on a rack in the refrigerator. Do not use your trusty wine refrigerator, it is too warm and humid. You need cold, dry conditions for dry ageing.
- Watch the meat carefully. It will start to dry out on the exposed meat section in particular on the ends. It will go a dark red colour.
- Check the meat for MOMC, slime and bad smell.[117] If it develops any such things, then discard it immediately.

The meat will age happily for up to 50-60 days in the right conditions. The meat just gets drier and darker in colour. For your first attempt, perhaps do not let it age for more than 20 days. Remember that the meat has already been aged somewhat. By the time you purchase it fresh from the butcher the meat is probably 10-14 days post kill. I do not factor this into my dry ageing timeline but it is worth knowing.

Remove the meat from the refrigerator. The meat will be dry, hard on the outside and very dark in colour. It may have some white mould. It should not smell bad. It should not be slimy or have the MOMC. Remove the fat cap, remove the meat from the bones in one piece. You will see immediately that the meat is darker red inside than normal and softer in texture. Note also that it is drier than fresh meat but is not dried.

Cut off the ends of the meat. Discard all the trimmings, they have no value and should not be eaten.[118]

---

117   There is no danger of critters. If you find them, then you are in real trouble.
118   At this point remember your dog. He or she will be very appreciative of the trimmings. The Rat got none. It is too evil and the meat trimmings were too good for it. The One True Dog however, appreciates such things.

If the meat has aged to plan you now have a piece of porterhouse which is darker, much more flavoursome and somewhat drier. Slice into thick steaks and cook. Do not overcook and serve at least at medium cooked, but preferably rare.

The resultant product is very tender and more richly beefy in taste than unaged meat. A good shiraz, horseradish and (perhaps a salad)[119] are all that is required.

---

119 Real charcutiers do not make friends with salad.

THE APPENDICES[120]

---

120 Do not stop reading here, there is good stuff in the Appendices.

THE TERMINOLOGY

The various cuts of pork and beef have different names from country to country and also within a country. It can make interpretation of a recipe very difficult. This is especially true of our North American friends, as George Bernard Shaw observed; *"England and America are two countries separated by a common language"*. The observation is also correct in the case of Australia and America.

Set out below are some of the terms you may come across:

Aitchbone	The hip bone which is exposed when the carcass is split laterally along the central line (spine) of the animal.
Back fat	Hard white fat which lies under the skin, above and on either side of the spine.
Blade	The muscle below the shoulder bone (scapula) in the shoulder but above the shoulder joint.
Boston Butt	The portion of the pork shoulder between the shoulder joint and scapula (USA).
Brisket	A cut which is from the rear end of the chest bones and the pectoral muscle.
Cheek	The muscle on either side of the animals jaw and can extend down the throat of the animal to where it joins the forequarter.
Chine bone	The spinal or vertebral column of the animal. In a split carcass, there will only be half on each side.
Chuck	The cut of meat cut from about the 5th rib and perpendicular to the backbone.
Chump	Derived from behind the loin toward the rear leg of the animal.
Connective tissue	The whitish or silvery tissue which surrounds muscles or which connects muscles to bone (tendon) or bone to bone (ligaments).
Coppa	See Boston Butt (USA).
Côte	A rack of pork (a section of pork ribs and loin) (French).
Échine	Shoulder but usually including blade bone and spare ribs (French).

Filet or filet mignon	A long tapered muscle which lies on either side of, underneath and behind the spine. (French)
Forequarter	Neck, shoulder, front legs and breast (chest) of the animal.
Girello	The eye of the round or topside (Italian).
Green bacon	Salted and cured pork belly (with or without its bones) but which has not been smoked (USA).
Ground meat	Minced meat (USA).
Hand	Under the throat, between the blade and down to the back of the animal. Essentially the lower part of the shoulder or forequarter (same as the picnic).
Headcheese	The terrine made from pork head meat (UK, USA).
Hock	The shank (closest to the body) of the leg either fore leg or rear leg.
Intermuscular fat	Fat between muscle groups or muscles; often quite thick and hard.
Intramuscular fat	Fat within a muscle, responsible for the feature called marbling.
Jambon	Rear leg, without the shank and trotter (French).
Joue	Cheek (French).
Jowl	See cheek.
Knuckle	The rear knee joint of the animal.
Picnic	A cut of meat (usually pork) from the shoulder, immediately below the Boston Butt (USA).
Poitrine	The chest (French).
Porterhouse	The large round muscle which runs parallel to and adjacent to the upper side of the spine. (The fillet is on the underneath and other side of the spine (chine) bones).
Primal	The primal cuts of a carcass are the first four basic subdivisions of butchery whereby the animal is divided into approachable portions – shoulder, loin, belly and leg.
Rump	From the rear end of the animal, on the top of the leg.

Shin	The leg of the animal, usually fore leg, often cut into rounds including the bone (osso-bucco) without the bone it is sold as shin or gravy beef (the latter is boneless).
Silverside	Adjacent to the topside (also called round).
Sirloin	See porterhouse.
Tenderloin	See filet, filet mignon (USA).
Tête	Head (French).
Topside	From the top end of the rear leg near the spine.
Trotter	Feet of the pig, from the ankle joint to the hoof.

THE MARKETS

If you are considering preparing charcuterie, then your local butcher is your new best friend. However, butcher shops are in decline and one may not be conveniently located. That answer is to shop at fresh produce markets. I like the colours, smells, noise and honesty of produce markets. I have been shopping at fresh produce markets for over 40 years, and still enjoy every visit enormously. Indeed I visit a fresh produce market at least weekly. When travelling, the fresh produce market is the thing that I most want to see for example, a street market in Paris, the mercat de la Boqueria in Barcelona, the Kretya Ayer wet market in Singapore, or the Queen Victoria Market in Melbourne - they are all endlessly fascinating to me. One does not have to be French to like a fresh produce market, but they do seem to do them rather well. The late, great Keith Floyd liked markets, especially French ones. He wrote:

> *"Watch a French housewife as she makes her way slowly along the loaded stalls... searching for the peak of ripeness and flavour... What you are seeing is a true artist at work, patiently assembling all the materials of her craft, just as the painter squeezes oil colors onto his palette ready to create a masterpiece."*

Floyd influenced most modern, so-called celebrity chefs. He was the first and his demise is a great loss.

Melbourne is favoured with extremely good fresh produce markets where a wide variety of meat, fish and other produce is available as follows:

Queen Victoria market (QVM).

The QVM has been in its present location for about 130 years. It is located on the corner of Elizabeth and Victoria Streets in Melbourne. It trades on Tuesdays, Thursdays, Fridays, Saturdays and Sundays. There is an excellent meat and seafood hall. Eels and fish roe are seen very occasionally.

If media reports are correct, it is to undergo a substantial renovation and expansion in the not too distant future. Hopefully the character of the QVM will be retained. See *www.qvm.com.au*

Preston market.

The Preston market is located in Cramer Street in Preston. The market trades every day except Sunday, Monday and Tuesday.

The meat and seafood is excellent. A good place for tuna, (in winter), eels (sometimes), pigs head (always) and fish roe (now and then). Frank The Butcher has a shop here.

See *www.prestonmarket.com.au*

Dandenong market.

The Dandenong market is located on 40 Cleeland Street, Dandenong and trades every day except Monday and Wednesday.

It has a very good meat and seafood hall (tuna can be found here in winter).

See *www.dandenongmarket.com.au*

Footscray market.

The Footscray market is located on the corner of Hopkins and Leeds Streets in Footscray. It is open every day except Monday and Sunday.

Great meat and seafood; often quite exotic seafood with a lot of live seafood (look for live eels available sometimes).

See *www.footscraymarketvictoria.com.au*

Oakleigh market.

The Oakleigh market is one of the smaller markets in Melbourne but some of the best seafood and meat can be found here.

Surrounding the market itself, which is very small, are several excellent butchers and fishmongers. The market is located at 12 Chester Street, Oakleigh and is open Friday, Saturday and Wednesday.

See *www.oakleighmarket.com.au*

Prahran market.

The Prahran market is open every day except Monday and Wednesday. It is located at 163 Commercial Road, South Yarra.

Very good meat and seafood.

See *www.prahranmarket.com.au*

Gleadell Street market.

The Gleadell Street market in Richmond is quite a unique open air market in Victoria, if not Australia. Apparently, it has been trading as a periodic and fresh produce market since approximately 1873.

Early every Saturday the street is closed off and the market is set up in much the same fashion as a French street market. It is a good place for fruit and vegetables, although meat, fish and cheese are also available.

Farmers markets.

There are also many farmers markets which are regular open air fresh produce markets where one purchases direct from the producer. Do not overlook them.[121]

---

121 See Australian Farmers Markets Association for details – farmersmarkets.org.au

THE SUPPLIERS

Here are some Australian suppliers of various products including knives, casings, Curing Salt and cultures:

1. Butcher at Home – *http://www.butcherathome.com.au*
2. Cellar Plus – The Artisan's Bottega, 317 Victoria Street, North Melbourne – *http://www.cellarplus.com.au*
3. Costante Imports, 377-379 Bell Street, Preston, Melbourne – *http://www.costanteimports.com.au*
4. Country Brewer – *http://www.countrybrewer.com.au*
5. Green Living Australia – *http://greenlivingaustralia.com.au*
6. Huon Distributors – *http://www.huondistributors.com.au*
7. Misty Gully Smokehouse – *http://www.mistygully.com.au*
8. The Redback Trading Company – *http://redbacktrading.com.au*
9. The Essential Ingredient, Prahran Market, Elizabeth Street, Prahran, Melbourne – *http://www.essentialingredient.com.au*
10. Smoked and Cured – *www.smokedandcured.com.au*
11. Ambello Bacteria Cultures – *www.ambellobacteria.com.au*
12. Home Make It – 4/158 Wellington Road, Clayton, Melbourne/265 Sprint Street, Reservoir, Melbourne – *www.homemakeit.com.au*

Bottling/preserving jars and equipment:

13. Oz Farmer Australia – *www.ozfarmer.com*
14. The Redback Trading Company – *http://redbacktrading.com.au*

Bulk (rendered) duck fat:

15. Luv-A-Duck, 228 Ingles St, Port Melbourne, Victoria – *http://www.luvaduck.com.au*

Smokers and smoking chambers:

16. Togar Ovens – *www.togarovens.com*
17. Hark Enterprises – *www.hark.com*
18. Bradley Australia – *www.bradley-smoker.com.au*

THE BIBLIOGRAPHY

There are a number of useful books on or related to charcuterie to which I have referred:

Author(s)	Title	Publisher
Boetticher, T. and Anor.	*"In the charcuterie".*	Ten Speed Press; 2013
Cottenceau, M.	*"Professional Charcuterie".*	Allen + Unwin; 1991
David, E.	*"French Provincial Cooking".*	Penguin Group; 1970
David, E.	*"Italian Food".*	Penguin Group; 1989
Demaio, P.	*"Preserving the Italian way".*	P. Demaio; 2008
Fearnley-Whittingstall, H.	*"The River Cottage Meat Book".*	Ten Speed press; 2007
Grigson, J.	*"Charcuterie and French pork cookery".*	Grub Street; 2010
Hasheider, P.	*"The complete book of butchering, smoking, curing and sausage making".*	Quarto Publishing Group USA Inc; 2016
Henderson, F.	*"The Complete Nose to Tail".*	Bloomsbury Publishing; 2012
Kowalski, M. and The Culinary Institute of America	*"The Art of Charcuterie".*	John Wiley & Sons, Inc; 2011
Kutas, R	*"Great sausage recipes and meat curing".*	The Sausage Maker, Inc; 2008
Lamb, S.	*"The River Cottage Curing and Smoking Handbook".*	Ten Speed Press, Crown Publishing Group; 2014
Livingstone, A. D.	*"Cold-smoking and salt-curing meat, fish and game".*	Lyons Press; 2011
Marianski, S, A. and R.	*"Meat smoking and smokehouse design".*	Bookmagic LLC; 2009

Marianski, S, and Marianski, A.	*"Curing and smoking fish".*	Bookmagic LLC; 2014
Marianski, S. and Marianski, A	*"Home production of quality meats and sausages".*	Bookmagic LLC; 2010
Marianski, S. and Marianski, A	*"The art of making fermented sausages".*	Bookmagic LLC; 2015
McGee, H.	*"On Food and Cooking; The science and lore of the kitchen".*	Hodder and Stoughton; 2004
McLagan, J.	*"Cooking on the bone".*	Grub Street; 2006
Mc Lagan, J.	*"Fat".*	Ten Speed Press; 2008
Reynaud, S.	*"Terrine".*	Phaidon Press Ltd; 2008
Reynaud, S.	*"Pork and Sons".*	Phaidon Press Ltd; 2007
Ruhlman, M. and Polcyn, B.	*"Charcuterie – The craft of salting, smoking and curing".*	W. W. Norton & Company; 2005
Ruhlman, M. and Polcyn, B.	*"Salami – The craft of Italian dry curing".*	W. W. Norton & Company, Inc; 2012
Turan, T.	*"Smoking, curing and drying".*	Apple Press; 2015
Vecchio, F. and Silva, E.	*"Charcutier.Salumiere. Wurstmeister."*	Self published, 2013
Weiss, J. and Mora, S.	*"Charcutería – The Soul of Spain".*	Surrey Books; 2014
Wildsmith, L.	*"Cured".*	Krause Publications; 2010

There are a number of other books to which I have referred, for interest, not necessarily for charcuterie:

Author(s)	Title	Publisher
Abbott, E.	*"The English and Australian Cookery Book"*.	Sampson Low, Son, and Marsden; 1864
Barrett, R.	*"You wouldn't be dead for quids"*.	Pan Australia; 1989
Beeton, I.	*"The book of household management Comprising information for the Mistress, Housekeeper, Cook, Kitchen-Maid, Butler, Footman, Coachman, Valet, Upper and Under House-Maids, Lady's-Maid, Maid-of-all-work, Laundry-Maid, Nurse and Nurse-Maid, Monthly Wet and Sick Nurses, etc. – also Sanitary, Medical & Legal Memoranda; with a History of the Origin, Properties, and Uses of all Things Connected with the Home Life and Comfort"*.	Oxford University Press; 2000
Bourdain, A.	*"Kitchen confidential"*.	Ecco/Harper Perennial; 2007
Connolly, J.J.	*"Layer Cake"*.	Grove Press; 2004
Floyd, K.	*"Floyd on Hangovers"*.	Penguin Books; 1993
Hazeley, J. A and Morris, J. P.	*"The Shed"*.	Ladybird Books; 2015
Kinnon Rawlings, M.	*"Cross Creek Cookery"*.	Simon & Schuster; 1996

Kurlansky, M.	*"Cod"*.	Vintage; 1999
Kurlansky, M.	*"Salt – A world history"*.	Vintage; 2003
Mallman, F.	*"Mallman on fire"*.	Workman Publishing Company, Inc; 2014
Mallman, F.	*"Seven Fires"*.	Artisan; 2009
Larousse Editors,	*"Larousse Gastronomique – Fish and Seafood"*.	Hamlyn; 2004
Larousse Editors,	*"Larousse Gastronomique – Meat, Poultry and Game"*.	Hamlyn; 2004
Portis, C.	*"True Grit"*.	Bloomsbury; 2011
Rayner, J.	*"The Ten (Food) Commandments"*.	Penguin Books, 2016
Saint-Ange, E. (Translated into English by Aratow, P)	*"La Belle cuisine"*.	Ten Speed Press; 2005
Schweid, R.	*"Consider the Eel"*.	Da Capo Press; 2004
Stein, R.	*"French Odyssey"*.	BBC Books; 2005
The Country Womens Association of Victoria	*'The CWA Cookery Book'*.	Magenta Press, 1990
Thompson, H.	*"Fear and Loathing at Rolling Stone: The Essential Hunter S. Thompson."*	Little Brown + Co; 2009
Thompson, J.	*"The Getaway"*.	Random House, Inc; 1990
Williams, J.	*"Back to the Badlands"*.	Harper Collins; 1993
Zola, E.	*'Le ventre de Paris'. ("The Belly of Paris")*.	Oxford University Press; 2007 (Translated by Nelson, B)

THE CONVERSION TABLES

Hopefully the structure of the recipes in this book will mean that you do not need to convert imperial measurements to metric. However if you do, the following is useful.

TEMPERATURE – F° TO C°

F°	C°
32	0
40	4
100	38
105	40
110	43
115	46
120	49
125	52
130	55
135	58
140	60
145	63
150	65
160	70
165	73
170	75
175	80

F°	C°
180	82
185	85
190	88
195	90
200	95
365	182
370	185
375	190
380	195
390	200
400	205
425	220
450	230
475	245
500	260
575	275
600	315

WEIGHT - IMPERIAL TO METRIC[122]

Imperial	Metric
½ ounce	14 g.
¾ ounce	21.26 g.
1 ounce	28.35 g.
1 ½ ounces	43 g.
1 ¾ ounces	49.61 g.
2 ounces	57 g.
2 ½ ounces	70 g.
3 ounces	85 g.
3 ½ ounces	100 g.
4 ounces (1/4 pound)	114 g.
4 ½ ounces	128 g.
5 ounces	142 g.
6 ounces	170 g.
7 ounces	198 g.
8 ounces	227 g.
9 ounces	255 g.
10 ounces	284 g.
10 ½ ounces	300 g.
28 ounces (1 ¾ pound, 1 pound 12 ounces)	794 g.
1 pound 13 ounces	822 g.
1 pound 14 ounces	851 g.
1 pound 15 ounces	879 g.
2 pounds	908 g.
2 ¼ pounds	1.02 kg
2 ½ pounds	1.14 kg
2 ¾ pounds	1.25 kg
3 pounds	1.36 kg
3 ¼ pounds	1.47 kg
3 ½ pounds (3 pounds 8 ounces)	1.59 kg
3 ¾ pounds (3 pounds 12 ounces)	1.70 kg
4 pounds	1.81 kg

---

122   F° to C° = F° − 32 x 5/9.

Imperial	Metric
4 ¼ pounds (4 pounds 4 ounces)	1.93 kg
4 ½ pounds (4 pounds 8 ounces)	2.04 kg
4 ¾ pounds	2.15 kg
5 pounds	2.27 kg
5 ½ pounds	2.50 kg
6 pounds	2.72 kg
7 pounds	3.18 kg
7 ½ pounds	3.40 kg
8 pounds	3.63 kg
9 pounds	4.08 kg
10 pounds	4.54 kg
11 pounds	4.98 kg
12 pounds	5.44 kg
13 pounds	5.90 kg
13 ½ pounds	6.12 kg
14 pounds	6.35 kg
15 pounds	6.80 kg
16 pounds	7.25 kg
20 pounds	9.07 kg
21 pounds	9.52 kg
25 pounds	11.34 kg

VOLUME – IMPERIAL TO METRIC[123]

Imperial	Metric (mls/litres)
¼ teaspoon	1 ml
½ teaspoon	2 ml
¾ teaspoon	3 ml
1 teaspoon	5 ml
½ fluid ounce 1 tablespoon	15 mls
1 fluid ounce 2 tablespoons ⅛ cup	30 mls

---

[123] 1 ounce = 28.35 grams. 1 pound = 453.59 grams.

Imperial	Metric (mls/litres)
1 ½ fluid ounces 3 tablespoons	45 mls
2 fluid ounces 4 tablespoons ¼ cup	60 mls
2 ⅔ fluid ounces 5 ⅓ tablespoons ⅓ cup	80 mls
3 fluid ounces 6 tablespoons	90 mls
4 fluid ounces 8 tablespoons ½ cup ¼ pint	120 mls
5 fluid ounces 10 tablespoons 1 cup plus 2 tablespoons	150 mls
6 fluid ounces 12 tablespoons ¾ cup	180 mls
7 fluid ounces 14 tablespoons ¾ cup plus 2 tablespoons	200 mls
8 fluid ounces 16 tablespoons 1 cup ½ pint	240 mls
10 ½ fluid ounces 21 tablespoons 1 cup plus 5 tablespoons	300 mls
11 fluid ounces 1 cup plus 5 tablespoons	325 mls
12 fluid ounces 1 ½ cups ¾ pint	360 mls
13 fluid ounces 1 ½ cups plus 2 tablespoons	385 mls
14 fluid ounces 1 ¾ cups	415 mls
15 fluid ounces	445 mls

Imperial	Metric (mls/litres)
16 fluid ounces 2 cups 1 pint	480 mls
20 fluid ounces 2 ½ cups 1 ¼ pints	600 mls
22 fluid ounces 2 ¾ cups	660 mls
24 fluid ounces 3 cups 1 ½ pints	720 mls
26 fluid ounces	780 mls
28 fluid ounces 3 ½ cups 1 ¾ pints	840 mls
32 fluid ounces 4 cups 1 quart	950 mls
36 fluid ounces 4 ½ cups 1 quart plus 4 ounces	1.06 litres
40 fluid ounces 5 cups 2 ½ pints	1.2 litres
48 fluid ounces 6 cups 3 pints 1 ½ quarts	1.41 litres
64 fluid ounces 8 cups 2 quarts ½ gallon	1.89 litres

124

---

124 1 tablespoon = 14.8 millilitres. 1 cup (8 fluid ounce) = 237 millilitres.

DRY MEASUREMENTS - IMPERIAL TO METRIC

Imperial	Imperial	Ounces	Metric
⅛ teaspoon or less	A pinch or 6 drops		0.5 g.
¼ teaspoon	15 drops		1 g.
½ teaspoon	30 drops		2 g.
1 teaspoon	⅓ tablespoon	⅙ ounce	5 g.
3 teaspoons	1 tablespoon	½ ounce	14 g.
1 tablespoon	3 teaspoons	½ ounce	14 g.
2 tablespoons	⅛ cup	1 ounce	28 g.
4 tablespoons	¼ cup	2 ounces	57 g.
5 tablespoons plus 1 teaspoon	⅓ cup	2.6 ounces	76 g.
8 tablespoons	½ cup	4 ounces	113 g.
10 tablespoons plus 2 teaspoons	⅔ cup	5.2 ounces	151 g.
12 tablespoons	¾ cup	6 ounces	170 g.
16 tablespoons	1 cup	8 ounces	225 g.
32 tablespoons	2 cups	16 ounces	454 g.
64 tablespoons	4 cups or 1 quart	32 ounces	907 g.

LIQUID MEASUREMENTS - IMPERIAL TO METRIC

Imperial	Pint	Quart	Gallon	U.S. Fluid Ounce	U.S. Table-spoon	Millil-itres	Litres	U.K. Ounces
1 cup	½	-	-	8	16	237	0.237	8.3
2 cups	1	-	-	16	32	473	0.473	19.2
4 cups	2	1	¼	32	64	946	0.946	40

THE EPILOGUE

Dear Reader,

You have read the book and hopefully tried some of the recipes. It is my fervent hope that now you are not afraid of charcuterie and will enjoy producing high quality charcuterie at home. Friends, family and associates will hold you in even higher esteem, if that is possible. Your entrance into a gathering, once quite unnoticed, will now be like walking into a roomful of meerkats. Enjoy the moment.

The science and history of this culinary backwater have become something of a fascination for me. I very much hope that it has been of interest to you. You are now a custodian of culinary practices which are in danger of extinction. Use your knowledge for good, not evil.

Allow me to close somewhere near to where I started, with Elizabeth David, this time writing in 1954 in *"Italian Food"*:

> *"This is, I think, a book for those readers and cooks who prefer to know what the original dishes are supposed to be like, and to be given the option of making their own adaptations and alterations according to their taste and their circumstances."*

Thank you for reading this modest work.

Happy ham and good gravlax.

P.J.B.

Melbourne, 2017.

Postscriptum:
I owe this book more than it owes me.

THE INDEX

THE INDEX

THE END

ATTRIBUTIONS

Lightning Source UK Ltd.
Milton Keynes UK
UKOW07n1357180917
309408UK00003B/7/P